M000033556

Opioid
Use Disorders

A Holistic Guide to
Assessment, Treatment & Recovery

Charles Atkins, MD

Copyright © 2018 Charles Atkins

Published by
PESI Publishing & Media
PESI, Inc.
3839 White Ave
Eau Claire, WI 54703

Cover Design: Amy Rubenzer
Editing: Marietta Whittlesey & Bookmasters
Layout: Bookmasters & Amy Rubenzer

Proudly printed in the United States of America

ISBN: 9781683731641

All rights reserved

Names: Atkins, Charles, author.
Title: Opioid use disorders : a holistic guide to assessment, treatment, and
    recovery / by Charles Atkins, MD.
Description: Eau Claire, WI : PESI, 2018. | Includes bibliographical
    references and index.
Identifiers: LCCN 2018033558 | ISBN 9781683731641
Subjects: LCSH: Opioid abuse. | Substance abuse--Alternative treatment.
Classification: LCC RC568.O45 A85 2018 | DDC 362.29/3--dc23 LC record available
at https://lccn.loc.gov/2018033558

PESI
Publishing
& Media
www.publishing.pesi.com

Books by Charles Atkins

NONFICTION

Co-Occurring Disorders: Integrated Assessment and Treatment of Substance Use and Mental Disorders
The Bipolar Disorder Answer Book
The Alzheimer's Answer Book

FICTION

Done to Death
Best Place to Die
Vultures at Twilight
Mother's Milk
Ashes, Ashes
The Prodigy
Go to Hell
Cadaver's Ball
Risk Factor
The Portrait

URBAN FANTASY FICTION PENNED AS CALEB JAMES

Haffling
Exile
Hound
Dark Blood

About the Author

Charles Atkins, MD, is a board-certified psychiatrist, published author, member of the Yale volunteer faculty, and national trainer. He is the chief medical officer for Community Mental Health Affiliates (CMHA), a multi-site agency headquartered in New Britain, Connecticut, that provides services to individuals with serious mental health and substance abuse problems.

Dr. Atkins writes both nonfiction and fiction, including plain-speak books on bipolar disorder and Alzheimer's disease (Sourcebooks), and a textbook, *Co-Occurring Disorders: Integrated Assessment and Treatment of Substance Use and Mental Disorders* (PESI). He has written hundreds of articles, columns, and shorts stories for professional and popular magazines, newspapers, and journals. He has been a regular contributor to the *American Medical Association's American Medical News*, a consultant to the *Reader's Digest Medical Breakthroughs* series, and his work has appeared in publications ranging from *The Journal of the American Medical Association (JAMA)* to *Writer's Digest Magazine*.

His website is www.charlesatkins.com

Dedication

To those who struggle with the disease of addiction, and to those who love you. There are a thousand roads to recovery, and where there is life, there is hope.

Table of Contents

Acknowledgments

I could never have written this book on my own. It's the result of years working with people with opioid use disorders, listening to them, and watching their struggles and triumphs. To those who taught me at Waterbury Hospital's West Main Behavioral Health. To Marie Johnston, who'd remind me, "They might be Jesus," when I got upset with a client who'd sold their medications. And to Lynn Zinno and Carol Genova, who managed chaos—and me—with grace and calm.

To my colleagues at Community Mental Health Affiliates in New Britain, from the CEO and executive team, to amazing case workers, program officers, therapists, nurses and nurse practitioners, psychiatrists, medical assistants, and patient navigators, it's a privilege to come to work and know that people are doing their best in the face of this epidemic. To the team who rally when it's time to do naloxone (Narcan®) distribution events, because people need to be educated and overdose kits need to be in the house. I also want to thank the expert readers who went through either the entire manuscript or portions to make sure I hadn't left anything out or had gotten something wrong: Dr. Rajesh Tampi, Mary Painter, Kristina Stevens, Lauren Doninger, Kim Karanda, Eileen Russo, and Dr. Kevin Sevarino.

To all those I've had the privilege to work alongside on the Connecticut Commissioners' Alcohol and Drug Policy Council, with special thanks to Julienne Giard, Melissa Sienna, Dan Rezende, Dr. Craig Allen, Karen Zaorski, Mark Jenkins, Dr. Kathie Maurer, Ally Kernan, Mark Jenkins, and everyone else who donates their time and comes to the table to try and make things better.

I need to give a nod to the strong team that helped pull this together, including my publisher Linda Jackson, editor Karsyn Morse, literary agent Al Zuckerman, and Marietta Whittlesey who tracked down permissions from around the world. To Liz Fitzgerald, my dear friend and the best editor I've ever known. To my family who tells me to slow down, which I ignore. And to my best friend and partner, Steve.

Finally, to all of those who sat down with me and shared their stories of courage, triumph, and at times, loss. It's been a privilege. I hope this book does justice to what you have entrusted in my hands.

Introduction

On the day I started this book, I learned that rocker Tom Petty's death was deemed an accidental multidrug overdose. Last week at a workshop I gave on the opioid epidemic a mother tearfully told me about the recent death of her son from heroin, and at my day job as a medical director for Community Mental Health Affiliates in Connecticut, I read yet another autopsy report that lists "accidental overdose with fentanyl" as the cause of death.

The overdose deaths—over 70,000 in 2017, the majority of which involved opioids—spiral upward, but that's just the tip of a deep-rooted opioid crisis in America. The drugs are cheap and more potent than ever. And the profit to be made off the suffering of so many is too hard to resist.

When I got asked to write a book on opioid use disorders, based on workshops I give, it seemed timely and important. Knowledge is power, and clinicians, family members, and people in all stages of recovery need to have clear information amid a confusing and rapidly evolving crisis.

I've worked with people with serious substance abuse and mental health problems throughout my career as a psychiatrist. What's happening is unprecedented, though not the first time in human history, or America's history, that an opioid epidemic has shaken a society. As overdose deaths surpass those from car accidents, and the numbers continue to rise, we need to act, and do so in ways that make a positive change.

This crisis has gathered attention. Likely due to the demographics of who becomes addicted, overdoses, and dies. Opioid use disorders cross all socioeconomic borders. From the rock star and movie star, to the homemaker who got hooked on pain pills, to the college student who felt invincible, to the woman with a history of sexual trauma who finds momentary relief in the oblivion of heroin to… As I look at the demographics of my own state, Connecticut, there have been overdose deaths reported by our medical examiner in every town, even tiny ones with populations of under a thousand.

By reading autopsies—it's part of my day job as a medical director—I've learned a lot. I've seen people die from taking no more than what was prescribed. These are mostly accidental deaths, though opioids are also implicated in many suicides and even deliberate poisonings. For reasons we'll discuss, people who thought they had the tolerance to handle what was in their bag of drugs or prescribed bottle of pills, are tragically mistaken. So too, I've read the final toxicology reports from intermittent users who thought they could do it "one more time." And in the past couple years I've seen the rise of super-potent fentanyls from China, often disguised as other things, that have been a death-dealer for anyone who uses street drugs. And while the bulk of our overdose deaths involve opioids, it's usually in combination with other sedating drugs and/or alcohol.

However, as I look at all the people affected, I see a tremendous opportunity to reach out and help. We have treatments that work, but they're often not readily available and there is still great confusion about the nature of opioids. While well-intended, the knee-jerk response to send everyone to an inpatient detox from opioids is usually the wrong one and a recipe for misfortune.

So too, getting the word out about overdose reversal kits, and more importantly the kits themselves, is a vital step, but only a step. To reverse an overdose saves a life in the moment, but if it's not coupled with helping that person make a change, it leaves them in withdrawal and looking for their next dose. One study out of Massachusetts showed that 10% of those rescued from an overdose are dead within 12 months.

The ray of light is that people can and do recover. I know as I've worked with many of them, as their psychiatrist, as a colleague, and as a friend. These are the people from whom I learn the most. I've included some of their voices in this book, both because their messages are important, and because they represent a powerful movement—with evidence behind it—that people in recovery can make all the difference to those still caught in the thrall of addiction. It's not just hearing someone say, "I've been there and gotten through it. You can too." But, "Hey, let's call that clinic together and I'll drive you there. We'll grab some coffees, and I'll hang out as long as you want." What's been dubbed the "soft handoff"—taking someone to a program, group, or rehab—can save a life.

CHAPTER 1

The Opioid Epidemic in America: How We Got Here and Why That Matters

- **Historical Overview**
- **The World Health Organization (WHO) Analgesic Ladder for Cancer Pain**
- **The Joint Commission, the Centers for Medicare & Medicaid Services, Big Pharma, and the Institute of Medicine Make Pain the Fifth Vital Sign**
- **Heroin Gets a Facelift**
- **The Rise of Fentanyl**

HISTORICAL OVERVIEW

The year 2017 saw over 72,000 overdose deaths in America. Because of the young ages of the victims and the large number, this pushed down life expectancy for Americans a second year in a row. The whys of this epidemic are varied and include aggressive marketing of opioids by pharmaceutical companies, the unique nature of how these substances affect our bodies and brains, and medical professionals who, in their desire to lessen pain, inadvertently colluded to create the current scenario through the over-prescribing of opioids for chronic pain. Others, such as drug families and organized cartels, have added fuel to the fire with the inundation of our cities and towns with inexpensive and potent heroin, and—more recently—fentanyl, which carry irresistible profits and predictable deaths.

This crisis, of which the overdose numbers are just the tip, began in the medicine cabinet. Over 70% of those who become opioid dependent begin with prescription pain medications, either prescribed (about 30%) or obtained from friends and family (over 40%). Americans consume over 90% of the world's pharmaceutical opioids with enough prescriptions written annually for everyone to have at least one bottle.

While this is not a historical text, it's useful to see how things evolved. Opiates, which refer to those drugs derived from the sap of the opium poppy (*Papaver somniferum*) have been known to have narcotic, sedating, and analgesic properties for thousands of years. In

Martin Booth's encyclopedic history, *Opium*, the first evidence of human involvement with the opium poppy came with the discovery of both cultivated seeds and pods in Neolithic sites in Switzerland that date back 6,000 years. The poppy's analgesic and euphoric properties were recognized by the ancient Egyptians, Greeks, and Romans. The Sumerian word for the poppy was the "joy plant." Even in ancient times, there was an awareness of the darker side to opium, that it could cause dependence, and death, and was often the preferred choice for assassins who could put their intended victim to sleep forever. So too, there are historic accounts of its use in suicide. This has a chilling echo today, as opioids laced with fentanyl have become a favored means to end one's life, and it's often difficult to discern what was accidental versus intentional.

Opium itself is not a single compound, but the poppy's sap contains dozens of different compounds, which include morphine, codeine, and thebaine. Prior to the development of the hypodermic syringe in the nineteenth century, the methods for ingesting opium were to eat it and then to smoke it, which became popular in 18th-century China.

In the early 19th century, morphine was isolated from opium by Friedrich Sertürner, and it became a godsend to surgeons and their patients, as an effective means to treat interoperative pain. The development of the hypodermic syringe provided a more effective way to deliver this rapid and potent medication. So too, other legitimate and important aspects of opioids, such as their anti-diarrheal properties, are credited with saving thousands—possibly millions—of lives from outbreaks of cholera and dysentery. But use of hypodermic needles rapidly spread to people who had become habituated to opium and morphine. Little was known about hygiene and bacteriology, so infections and spread of illnesses such as hepatitis, became common.

Opioids, those compounds that are synthesized in labs and act on the body's opiate receptors, are more recent developments and include methadone, oxycodone, fentanyl, and many others. (Throughout this book I'll use the word "opioid" to refer to all substances that bind to opiate receptors and create typical effects: pain relief, sedation, euphoria, constipation, and so forth.)

The Civil War, with its devastating morbidity and mortality, produced thousands of habitual users, as injured and shell-shocked soldiers ("the soldier's sickness") became dependent on morphine. With no regulations, tincture of morphia and laudanum found their way into popular patent medications, which often included cocaine, cannabis, high-content alcohol, and even chloral hydrate. Laudanum, cocaine, morphine, and raw opium could be purchased at pharmacies without a prescription. Claims on medications with names like Wizard and Snake Oil were enthusiastically inclusive as to what they could cure, from a colicky baby, rheumatoid, toothaches, kidney problems, diarrhea, and gout, to female troubles. Or as a bottle of Dr. J. Collis Browne's Chlorodyne, first produced in 1857 and available into the 1970s in England, proclaimed, "A medicine chest in itself." Morphine and laudanum-rich cocktails, such as Mrs. Winslow's Soothing Syrup, were specifically targeted to help mothers keep their teething infants and young children placid and calm. And in some instances, dead.

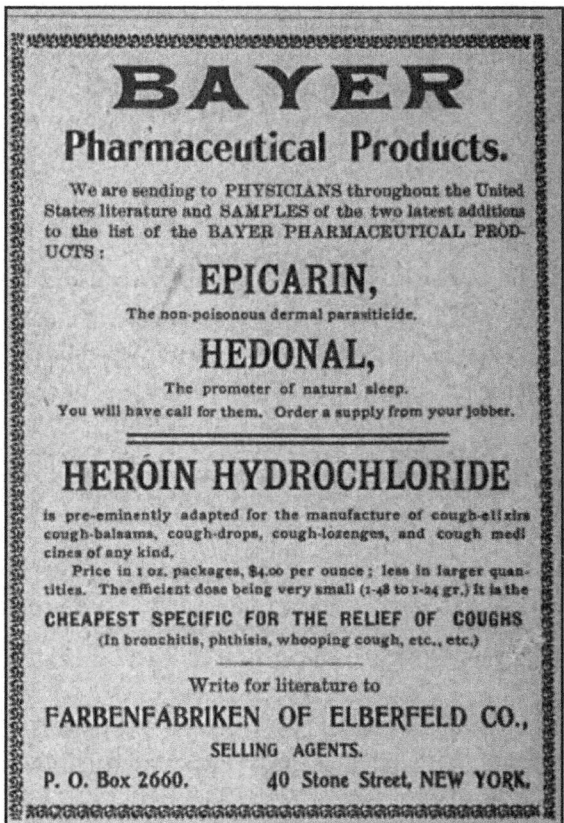

With free access to opiated patent medications and no legislation around the prescribing of opium and its derivatives, it's no surprise that our current opioid crisis is not our first.

At the start of the 20th century, it's estimated that there were 250,000 habitual users in the United States, with a disproportionate number of them being "genteel" women. From a global perspective, these numbers pale compared to the extreme opium problems of China in the 19th and first-third of the 20th century, where, at its height, one-tenth of the population were dependent.

In 1895, Bayer Pharmaceuticals brought heroin to market—it had first been synthesized from morphine in the middle of the century—as a potent pain reliever and cough suppressant. It was said to be a safe alternative to morphine and could be used to wean someone off it. It was widely available without a prescription and came in pill, liquid, and lozenge forms, some specifically targeted to children. It was subsequently pulled from the shelves and deemed illegal in 1924.

In 1906, the Pure Food and Drug Act laid the groundwork for what would eventually establish the Food and Drug Agency (FDA). Initially this legislation ensured accurate labeling of foods and medications. Included was the identification of 10 drugs with "dangerous" and "addictive" properties; these were: "alcohol, morphine, opium, cocaine, heroin, alpha or beta eucaine, chloroform, *Cannabis indica,* chloral hydrate or acetanilide, or any derivative or preparation of any such substances contained therein." While the law did not outlaw any of these compounds, it did require that they be clearly labeled, including the amount.

In 1914, the Harrison Narcotic Tax Act passed and required that anyone involved in the production or distribution of opioids and cocaine obtain a license to do so. It added that physicians could continue to prescribe opiates, but because addiction was not considered a disease, they were forbidden to prescribe it for maintenance. Pharmacists and physicians who did not comply were imprisoned, as were many of those dependent on opioids. This, as might be expected, had a chilling effect on the willingness of doctors to prescribe.

Those two pieces of legislation, along with public indignation, are widely credited with stemming the opioid epidemic of the late 19th and early 20th century, but also with the creation of a black market in heroin and morphine to supply the daily needs of those addicted and unable to stop.

THE WORLD HEALTH ORGANIZATION (WHO) ANALGESIC LADDER FOR CANCER PAIN

In 1986, WHO published a three-step analgesic ladder for the treatment of cancer pain. It was found to be inexpensive and managed pain in 70–90% of patients. It had three steps: use of a non-opioid (aspirin and nonsteroidal), weak opioids, and if pain was not adequately controlled, a strong opioid. All steps mentioned the use of pharmacologic adjuvant treatments and recommended the use of pain scales.

There were a number of guidelines:

- Use oral medications when possible.

- Establish a regular dosing interval.

- Evaluate pain based on intensity and using a scale.

- Dosing is individual and based on the patient.

- A written plan of care is developed around pain management and includes details on the dosage schedule to control pain.

While specifically developed to address the under-treatment of cancer pain, the WHO ladder found its way into the treatment of all types of pain, including chronic pain.

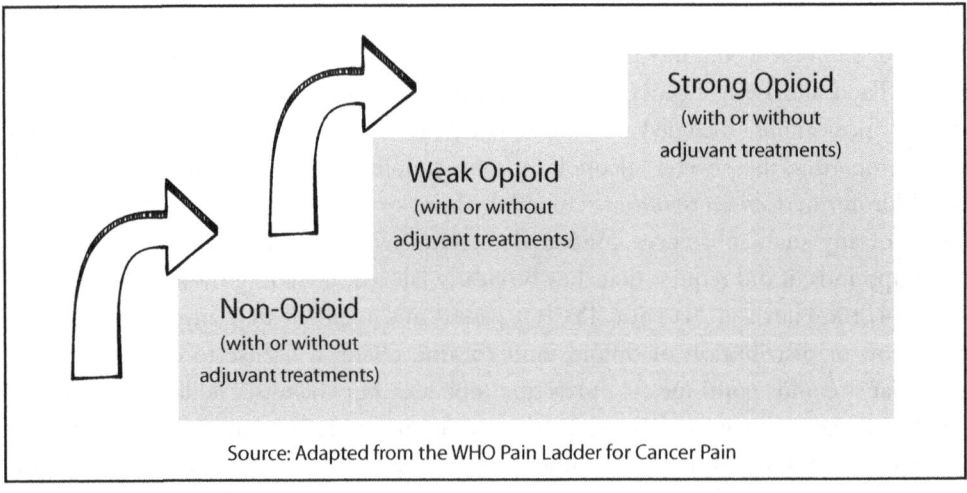

Source: Adapted from the WHO Pain Ladder for Cancer Pain

The Joint Commission, the Centers for Medicare & Medicaid Services, Big Pharma, and the Institute of Medicine Make Pain the Fifth Vital Sign

In his wonderfully researched book, *Dreamland*, Sam Quinones connects the dots between WHO's pain ladder, which was for the humane treatment of cancer pain, to the liberal and widespread use of opioids for chronic pain of all sorts in the 1990s and early 2000s. The Joint Commission developed standards around pain and aggressively ensured that the thousands of hospitals and clinics it surveyed complied. Medicare reimbursement became tied into an agency's ability to assess and treat pain, and physicians and nurses were encouraged to view pain as the fifth vital sign, alongside pulse, temperature, blood pressure, and respiration rate. Pain scales, often with emoji-like faces, which ranged from a serene smile to an agonized grimace, were developed. At every visit, emergency room encounter, or on hospital rounds, patients would point to the face, or the number on a 10-point scale, and could expect to receive medication that would move them closer to the pain-free happy face.

At the same time, pharmaceutical companies developed and brought to market potent synthetic opioids, including long-acting, slow release agents (MS Contin, OxyContin, and others), which were promoted and aggressively marketed to physicians as having minimal addictive properties, based largely on a 1980 letter by Jane Porter and Hershel Jick to the editor of the *New England Journal of Medicine*. These claims were unfounded, but widely disseminated by the drug companies and embraced by physicians and patients seeking relief from their back, joint, fibromyalgia, and other chronic pain conditions. Over the course of a decade, what had once been ingrained in the minds and practices of every physician—prescribe opioids only when absolutely needed and for the shortest time possible—had been replaced by the erroneous belief that opioids were safe and mostly free of addictive potential.

From the moment OxyContin became available, people who misused opioids quickly understood that its long-acting properties, which were supposedly a deterrent to the development of tolerance and withdrawal, could be sidestepped and the full amount of the medication obtained at once by crushing the pills to snort them or dissolving them in water to inject them. Pain management clinics, fueled by pain as the fifth vital sign, sprouted up around the country, and "pill mills" where physicians, some well-intended and some unscrupulous, wrote a 100 or more prescriptions a day and seeded a new wave of opioid dependence and addiction that cut across all socioeconomic racial, and cultural divides. No longer were opioids a "skid row" or jazz club problem, but sons and daughters of doctors, lawyers, politicians, and plumbers all got hooked.

Heroin Gets a Facelift

After the earlier opioid epidemic of the 19th and early 20th century, opioid users became vilified and characterized as dope fiends. There were added dimensions of racism toward African Americans and the Chinese, even though the largest group of those on opiate-rich patent medications and laudanum were white women of the middle class and Civil War veterans.

In the middle of the 20th century up until the 1980s, illicit heroin came into this country from Afghanistan, Bangladesh, and other Asian countries. It was often cut (diluted) multiple times to increase profit and was mostly found in large cities. Its users were outside mainstream America, from beat writers like William S. Burroughs (*Naked Lunch, Junkie*), Jazz musicians like Billie Holiday and Willie Parker, to Bowery bum characterizations of a heroin user. Per the DEA, the average potency of the powdered heroin available on the street was about 3–12%. For habitual users, this barely prevented withdrawal.

But then something changed, as pain had turned into the fifth vital sign and oxycodone and other prescription opioids became readily available, the supply and type of heroin also shifted. No longer was it China White and other powdered products from Asia, but black-tar heroin arrived from small-town Mexico, along with much purer forms of white and brown powder. These were uncut, had a purity of 70–90%, were inexpensive— often costing much less than the pills—and with a phone call, it would get delivered to your door like a pizza. As might be predicted, this radical and rapid increase in potency led to a rise in overdoses as black-tar heroin, and other higher-potency products, spread across America with a broad-customer focus, which now included the suburbs.

THE RISE OF FENTANYL

Between 2002 and 2018 we have seen fentanyl(s), a large family of synthetic opioids, go from being rare substances of misuse to become the gas thrown onto the flame. In Connecticut, autopsy toxicology data from the chief medical examiner shows that between 2002–2017 fentanyl has gone from contributing to 4% of overdoses to 65%. In Florida, there were 251 fentanyl-related deaths in 2012 and 911 in 2015, a 263% increase. One local addiction treatment facility that started to test for the presence of fentanyl found it in 70% of their new admissions.

The Drug Enforcement Agency (DEA) also credits fentanyl with the current surge in the opioid epidemic. They cite the National Forensic Information Lab System (NFLIS) data

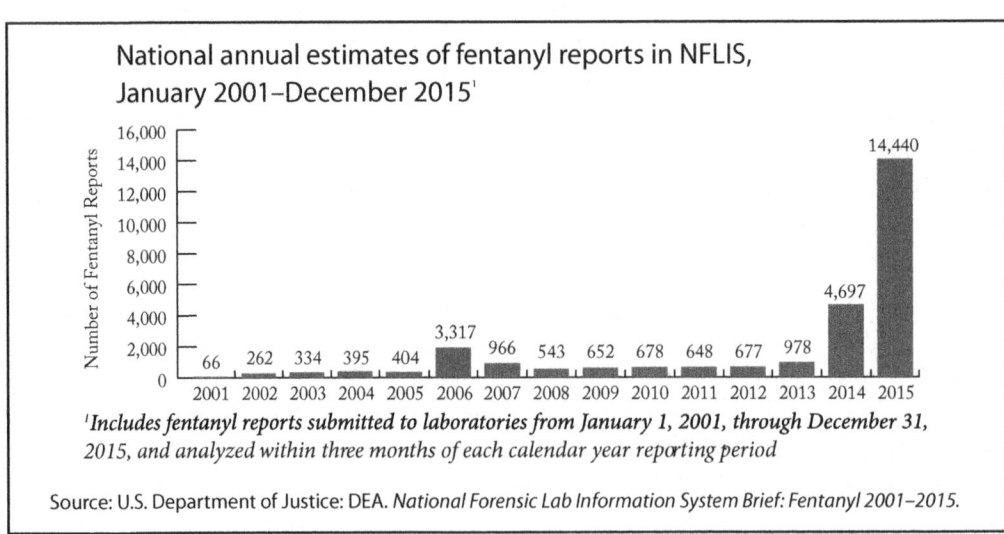

National annual estimates of fentanyl reports in NFLIS, January 2001–December 2015[1]

[1]*Includes fentanyl reports submitted to laboratories from January 1, 2001, through December 31, 2015, and analyzed within three months of each calendar year reporting period*

Source: U.S. Department of Justice: DEA. *National Forensic Lab Information System Brief: Fentanyl 2001–2015.*

that shows a precipitous rise in fentanyl-positive drugs that have been seized and analyzed by law enforcement.

Logical questions to consider with fentanyl, which will help us orient to the mind of the user, as well as the dealer, include:

Why would someone take a drug that they know could kill them? To which someone who uses will tell you, "That's the drug you want. If you know there's this super-potent dope in a certain town, you and your friends are getting in a car to go get some." As a friend of mine in recovery said, "When you're in the middle of your addiction you don't consider that you might overdose. It's not in your consciousness." Or as another client shared with her therapist, "You want it because that's the good stuff, and those other people died because they couldn't handle it, but I'll be okay."

Why would a dealer deliberately supply their customers with what could easily be a fatal dose? The answer to this question is pure economics and chilling. A kilogram of fentanyl obtained over the dark web from China and shipped via USPS costs between $3,000–$10,000. Each kilogram contains one thousand grams. Each gram contains one thousand milligrams. A milligram of highly potent fentanyl is what's typically found in a laced bag of heroin or counterfeit pain pill. Each bag of dope retails for $4–$10 based on location and supply. Here's the math: 1,000 (grams) × 1,000 (milligrams) = 1,000,000 potential doses × $4 to $10 = 4 to 10 million dollars on your $3,000–$10,000 investment. With the potential for profits of that magnitude, it's easy to understand how we have arrived at this current crisis and deadly epidemic.

Opioids: Definitions, Neuroscience and the Hijacking of the Brain's Reward System

- **Overview**
- **Terms and Definitions**
- **Scheduled Drugs**
- **Neurodevelopment and the Hijacking of the Dopamine Reward System**
- **The Dopamine Reward System (Meso-Limbic Pathway)**

Overview

As we delve into the many ways opioids affect our brains and bodies, we need to cover some basic concepts and definitions. Each of these compounds can be thought of as having a unique fingerprint, which includes how strong it is (potency), its duration of action, and how tightly it binds to opiate receptors. This is further complicated by the individual using the drug, their genetics, how they use opioids (oral, intranasal [snorted], intravenous, subcutaneous, smoked, transdermal), their tolerance, and their duration and patterns of use.

Terms and Definitions

Potency: The relative strength of one opioid when compared to another in a milligram for milligram way. This is standardized with one milligram of morphine. This takes on significance when considering drugs laced with fentanyl, which can range in potency from 50 times more potent than morphine to, in the case of carfentanil (the elephant tranquilizer), up to 10,000 times.

Morphine Milligram Equivalents (MME): Using the concept of potency, we can calculate MMEs. The chart on page 11 includes relative potencies as they relate to 1mg of morphine. The following are some sample conversions. There's tremendous

9

variability in how different people metabolize opioids, so the numbers are inexact. Also, how a substance is used, oral vs. intravenous, affects its potency, duration, and length of action. For instance, oral morphine is one-third as potent as intravenous morphine.

- 50mg of hydrocodone = 50MME

- 12mg of methadone = 50MME

- 60mg of oxycodone = 90MME

Morphine equivalents have been used to study overdose and other risks associated with opioids.

- Veterans who died from an overdose were on an average of 98MME/day.

- Doses as low as 50MME carry an increased risk for overdose.

- Doses of > 90MME are associated with high overdose risk.

Duration of Action: This is the length of time one experiences the effects of a substance. With opioids, it helps to break this into two components: How long does the substance provide analgesia (pain relief), and how long can it keep someone who is opioid-dependent from going into withdrawal? These can be quite different. For instance, methadone can be used to treat pain, and it lasts four to six hours; but it can be taken once a day to prevent withdrawal. The same is true for the partial agonist buprenorphine, which, when used for moderate to severe pain, needs to be administered three to four times a day; but to treat an opioid use disorder, it can be taken once a day, though many prefer to split their daily dose in two.

Half-Life (T½): This describes how long it takes for the body to eliminate 50% of a substance. To clear over 90% of a medication involves five half-lives. The first clears 50%; the second, 25%; the third, another 12.5%; and so forth. Half-lives of opioids vary greatly, from heroin and certain fentanyl(s), with half-lives on the order of a few hours or less, to methadone and buprenorphine—used to treat opioid use disorders—that have half-lives on the order of 48 hours.

Half-lives carry predictive value when trying to gauge when a person will go into withdrawal. For people who are opioid dependent, half-lives and length of duration become a central focus of their existence, as they must obtain their next dose to avoid withdrawal.

Endogenous Opiates: We produce natural opiates. This turned into the buzz phrase "runner's high" when talking about the release of endorphins, dynorphins, and enkephalins during intense exercise and other pleasurable activities, such as sex. Endogenous opiates, along with dopamine, play pivotal roles in the brain's reward system, which, from an evolutionary perspective, evolved so that we'd experience both food and sex as enjoyable. When outside opioids are taken over an extended period, the body decreases production of all products related to endogenous opiates

Opioid Potencies

Substance	How Used	Dosing Frequency and Half-Life (T½)*	Type	Potency* in Morphine Milligram Equivalents Oral Morphine = 1
Buprenorphine (Subutex®)	Sublingual (under the tongue)	Once or twice daily, more frequently if used for pain T½ = 16–36 (sublingual)	Partial agonist	30
Buprenorphine/ naloxone (Suboxone®, Zubsolv®, Sublocade™)	Sublingual, also available as a long-acting injectable (monthly/ Sublocade™)	Once or twice daily, more frequently if used for pain T½ = 16–36 (sublingual)	Partial agonist combined with an antagonist	30
Codeine	Oral	Every 3–6 hours T½ = 2.9–3.6	Agonist	0.15
Fentanyl (prescription) (Actiq®, Duragesic®, Sublimaze®)	Transdermal/ patch, oral (lozenge), injection	Oral: unclear Injection: every 4 hours Patch: every 72 hours T½ = 3.7–4.1	Agonist	Transdermal 2.4–7.2
Fentanyl (illicit/street) (Acetyl fentanyl, butyl fentanyl, feranyl fentanyl, ocfentanil, 3-methyl fentanyl, valeryl fentanyl, sulfentanil, carfentanil—the elephant tranquilizer)	Available in a variety of forms, often disguised as a pill or sold as heroin	Short acting to ultra-short acting Variable T½, some less than 2 hours	Agonist	50 to more than 10,000 times more potent than morphine for carfentanil
Heroin	Snorted, injected, smoked	Every 4–8 hours T½ = +/– 4 hours	Agonist	Dependent on the purity
Hydrocodone (Vicodin®, Lortab®, Lorcet®)	Oral	Every 4–6 hours T½ = 4.2–8	Agonist	1
Hydromorphone (Dilaudid®)	Oral, rectal (suppository), intravenous	Every 3–4 hours T½ = 2.4–3	Agonist	4

(Continued)

Substance	How Used	Dosing Frequency and Half-Life (T½)*	Type	Potency* in Morphine Milligram Equivalents Oral Morphine = 1
Methadone (Dolophine®, Amidone, Methadose™)	Oral	Once a day T½ = 27–39 hours	Agonist	Dosage base 1–20mg/day = 4 21–40mg/day = 8 41–60mg/day = 10 ≥61–80mg/day = 12
Meperidine (Demerol®)	Oral, Intravenous	Every 2–3 hours T½ = 3.2–4	Agonist	0.1
Morphine (Kadian®, Avinza®)	Oral, intravenous	Immediate release: every 3–4 hours Slow release: every 8–12 T½ = 1.9–2.4	Agonist	1
Opium	Smoked	Every 4–6 hours T½ = 2–3	Agonist	1
Oxycodone (OxyContin®, Roxicodone®, Roxicet™, Percocet®, Percodan®, etc.)	Oral	Immediate release: every 3–4 hours Sustained release (OxyContin): every 8–12 hours T½ = 2.1–3.1	Agonist	1.5
Propoxyphene (Darvocet®, Darvon)	Oral	Every 3–4 hours T½ = 6–12	Agonist	.05
Sufentanil	Intravenous	Every 2–4 hours T½ = +/– 2.5	Agonist	500
Tramadol (Ultram®, ConZip™, Ryzolt®)	Oral	Every 4–6 hours T½ = 4.5–7.5	Agonist	0.1

*Potencies and half-lives are averages and do not account for individual variation.

(receptors and the molecules themselves). Studies in both humans and animals show that when ingested opioids are stopped, the production of endogenous opioids does not resume quickly, and might never returns to its prior status. This has implications for the experience of protracted post-acute withdrawals, and the high likelihood for relapse, even after extended lengths of abstinence.

Opioid Receptors: Opioids bind to specific receptors throughout the body in a lock-and-key way. This is a useful model to keep in mind as we discuss how various opioids bind, inhibit, antagonize, block, and otherwise compete for the receptor.

Receptor Types:

- Delta—Produces analgesia. Enhances mood (anxiety and depression).

- Mu—Produces analgesia. Enhances mood. Activates central dopamine reward system. Euphoric effects. (The mu receptors are those most associated with the rewarding effects of opioids.)

- Kappa—Stress-induced analgesia. Associated with emotional changes, including sadness/dysphoria. Of interest to researchers as it is less associated with some of the actions of the mu receptor, including respiratory depression and mood enhancement.

- Like-1 (ORL1/nociceptin)—Most recently identified receptor type.

Analgesia: Relief from pain.

Narcotic: This carries two broad meanings. It refers to opioids and their ability to dull the senses, alleviate pain, and in high enough doses induce sleep, coma, and death. Another broader definition refers to any drug, such as illicit opioids, cannabis, cocaine, and the like, which are regulated and restricted due to their potentials for addiction and abuse.

Dependence: This term carries both psychological and physiologic meanings. In regard to opioids, dependence occurs when an individual stops the substance and within an expected time frame experiences withdrawal symptom. The withdrawal resembles a serious case of the flu accompanied by mild to profound emotional distress. Dependence and tolerance to opioids can develop within weeks of habitual use.

Tolerance: Over time, individuals who habitually take opioids will require higher doses to achieve the same effect. For some, who initially turned to opioids for their euphoric, antidepressant, and anxiolytic effects, these may no longer be achievable. Tolerance is a major cause of progression in patterns of usage. Typically, people begin with pills, then progress to snorting, skin-popping (shooting drugs under the skin), and intravenous use, or to the deliberate pursuit of potent, and dangerous, fentanyl.

For pain relief, tolerance means a person needs to take a higher dose to achieve the same effect.

Opioid Agonist/Pure Agonist: These substances act directly on the opiate receptor and have no ceiling effect. This means that if taken in high enough doses, a person will eventually stop breathing. Pure agonists include: heroin, oxycodone, fentanyl, morphine, opium, methadone, and hydromorphone, among others.

Partial Opioid Agonist: This substance provides some of the typical opioid effect (pain relief, prevention of withdrawal symptoms), but when taken in higher doses it has a ceiling effect and will not lead to respiratory depression unless combined with other central nervous system depressants, such as alcohol, benzodiazepines, and certain sleeping medications. Buprenorphine (Suboxone, Subutex, Zubsolv) is a partial opioid agonist.

Opioid Blockers: These substances bind/block the opiate receptor and prevent other opioids from being able to bind. Naltrexone and naltrexone XR (Revia and Vivitrol) are opioid blockers, but are not opioids. The medication buprenorphine, which is also a partial agonist, has some blocking capabilities as well.

Antagonists: Like a blocker, these substances occupy the receptor so that if a person takes an opioid it cannot bind to the site. Their antagonist property is that they can displace an opioid from the receptor. Naloxone (Narcan), the medication used to reverse overdoses, is an opioid antagonist. Naltrexone and naltrexone XR (Revia and Vivitrol) also have antagonist properties, and when used as a form of medication-assisted treatment (MAT, discussed later) the individual must be fully detoxed from opioids prior to their initiation. If they are not, the medication will precipitate withdrawal.

SCHEDULED DRUGS

Controlled substances in the United States are scheduled by the DEA according to their perceived risk for dependence and misuse. A complete alphabetical list can be accessed online through the DEA at: https://www.deadiversion.usdoj.gov/schedules/orangebook/c_cs_alpha.pdf

Schedule I drugs: These are substances deemed by the government to have no medical purpose and a high potential for abuse. They include heroin, LSD, cannabis, peyote, and 3,4-methylenedioxymethamphetamine (ecstasy/Molly).

Schedule II drugs: These are prescription medications that carry a high risk for tolerance, dependence, and misuse. They include: oxycodone, codeine, hydrocodone, morphine, fentanyl, sufentanil, and stimulants prescribed for ADHD.

Schedule III drugs: These substances are considered to have moderate to low risks for tolerance, dependence, and abuse. They include medications with less than 90mg of codeine per dose, ketamine, anabolic steroids, and testosterone.

Schedule IV drugs: These are considered to have a low risk for dependence. However, this is inaccurate as the list includes the benzodiazepines and prescription sleeping medications, as well as tramadol, all of which are known to have significant risks for dependence, tolerance, and misuse. In combination with opioids these have contributed to tens of thousands of deaths.

Schedule V drugs: These are considered to have the lowest risk for dependence, and include substances to treat diarrhea and cough, such as prescribed Robitussin® with codeine, and diphenoxylate (Lomotil®)—a potent antidiarrheal.

Neurodevelopment and the Hijacking of the Dopamine Reward System

At birth, we have more brain cells (neurons/gray matter) than at any point in our lives. As we develop and learn to suckle, crawl, walk, use a toilet, and talk, our brain cells form connections and pathways through their axons and dendrites (synapses). Nerve cells that are not used die back, as do unused axons and dendrites (synaptic pruning). As behaviors become reinforced, the high-fat white matter (myelin) wraps around the circuitry like an electric insulator to enhance the speed and efficiency of firing and transmission. An expression that describes this process is, "Nerves that fire together, wire together."

This tremendous neural opportunity accounts for why children at young ages can learn to speak multiple languages, play musical instruments, and master skills at sports that they will never have the same facility to acquire when they are adults.

This process of neural development, pruning back of gray matter and reinforcement of white matter, continues through adolescence and into young adulthood. The last portions of the human brain that become fully wired are the frontal and prefrontal cortices. These are portions of the brain that involve:

- Reasoning and problem solving, which include the synthesis of diverse sensory, emotional, and other information, such as prior experience.

- Perception, how we perceive the world and others.

- Reflective delay, which is the balance between impulsive action and weighing possible consequences. "Gee, I'd love to jump that fence and go for a swim, but maybe I shouldn't because I could get arrested."

The above bulleted items are the final pieces of learning on our way to becoming fully formed adults. These are the developmental tasks adolescents and young adults have not yet completed. These account for much of the behavior we see in young people, where reasoning is often more black and white, extreme, creative, and volatile. This is further complicated by the fact that once we've hit puberty, we have adult levels of sex hormones and the physical, behavioral, and emotional changes that come with higher levels of testosterone for boys, and the cyclic patterns of estrogen and progesterone for girls. A metaphor for this surge of hormones in a not-fully-developed brain might be like having a Maserati with no brakes.

THE DOPAMINE REWARD SYSTEM (MESO-LIMBIC PATHWAY)

The underpinnings of addictive disorders, ones where a person compulsively engages in a behavior despite known negative consequences, are tied to deep-brain structures, which provide the experience of pleasure (hedonic impulse) through the release of the neurotransmitter, dopamine. Referred to as the "reward system," or meso-limbic pathway, this neural circuitry likely evolved so that we would experience pleasure from a good meal, from sex, and from human interaction—things vital to our survival. As these connections between behavior and reward are made, they develop into deeply rooted memories and the desired activities (eating, procreation, and forming and maintaining relationships) are reinforced.

However, substances that we experience as pleasurable, including nicotine, alcohol, opioids, cocaine, methamphetamine, and so forth, activate these dopamine-rich cells through various mechanisms. In the case of opioids, these dopaminergic neurons have receptors that clearly recognize the morphine molecule, and ones that look similar. Once bound to these receptors, dopamine is released, and we experience euphoria and other pleasurable emotional and physiologic symptoms, which can include sexual arousal, and diminished anxiety and depression. In time, what starts as a learning process, "Gee, snorting oxycodone feels awesome," creates cellular (synaptic) changes to where the snorting of oxycodone is a hardwired memory.

The earlier someone accesses the reward system for things other than food or sex the more deeply entrained memories become to continue to engage in these pleasurable activities. Studies show that, regardless of the substance, early use carries a greater risk for later substance-use disorder. So too, from a public health perspective, the later you can delay any substance use, including tobacco, the lower the risk that a person will develop a use disorder. While the notion of "gateway drugs" has its detractors, there are few who find their way to habitual opioid use and misuse, who didn't have early experience with alcohol, marijuana, and/or nicotine, including vaping.

CHAPTER 3

The Face of the Epidemic and Those at Greatest Risk

- **Overview and Statistics**
- **Risk Factors for Developing an Opioid Use Disorder**
- **Adverse Childhood Experiences Score (ACES)**
- **Overdose Statistics**
- **Those at the Greatest Risk for Overdose**

OVERVIEW AND STATISTICS

Our current opioid and overdose epidemic, for a variety of reasons, has hit middle- and small-town America hard. This is not a problem of just inner cities, or people from lower socioeconomic status. It's the high school football player, his mother, grandmother, and the girl who babysits his kid sister. A review of the medical examiner's website from my home state of Connecticut shows nearly every town, including tiny hamlets, have had recent overdose deaths. Rich and poor alike are fair game, and the infusion of potent, inexpensive, and lethal fentanyl has fanned the current fire.

While overall trends in drug use have decreased since a peak in the 1960s opioids are the exception. In SAMHSA's 2016 National Survey on Drug Use and Health (NSDUH), it was reported that 11.8 million Americans aged 12 and older (4.4% of the total population) misused opioids. The majority, 11.5 million (97.4%), misused prescription medications, while a much smaller number, 948,000 (8%), misused heroin. And some used both.

While over 90% of people who meet criteria for a substance-use disorder will never seek treatment, these numbers are different for those who misuse opioids. NSDUH data show one in five people with an opioid use disorder received some form of treatment for it in the preceding 12 months. This broke down to 37.5% of heroin users and 17.5% of people with prescription pain medication misuse. These higher numbers reflect the severity of opioid use disorders, and the desperation they can engender. Opioids are unique among drugs. They have the power to bring euphoric highs, but as they wear off, they punish the user with a crushing withdrawal. The answer to the *dope sickness*, is the next pill line, or needle; in what can be a very short time, tolerance, dependence, and the cycle of addiction become rooted.

As is shown in the chart below, the majority of people with opioid use disorders use prescription pills. This speaks to the truism that opioid use disorders start in the medicine cabinet and not on the street. The following chart, based on 2013 NSDUH/SAMHSA data, pulls this into clarity, where over 50% of people who misused opioids got them for free from a friend or family member. These numbers have remained consistent with more recent surveys.

Heroin use has seen a steady increase since 2002. This is fueled by more stringent and restrictive prescribing guidelines for pain medications, the low cost of heroin—often laced with fentanyl—and an overall increase in the number of people who misuse opioids.

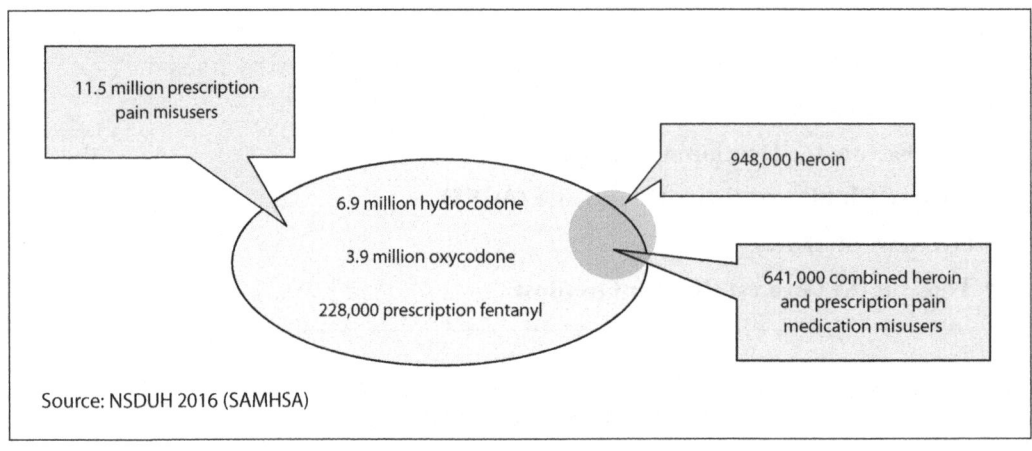

Source: NSDUH 2016 (SAMHSA)

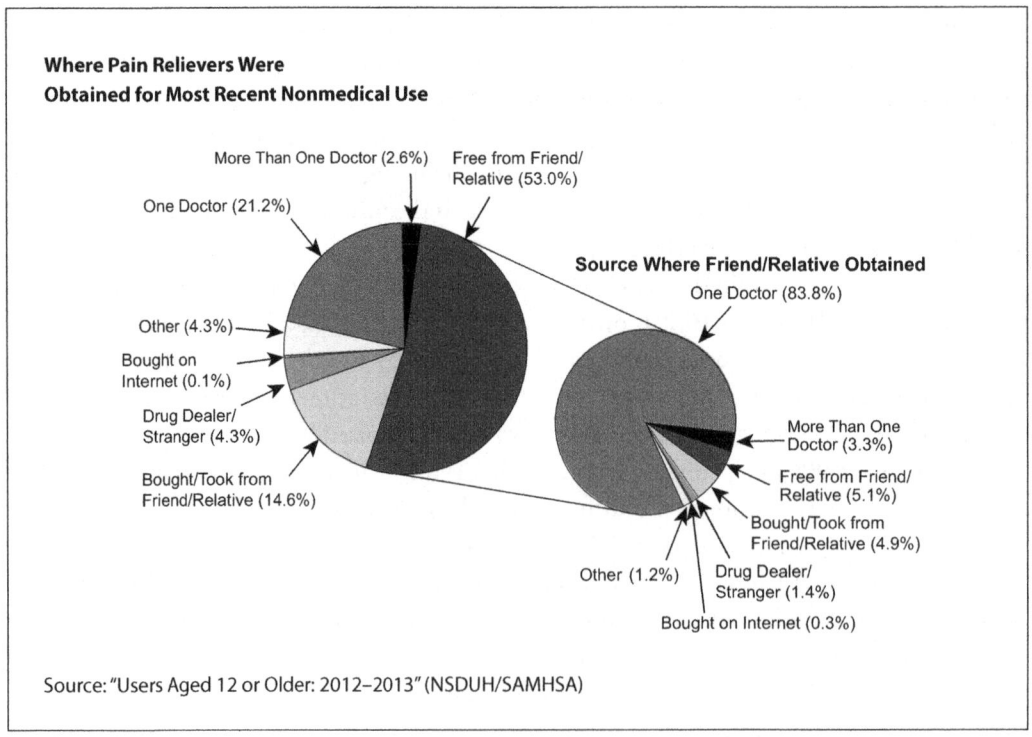

Source: "Users Aged 12 or Older: 2012–2013" (NSDUH/SAMHSA)

The most dramatic increases have been among young adults ages 18–25. Other key statistics include:

- 2016 saw 63,600 overdose deaths, with 42,419 involving opioids.

- From 1999–2016, the rate of overdose death increased from 6.1 per 100,000 people to 19.8.

    - Over this same period the rate for men increased from 8.2 to 26.2, and for women from 3.9 to 13.4.

- Those with the highest rates of death were aged 25–34 (34.6 per 100,000), 35–44 (35.0), and 45–54 (34.5).

- From 1999–2016, rates of overdose death involving synthetic opioids other than methadone (fentanyl, tramadol) increased from 0.3 per 100,000 to 6.2 per 100,000.

Risk Factors for Developing an Opioid Use Disorder

There is no single profile of a person with an opioid use disorder, though there are trends. Opioid use disorders cross all socioeconomic, racial, and age barriers. While certain groups carry an increased risk, there are many grieving parents who correctly identify that their dead son or daughter had no obvious risk factors, other than associating with friends who were getting high and introduced them to opioids.

Risk factors include:

- Gender. Men are twice as likely to develop any substance-use disorder than women, although with respect to opioids, women have been catching up.

- People with mental health problems are at greater risk for all substance-use disorders.

- People with a high number of adverse childhood experiences (ACEs). This is a list of 10 adverse events experienced before the age of 18 (see the following questionnaire). The number a person has experienced is their ACEs score.

- People prescribed opioids for an injury.

- Early age of substance initiation. Data shows that regardless of the substance, including tobacco and vaping, the younger a person begins to use, the greater their risk for developing a later substance-use disorder, including opioid use disorders.

- People prescribed opioids before the age of 18 are at increased risk for opioid use disorders.

- People on long-term use of opioids for chronic (non-cancer or palliative) pain are at increased risk.

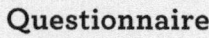
Adverse Childhood Experiences (ACEs)

Know Your ACEs Score

Prior to your 18th birthday:

1. Did a parent or other adult in the household often or very often: Swear at you, insult you, put you down, or humiliate you? Or act in a way that made you afraid that you might be physically hurt?

    No___ If Yes, enter 1 ___

2. Did a parent or other adult in the household often or very often: Push, grab, slap, or throw something at you? Or ever hit you so hard that you had marks or were injured?

    No___ If Yes, enter 1 ___

3. Did an adult or person at least five years older than you ever: Touch or fondle you or have you touch their body in a sexual way? Or attempt or actually have oral, anal, or vaginal intercourse with you?

    No___ If Yes, enter 1 ___

4. Did you often or very often feel that: No one in your family loved you or thought you were important or special? Or your family didn't look out for each other, feel close to each other, or support each other?

    No___ If Yes, enter 1 ___

5. Did you often or very often feel that: You didn't have enough to eat, had to wear dirty clothes, and had no one to protect you? Or your parents were too drunk or high to take care of you or take you to the doctor if you needed it?

    No___ If Yes, enter 1 ___

Copyright © 2018 Charles Atkins. *Opioid Use Disorders*. All rights reserved.

6. Were your parents ever separated or divorced?

    No___ If Yes, enter 1 __

7. Was your mother or stepmother: Often or very often pushed, grabbed, slapped, or had something thrown at her? Or sometimes, often, or very often kicked, bitten, hit with a fist, or hit with something hard? Or ever repeatedly hit over at least a few minutes or threatened with a gun or knife?

    No___ If Yes, enter 1 __

8. Did you live with anyone who was a problem drinker or alcoholic, or who used street drugs?

    No___ If Yes, enter 1 __

9. Was a household member depressed or mentally ill, or did a household member attempt suicide?

    No___ If Yes, enter 1 __

10. Did a household member go to prison?

    No___ If Yes, enter 1 __

Now add up your "Yes" answers: _____ This is your ACEs score.

Copyright © 2018 Charles Atkins. *Opioid Use Disorders*. All rights reserved.

ACEs scores of 4 or more (and it doesn't matter which 4) carry higher rates for various physical and emotional problems, including substance use, obesity, and suicide. As scores go higher, so too does the risk for an opioid use disorder. The Centers for Disease Control (CDC) maintains a robust ACES website that tracks dozens of variables related to physical, social, and mental health: https://www.cdc.gov/violenceprevention/acestudy/index.html.

OVERDOSE STATISTICS

According to the CDC there has been a fivefold increase in overdose deaths involving opioids between 1999–2016, with 42,249 reported in 2016. In the same year, total overdose deaths were reported at an all-time high at 64,070. This record was broken with over 70,000 in 2017.

There is tremendous state-to-state variability in overdose rates, the five highest in 2016 being: West Virginia, Ohio, New Hampshire, Pennsylvania, and Kentucky.

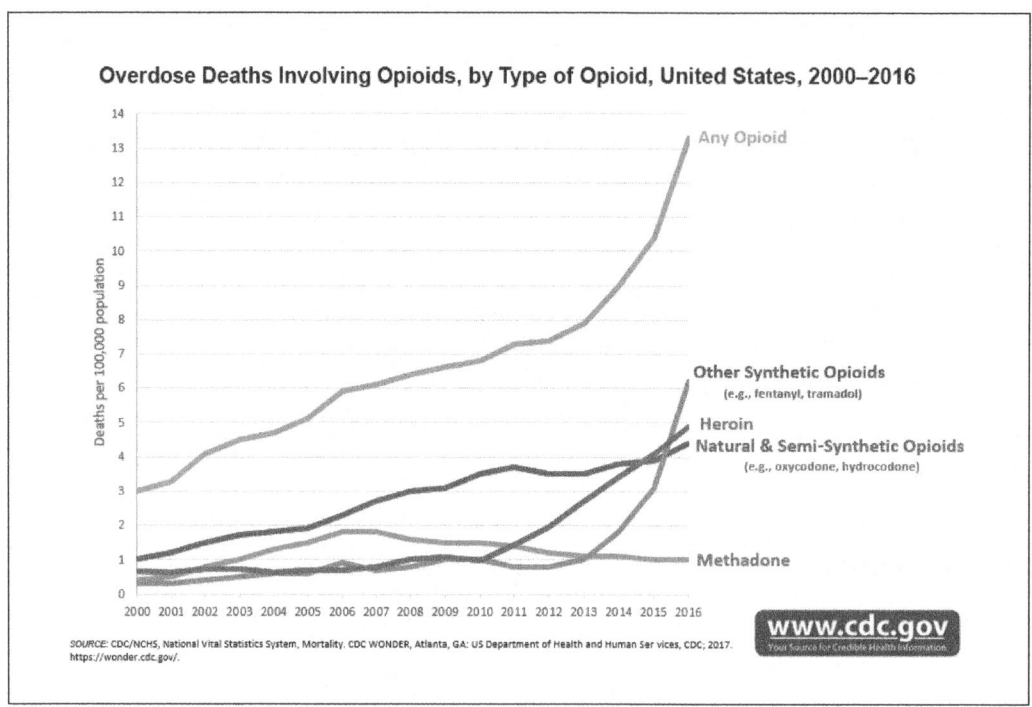

THOSE AT THE GREATEST RISK FOR OVERDOSE

As we review the statistics, clear trends emerge on those at highest risk:

- People with opioid use disorders who have been incarcerated. People who have been incarcerated typically have lost their tolerance and are at great risk for relapse and fatal overdose following their release. Few states and facilities offer treatment for individuals with opioid use disorders while they are in jail or prison. Current practices, which are not ideal, include rapidly detoxing individuals with methadone when they are incarcerated. The notable exception is that pregnant women may be maintained on MAT until after they deliver.

- People leaving detox and residential facilities. Here again, if the person has been taken off all opioids and is not on a blocker, the risk for relapse and overdose is high. There may be an added risk for those who leave treatment early and/or against medical advice.

- People with mental health problems. Overdose deaths are higher in individuals with opioid use disorders combined with one or more mental health diagnoses.

- People on higher doses of prescribed opioids. Greater than 90MMEs/day is associated with greatly increased risk for overdose death.

- People who take prescription opioids in combination with other central nervous system depressants, including the benzodiazepines, alcohol, and prescription sleeping medications.

- People with a prior history of an overdose reversal. A recent study from Massachusetts reported that 10% of people who had received an overdose reversal with naloxone (Narcan) were dead within 12 months.

- New users. People who are naïve to opioids who inadvertently take a lethal dose.

CHAPTER 4

Making the Diagnosis: The DSM-5 and Beyond

- **Overview**
- **The Diagnosis**
- **WHO's Criteria, International Classification of Diseases-10 (ICD-10), for Substance Dependence (Opioids and Other Substances)**
- **The DSM-5® and Opioid Use Disorders**
- **Signs and Symptoms of Opioid Withdrawal, and Opioid Use**
- **Opioid Overdose**

OVERVIEW

In this chapter we'll review the broad strokes for making a diagnosis of an opioid use disorder. We'll review the signs and symptoms of withdrawal, intoxication, and overdose, which include physical, emotional, and behavioral components.

For clinicians, people with opioid use disorders, and their families, a basic understanding of symptoms can alert you to signs of a relapse, withdrawal, intoxication, and a potential overdose. I wish I knew earlier in my career how opioid withdrawal manifests, as I would have been better equipped to help people who were suffering.

At this point, I can walk into any emergency room or inpatient unit and identify the person who is opioid-dependent but has not divulged that to the treatment team. They're at the nurse's station begging for something to help them feel better. Their pupils are bright and wide, their nose and eyes are runny, and they've wrapped a sheet around their shoulders to try and stop the chills, as sweat streams down their face. They're anxious, desperate and miserable, and complain of a variety of physical symptoms, from abdominal cramps and muscle aches to nausea, vomiting, and diarrhea.

As you read this, in the context of a book on opioids, you might think, "of course they're in withdrawal." But in that busy emergency room, or inpatient medical or psychiatric unit, their symptoms are written off to other things, including that old chestnut: "drug-seeking behavior." Recognizing withdrawal and other states, such as an overdose, may not always be obvious, especially when it's not known that the person uses opioids. But when a person with undiagnosed and untreated withdrawal signs out against medical advice from an emergency room or hospital ward, after they've been admitted for a life-threatening bacterial endocarditis or a methicillin-resistant cellulitis, the outcome is often tragic.

THE DIAGNOSIS

The two major diagnostic systems in use in the United States are the WHO ICD-10, and the American Psychiatric Association's DSM-5—which will be summarized. (For the actual DSM-5 criteria, the reader is referred to that manual.) With both systems, in the absence of adequate information to make the requisite number of criteria for a diagnosis, clinical judgment can tip things one way or another. This becomes useful in various scenarios:

- The person denies use, despite compelling objective data to the contrary: track marks, opioid-positive drug screen, old records documenting an opioid use disorder.

- The person has an altered mental status, is unresponsive, or comatose, and there is adequate corroborating information to make the diagnosis.

WHO's CRITERIA, INTERNATIONAL CLASSIFICATION OF DISEASES-10 (ICD-10), FOR SUBSTANCE DEPENDENCE (OPIOIDS AND OTHER SUBSTANCES)

Three or more must have been present at the same time during the previous 12 months for a diagnosis:

- Strong urges or compulsions to use the substance.

- Trouble controlling substance-based behaviors, such as amount of use, duration of use, and initiation of use.

- Withdrawal symptoms develop when the substance is not taken, or taken in a lower amount. And/or use of the same, or a similar substance, to decrease withdrawal symptoms, such as:

  - Purchasing illicit buprenorphine to decrease withdrawal from heroin or another opioid.

  - A person with an alcohol-use disorder who needs an "eye opener" to stop the shakes.

- Tolerance. Higher amounts are needed to achieve a similar effect. (Especially true for opioids and alcohol.) This can be extreme to where a tolerant individual now requires a dose that might kill a nonuser.

- Usual pursuits and interests are decreased or stopped altogether due to time needed to obtain the substance, or to recover from its effects.

- A parent who nods off (falls asleep/goes unconscious due to the opioids) and is unable to attend to their newborn.

- Loss of employment due to being high on the job or not showing up at all.

- Substance use continues despite awareness of negative consequences, such as recurrent overdoses, liver damage, cognitive impairment, or other physical harm. (Here the distinction is added that the individual is aware of the existence and extent of the damage.)

THE DSM-5 AND OPIOID USE DISORDERS

In the United States, the American Psychiatric Association's DSM-5 continues to be the standard diagnostic manual for psychiatric and substance-use disorders. DSM diagnoses are then paired with ICD-10 (WHO) alphanumeric codes. There are 11 criteria for opioid use disorders in the current manual that cover the physiologic, cognitive, and behavioral symptoms. Of note, the two criteria related to physiologic tolerance and dependence should not be counted toward a diagnosis in a person prescribed opioids for pain or another medical condition, and taking them appropriately.

Major changes between the DSM-IV-TR and the DSM-5 are as follows:

- The terms "abuse" and "dependence" have been replaced by severity criteria of mild (2–3 criteria), moderate (4–5), and severe (6 or more).

  - Mild corresponds to the ICD-10 code for "abuse."

  - Moderate and severe code for "dependence."

- The criterion related to legal problems due to opioid misuse has been eliminated.

- A criterion has been added for cravings/urges to use.

SIGNS AND SYMPTOMS OF OPIOID WITHDRAWAL, AND OPIOID USE

Withdrawal is often likened to a severe case of influenza (the flu). In many ways the signs and symptoms of use and withdrawal are opposites. The following table lays out the common signs and symptoms of both. Metrics, such as the Clinical Opioid Withdrawal Scale (COWS) and Subjective Opioid Withdrawal Scale (SOWS), to measure signs and symptoms of withdrawal will be reviewed in the MAT chapter.

Signs and Symptoms of Opioid Withdrawal and Intoxication

Signs and Symptoms	Withdrawal	Intoxication
Gastrointestinal	Nausea, vomiting, cramping, diarrhea	Constipation (can be severe and progress to bowel obstruction)
Pupil size	Wide pupils (can obliterate the colored part [iris] of the eye [mydriasis])	Pinpoint pupils (miosis)
Respirations	Rapid rate	Decreased rate (in overdoses it can become loud, snoring, gasping and eventually stop altogether)
Skin	Sweating, gooseflesh	Dry (there may be scratching and evidence of needle marks [tracks] scars from old abscesses, or redness from active cellulitis)
Tremor	Yes	No
Bone or joint aches	Yes	No
Runny nose	Yes	No
Tearing	Yes	No
Yawning	Yes	Possible (may be sleepy, nodding off)
Mood	Anxious, depressed, irritable, angry	Calm, happy, euphoric
Behavior	Restless, agitated	Calm to sleepy, depending on dose and tolerance
Level of alertness	Alert	From normal, to nodding off, to unconscious, unarousable, and comatose
Hot and/or cold flushes	Yes	No
Muscle twitches	Yes	No
Cravings/Urges to use	Yes	Variable

Copyright © 2018 Charles Atkins. *Opioid Use Disorders*. All rights reserved.

OPIOID OVERDOSE

An opioid overdose is a medical emergency that, if not treated—typically with naloxone (Narcan)—can result in coma, respiratory and vascular collapse, and death. Signs and symptoms of an overdose, especially in the setting of potent fentanyl, oxycodone, heroin, and mixed-drug overdoses, can occur in a matter of minutes.

- Breathing becomes shallow, gasping, snoring, and then ceases.

- Lips and nail beds can turn blue or gray from the lack of oxygen.

- The person becomes increasingly lethargic and sedated. Speech may be slurred and they may act confused. This can progress to unresponsiveness, unconsciousness, and coma.

- Pupils are pinpoint.

- Muscular rigidity, especially of the torso, in some instances.

CHAPTER 5

Opioids and Pain Management

- My Only Relief Is a Tiny Blue Pill
- Overview
- What Is Pain?
- Emotional and Physical Components of Chronic Pain
- Chronic Pain, Opioids and the Path to Tolerance, Dependence, and Addiction
- The Opioid Myth and Mystique
- Facts and Figures on Chronic Pain and Opioids
- The *CDC Guideline for Prescribing Opioids for Chronic Pain—United States, 2016*
- Non-Pharmacologic and Integrative Approaches to Pain
- Case Study and Discussion

MY ONLY RELIEF IS A TINY BLUE PILL
ELEANOR A. SORENSEN'S STORY

As a recovering addict who deals with chronic pain, I can say there's a fine line to becoming a martyr. How and when does one decide that their quality of life is so bad that they're willing to go back to what it was that almost killed them the first time?

I am a much stronger person today. I have a great network of people in my life. I am responsible for myself today. Using just isn't in my thought process anymore and I think I'm at a great place in my recovery.

However, this chronic pain that I deal with because of two rods that were placed in my back when I was 12, and the spinal stenosis and bone deterioration that they won't operate on because of the rods ... I've held out so long 'cause I just don't want to take another opiate and become dependent on them. But then there's the pain. The pain that interrupts my sleep, that inhibits me from being able to get up and walk first thing in the morning. The pain that drives me to tears 'cause it's so constant, and I don't get a break from it and I don't know what else to do but to cry 'cause I've gotta release it somehow. The pain that I fear may drive me completely mad if I don't get a break from it. But ... the only relief I can find comes in the form of a tiny, little blue pill, prescribed by my doctor who is fully aware that I am an addict.

OVERVIEW

As discussed in Chapter 1, the evolution of our current opioid epidemic is due in a large part to the overprescribing of oxycodone, hydrocodone, and other opioids for the treatment of chronic pain. This occurred in the absence of evidence to support the long-term use of these highly addicting compounds for conditions such as back pain, arthritis, sciatica, and migraines. There continue to be no good studies to support this practice and substantial evidence that supports the dangers of chronic opioid use: dependence, tolerance, diminished quality of life, diminished functional capacity, opioid-induced hyperalgesia, risk for overdose and death. While the above is true, it's important to remember that opioids are potent tools in the treatment of cancer and end-of-life palliative care. This distinction became blurred, as pain of any sort turned into the fifth vital sign, and it became the right of every patient and the duty of every physician to medicate the hurt away until the face on the 10-point scale was smiling and serene.

Additionally, in this chapter we'll review non-pharmacologic and integrative—what used to be called "complementary and alternative medicine" (CAM)—strategies shown to be effective in reducing pain, including physical therapy, cognitive behavioral therapy (CBT), mindfulness, prayer, and exercise.

What Is Pain?

To start, we need to understand pain. On the surface there might appear to be a simple answer, but our experience of pain is complex. It involves both what is perceived through pain receptors at the site of injury, as well as the pathways by which the experiences of pain—both emotional and physical—are transmitted and processed in our brains.

There is acute and chronic pain. In the first we can usually identify its source, such as a splinter or touching a hot stove. Special nerve endings (nociceptors) are triggered and transmit the information up our spinal column to related areas in the brain. This gets processed as a warning and we remove the splinter before it becomes infected or take our hand off the burner. With chronic pain (three months and beyond—some experts put this as greater than six months), the underlying source may or may not be identifiable, and the experience of daily pain, its severity and duration, can negatively impact a person's quality of life and ability to function. Chronic pain, as opposed to acute, persists beyond when one would expect healing to have occurred, and can be thought of as a medical condition, as opposed to a symptom of an injury.

Another dimension of pain to consider is that it is subjective. There are no machines or tests to accurately measure its severity. Pain is what the person experiencing it says it is. Which brings us to suffering. A person can experience moderate to severe pain with or without suffering. "I just have to deal with it," versus, "I can't stand this."

Types of pain can be lumped into three large categories:

Nociceptive (mechanical)	Pain from identifiable injury, such as a burn, cut, or broken limb.
Neuropathic (radiating/ radicular pain)	Pain from a lesion or abnormal firing of the sensory nervous system, such as from a compressed or injured nerve. The pain may be experienced at the site of injury or along the path of a particular nerve, as is seen with sciatica, compressed discs, and other radiating pain syndromes (radicular pain).
Mixed Nociceptive/ Neuropathic	This is where both forms of pain occur simultaneously. A person with a disc injury may experience pain both at the site of the compression and along the path(s) of the affected nerve(s).

EMOTIONAL AND PHYSICAL COMPONENTS OF CHRONIC PAIN

Chronic pain, depending on its source and site, can contribute to a host of negative health and emotional outcomes. These include insomnia, diminished appetite and weight loss, anxiety, depression, decreased physical activity, suicidality, and impaired social and occupational functioning. All the above may lead a person to seek sedating, numbing, and mood-enhancing medications even if the benefits are short-lived.

CHRONIC PAIN, OPIOIDS AND THE PATH TO TOLERANCE, DEPENDENCE, AND ADDICTION

Through some behavioral lenses, opioids are both positive and negative reinforcers. A person in pain takes an opioid and experiences the reward of having the pain relieved, as well as mood-altering effects, which can include euphoria and calm. Over time, the same dose is no longer effective as tolerance develops. To again experience relief and a sense of well-being, the person takes a higher dose, but soon becomes faced with the additional dilemma of withdrawal. To prevent this negative outcome, an opioid must be taken (negative reinforcement). As doses escalate it becomes unclear as to what is being treated, an underlying pain syndrome, which may or may not have resolved, or opioid dependence.

To further complicate things is the development of opioid-induced hyperalgesia (OIH). This is a magnified pain sensitivity common with people on long-term opioids. Not only is the person now dependent on opioids, but the underlying experience of pain is magnified. The underlying cause(s) of OIH are not fully understood, but likely involve neurophysiologic changes that occur with people on long-term opioids.

THE OPIOID MYTH AND MYSTIQUE

There is a general, and misguided, belief among the public and even healthcare providers, that opioids are the most effective medications for severe and chronic pain. They are not. A combination of acetaminophen and ibuprofen is. However, opioids, with their additional mood-altering and euphoria-inducing benefits, are important and crucial in the treatment of cancer, end-of-life palliative care, and acute pain syndromes (post-surgery, post-trauma).

As we look at the relative risks and benefits of opioids, combined with minimal evidence to support their efficacy to treat chronic pain, a balance must be struck. So too, the non-steroidal pain medications (NSAIDs), and aspirin, are not free from potential side effects and adverse reactions. They can all cause gastrointestinal symptoms, including ulcers and kidney problems. Acetaminophen (Tylenol®) should be avoided in someone with liver disease and can be dangerous, and even fatal, when taken as an overdose. NSAIDs elevate the risk of cardiovascular events.

This chapter will look at recent guidelines from the CDC for the prescribing of opioids. While geared toward physicians and others licensed to prescribe opioids, these represent the current direction and, with minor variations, are supported by other consensus groups. While the days of getting 30 hydrocodone after having wisdom teeth pulled or having a pain-management doctor write a prescription for 90 long-acting oxycodone with two refills, are not over, they are on the wane. New statutes in many states limit the size of prescriptions, especially when starting a medication, and require the prescriber to check the Prescription

Drug Monitoring Program (PDMP) at initiation of an opioid (some now have this with any controlled substance) and periodically thereafter.

Facts and Figures on Chronic Pain and Opioids

Most people who currently misuse opioids began with prescription medications, whether prescribed or obtained from friends, family, or another source. For many, this started with opioids prescribed for pain. It also brings us to the baby-and-the-bathwater issue that opioids are important and powerful medications with legitimate uses. For those who begin with appropriately prescribed pain medication and advance to misuse, the line is often blurred.

Studies that have compared the efficacy of opioids to nonsteroidal medications have shown the following (efficacy is typically defined as a 50% reduction in pain):

- Dental pain
    - A review of the literature in the *Journal of the American Dental Association* found that following wisdom tooth extraction, a combination of 325mg of acetaminophen combined with 200mg of ibuprofen gave better pain relief than oral opioids.

- Back pain (including sciatica with pinched nerve, and degenerative disc disease, including herniation)
    - Patients on opioids were more likely to progress to surgery than those on nonsteroidals.
    - Patients started on opioids were more likely to remain on them for years.

- Kidney stone (often considered one of the most severe forms of pain)
    - The Cochrane report showed both opioids and nonsteroidals were effective, though a greater number of studies reported lower pain scores for the nonsteroidals.

- Chronic pain
    - More than 9 million Americans are being treated with opioids for chronic pain.
    - Numerous studies and literature reviews have found no good evidence to support the long-term (greater than four months) efficacy of opioids for chronic pain.

- Veterans
    - As many as 50% of male and 75% of female veterans report pain in primary care settings.

To address the appropriate prescribing of opioids for non-cancer, non-palliative, and non-end-of-life pain, several entities have published guidelines. The following 12 guidelines are from the *CDC Guideline for Prescribing Opioids for Chronic Pain—United States, 2016.*

(Handout)

Prescribing Opioids for Chronic Pain

The CDC recommendations for prescribing opioids for chronic pain outside of active cancer, palliative, and end-of-life care.

Determining When to Initiate or Continue Opioids for Chronic Pain

1. Non-pharmacologic therapy and non-opioid pharmacologic therapy are preferred for chronic pain. Clinicians should consider opioid therapy only if expected benefits for both pain and function are anticipated to outweigh risks to the patient. If opioids are used, they should be combined with non-pharmacologic therapy and non-opioid pharmacologic therapy, as appropriate.

2. Before starting opioid therapy for chronic pain, clinicians should establish treatment goals with all patients, including realistic goals for pain and function, and should consider how therapy will be discontinued if benefits do not outweigh risks. Clinicians should continue opioid therapy only if there is clinically meaningful improvement in pain and function that outweighs risks to patient safety.

3. Before starting—and periodically during—opioid therapy, clinicians should discuss with patients known risks and realistic benefits of opioid therapy and patient and clinician responsibilities for managing therapy.

Opioid Selection, Dosage, Duration, Follow-Up, and Discontinuation

4. When starting opioid therapy for chronic pain, clinicians should prescribe immediate-release opioids instead of extended-release/long-acting (ER/LA) opioids.

5. When opioids are started, clinicians should prescribe the lowest effective dosage. Clinicians should use caution when prescribing opioids at any dosage, should carefully reassess evidence of individual benefits and risks when increasing dosage to = 50 MME/day, and should avoid increasing dosage to = 90MME/day, or carefully justify a decision to titrate dosage to = 90MME/day.

6. Long-term opioid use often begins with treatment of acute pain. When opioids are used for acute pain, clinicians should prescribe the lowest effective dose of immediate-release opioids and should prescribe no greater quantity than needed for the expected duration of pain severe enough to require opioids. Three days or less will often be sufficient; more than seven days will rarely be needed.

Copyright © 2018 Charles Atkins. *Opioid Use Disorders*. All rights reserved.

7. Clinicians should evaluate benefits and harms with patients within one to four weeks of starting opioid therapy for chronic pain or of dose escalation. Clinicians should evaluate benefits and harms of continued therapy with patients every three months, or more frequently. If benefits do not outweigh harms of continued opioid therapy, clinicians should optimize other therapies and work with patients to taper opioids to lower dosages or to taper and discontinue opioids.

Assessing Risk and Addressing Harms of Opioid Use

8. Before starting—and periodically during continuation of—opioid therapy, clinicians should evaluate risk factors for opioid-related harms. Clinicians should incorporate into the management plan strategies to mitigate risk, including considering offering naloxone when factors that increase risk for opioid overdose, such as history of overdose, history of substance-use disorder, higher opioid dosages (= 50MME/day), or concurrent benzodiazepine use, are present.

9. Clinicians should review the patient's history of controlled substance prescriptions using state PDMP data to determine whether the patient is receiving opioid dosages or dangerous combinations that put him or her at high risk for overdose. Clinicians should review PDMP data when starting opioid therapy for chronic pain and periodically during opioid therapy for chronic pain, ranging from every prescription to every three months.

10. When prescribing opioids for chronic pain, clinicians should use urine drug testing before starting opioid therapy and consider urine drug testing at least annually to assess for prescribed medications as well as other controlled prescription drugs and illicit drugs.

11. Clinicians should avoid prescribing opioid pain medication and benzodiazepines concurrently whenever possible.

12. Clinicians should offer or arrange evidence-based treatment (usually MAT with buprenorphine or methadone in combination with behavioral therapies) for patients with an opioid use disorder.

All recommendations are category A (apply to all patients outside of active cancer treatment, palliative care, and end-of-life care) except recommendation 10 (designated category B, with individual decision making required); see full guideline for evidence ratings.

Copyright © 2018 Charles Atkins. *Opioid Use Disorders.* All rights reserved.

Non-Pharmacologic and Integrative Approaches to Pain

To finish out this chapter we'll discuss non-pharmacologic and integrative approaches to pain. This is not an exhaustive list and it's a good idea to ask your clients about what things they've tried, or currently use, to reduce pain. This open-ended approach and willingness to discuss wellness strategies, spirituality, and complementary and alternative therapies—which may include nutritional and herbal supplements—both validates their efforts at self-efficacy and provides an opportunity to explore and learn about emerging and, in some cases, ancient techniques to manage pain. It's important to remember that when discussing integrative therapies, it's not a question of one or the other, but both. Careful assessment of the cause(s) of pain, which may involve traditional western techniques such as imaging studies, should not be forgotten. The non-steroidal may be essential to handle pain from the acute injury while yoga, meditation, or CBT improves functioning and further diminishes the pain.

The evidence for integrative medicine in the treatment of chronic pain grows. This includes positive studies and meta-analyses (pooling of data from multiple studies) that demonstrate the benefits of:

- Cognitive behavioral therapy (CBT)

- Meditation

- Exercise

- Physical therapy

- Yoga

- Chiropractic

- Tai chi

- Qigong

- Acupuncture

- Prayer and spirituality

- Biofeedback

- Hypnosis

- Reiki

- Nondrug strategies to enhance restorative sleep

When making recommendations it's important to match the individual with what they are willing and able to do, as well as the condition(s) to be addressed. High-impact aerobics would not be a good choice for someone with knee problems. Is this someone who can commit to time in the gym, or daily meditation sessions? Does this person have the financial resources to see an acupuncturist or massage therapist? If not, perhaps there's a local school that has a student clinic with discounted or free services. Do they have insurance that covers a chiropractor?

Cognitive Behavioral Therapy

CBT is an effective strategy to manage the challenges associated with chronic pain, improve quality of life and functioning, and decrease the experience of pain. It employs an active, problem-solving approach. A manualized CBT specifically for veterans with pain identifies five key components to the therapy:

1. Exercise—walking program to increase involvement with valued activities.

2. Pacing—how to accomplish tasks in a thoughtful and sensible way.

3. Relaxation training—techniques to decrease stress and muscle tension.

4. Cognitive restructuring—identify unhelpful thoughts and increase balanced thinking.

5. Behavioral activation—increase engagement in rewarding and meaningful activities.

The entire therapist's manual, which includes handouts and worksheets, is available for free from the Department of Veterans Affairs at: https://www.va.gov/PAINMANAGEMENT/docs/CBT-CP_Therapist_Manual.pdf

Mindfulness Meditation

There is a robust literature on the benefits of mindfulness meditation. In the treatment chapter, we'll find mindfulness (at times going under different names such as "grounding technique") woven into many therapies including dialectic behavior therapy (DBT) and most manualized trauma treatments. The first contemporary researcher to explore the benefits of mindfulness meditation to address pain, including chronic and cancer pain, was Jon Kabat-Zinn. He lays out the framework for his eight-week mindfulness-based stress reduction program (MBSR) in his book, *Full Catastrophe Living: Using the Wisdom of Your Body and Mind to Face Stress, Pain, and Illness.*

Mindfulness meditation involves pulling oneself into the present moment, repeatedly. Various techniques are employed to develop this skill and quiet our chatty minds. In regard to pain, the meditator learns to observe the pain, but not to cling to it, as that moment comes and goes. In a mindfulness practice, the meditator learns to embrace their pain as an essential part of their experience. By relaxing into the pain, not avoiding it and not clinging to it, suffering is reduced. Beyond pain, studies show the benefits of mindfulness meditation in a broad range of behavioral-health domains, which include depression, anxiety, PTSD, and insomnia.

For those wishing to pursue a mindfulness practice, there needs to be a time (or times) set aside each day. In MBSR this is at least a 45-minute commitment six days/week. A standard meditation lasts 30 minutes. Formal exercises include:

- Seated meditation

- Meditation lying down

- Walking meditation

- Gentle stretching and movement with the breath (Hatha yoga)

While mindfulness starts in our heads, there is a rich body of evidence that supports the mind-body connection of a meditative practice and its ability to effect positive changes at cellular, chemical, and organ/organism levels. Evidence includes:

- Brain imagining studies that compared meditators to non-meditators showed increased gray matter in both deep-brain structures (hippocampus) and the frontal and pre-frontal cortices.

- Brain waves of meditators captured on electroencephalograms (EEGs) have increased alpha and theta waves, which correspond to states of rest and relaxation.

- Meditators after eight weeks of MBSR showed enhanced immune response over controls when given the influenza vaccine.

- There were diminished inflammatory proteins in people with breast and prostate cancer after MBSR—these results were still positive after one year.

- Meditators had decreased cortisol levels. (Cortisol is an integral part of our stress response. Animals and humans under chronic stress, and people with anxiety disorders and panic, have elevated levels of cortisol.)

- Meditators also had higher levels of serum nitrites and nitrates (anti-atherosclerotic plaque agents).

Exercise

Studies on the positive effects of exercise include both physical and emotional outcomes. Regular exercise improves strength, mobility, endurance, and flexibility. After a workout, feelings of accomplishment, well-being, and calm can have a direct and immediate effect on underlying anxiety, depression, and other negative emotional states. There is evidence to support the benefits of exercise in a myriad of conditions, such as low-back pain, fibromyalgia, migraine, arthritis, neck pain, heart disease, stroke, obesity, disturbed sleep from many causes, and even in delaying the onset of Alzheimer's.

Different forms of physical exercise have been reviewed and there is no clear indication for one form—aerobic, strength, martial arts including qigong, yoga, sports—over another. The length of time someone exercises does appear to matter, and the benefits may diminish under a half-hour session. My general rule is to encourage 45 minutes per day, and don't let two days go by in a row without doing something. This is a bit more than the American Heart Association and CDC's recommendations of 150 minutes/week of moderate exercise or 75 minutes/week of vigorous exercise to decrease the risk of heart attack and stroke.

Caution is advised prior to starting any exercise regimen, and direction from a physician, physical therapist, or other professional may be warranted. Key to studies that have shown positive benefits from exercise indicate that it needs to be ongoing and of adequate duration. Knowing about the benefits of exercise does little, but getting to the gym or doing some form of physical activity 45 minutes a day does a lot. As with all wellness activities, the establishment of routines—new habits—is important. How will you, or your client, weave exercise into what may be an already busy schedule? Is this someone who needs to go to a gym and get the added benefits of socialization? Or is this someone who does better at home with a yoga tape, stepper, or series of P90X videos? Perhaps they have a dog and the two of them could go for mutually satisfying brisk walks.

Finally, for people with opioid use disorders, exercise carries another theoretically important factor. When people take opioids in a chronic way, there is a reduction in both opiate receptors and the naturally occurring opioids discussed, which include the endorphins, dynorphins, and enkephalins. Exercise is associated with increased levels of endorphins, both in the central and peripheral nervous systems. While not well studied in people with opioid use disorders, one strategy for someone tapering off an opioid—including replacement therapies—would be to get moving … literally.

Physical Therapy

Physical therapy (PT) aids in the recovery from a wide range of both acute and chronic conditions that are often accompanied by pain. Strategies incorporate strength and range-of-motion exercises to improve overall functioning. As with exercise, practice and repetition are key.

PT may utilize other noninvasive strategies, such as transcutaneous electrical nerve stimulation (TENS), to try and lessen perceived pain.

A 20-year-old with Chronic Pain & Endometriosis

Jen is a 20-year-old premed sophomore at Q University. She is referred to the university's mental health clinic by her new gynecologist, Dr. Draven. He bought the practice from Jen's prior gynecologist, who retired. Dr. Draven became concerned when he reviewed Jen's profile on the state's PDMP. It showed monthly prescriptions for oxycodone over the last two years—all written by her previous gynecologist. But most of her refills had occurred two to seven days prior to when they should have run out. He also noted that Jen had contacted his office multiple time requesting early renewals.

At her most recent visit, she complained of severe and disabling endometriosis, for which she stated oxycodone was the only effective medication. "I barely make it out of bed." She is currently on 120mg/day and admits that, when the pain is severe, she may take "an extra pill or two."

Jen is unhappy to be at the mental health clinic and appears to be suffering with a cold. She only kept the appointment so she can be "cleared" to continue with her Oxycodone—which has nearly run out—and she has been told there will be no more early refills. She states that she's had to cut down to make them last.

She reports that she was first given oxycodone when she was 16, following a horse-riding accident where she sustained a complex wrist fracture. She took the medication for two weeks and then discontinued them without difficulty.

For complaints of severe menstrual pain and non-menstrual pelvic pain, which were later diagnosed via laparoscopy as endometriosis, she was put on nonsteroidal medication, then low-dose codeine/Tylenol, both of which she found ineffective. She has been on a variety of hormonal therapies to suppress and control her menses but has found these have not managed her symptoms or her pain. At 17, her previous gynecologist switched her to oxycodone three to four times daily. Over the years the dosage has been increased to its current level.

Jen has no significant psychiatric history. She briefly attended family therapy at the time of her parents' divorce when she was 12. She graduated from Fairfield High School with a 3.9 GPA and has been on the dean's list her first three semesters at Q. She is the middle of three girls and, following her parents' divorce, mostly stayed with her mother and sisters. Her father remarried within a year of the divorce. She speaks with both of her parents weekly by phone and likes to visit her father and stepmother at their lake house in Washington, Connecticut.

Jen denies use of illicit drugs, though she has tried cannabis. She admits to occasional use of alcohol at parties and family gatherings. She states she does not drink to get drunk or use her pain medication to get high. A urine toxicology is negative for all substances except oxycodone and its metabolites.

On her mental status examination, she presents as an articulate, well-groomed young woman. She denies symptoms of serious depression (PHQ-9 is a 4) or anxiety, but she is concerned that she will not get "cleared" for her oxycodone and reports she does not know how she'll deal with the resultant pain, which she rates as a 9–10 on a 10-point scale. Her affect is anxious, and she has cold-like symptoms—runny nose and eyes. At times she does appear to be in physical distress, and she repeatedly asks how much longer the evaluation will take. There is no evidence of psychosis. She is not suicidal or homicidal.

DISCUSSION

Jen presents to a university mental health clinic to be assessed for a possible substance-use problem by her gynecologist. Her goal is to be "cleared" with the desire to continue her opioids without interruption.

The first question is, does she meet criteria for an opioid use disorder? In the DSM-5 the criteria for tolerance and withdrawal do not apply if a person is taking medications in an appropriate and prescribed way. It's clear from her withdrawal symptoms, runny nose, and flu-like symptoms that she has developed a dependence on opioids, and that she's been progressively needing more. Her high dose (≥100 MMEs) speaks to tolerance and risk.

What could be considered signs of misuse include:

- Prescriptions running out too soon.

- Taking "an extra pill or two."

- Multiple calls to her gynecologist for early refills.

- Her anxiety and desire to end the session may represent signs of craving, or at least her need to take a pill to decrease her withdrawal symptoms.

- The PDMP showing a consistent pattern of early refill.

However, she continues to function at a high level in school, does not report stopping important activities because of her opioid use, and describes no high-risk behaviors related to the opioids. She also does not believe that her use of prescribed opioids is a problem and she has made no efforts to cut down or stop (level of motivation to decrease or stop opioid use is low).

The above case could go either way in terms of a diagnosis. Regardless, Jen is in trouble and the next, and perhaps more important, question is: Do the benefits of opioids for her chronic pain condition outweigh the risks? Potential benefits can be broken down into three domains:

1. Pain relief: She states opioids are the only thing that have been effective.

2. Functioning: Currently functions at a high level, but reports being unable to function when the endometriosis pain is severe, prior to her menses.

3. Quality of life: Does not report current quality-of-life problems.

The risks of long-term, high-dose opioid use are substantial, and include development or worsening of a use disorder, increased tolerance, respiratory depression, accidental overdose, and death. Moreover, her dosage has escalated over time and she continues to report high levels of pain, which raises the question of opioid-induced hyperalgesia.

As we look at the CDC guidelines, we see that in this instance, as with many people, the chance for early intervention has passed. We're working with a person with true suffering and pain, who has been prescribed medications by a physician and now has a twofold problem. The medical condition and opioid dependence.

Strategies that would be recommended with Jen include:

- Help her establish goals about her use of opioids and pain. Is the goal to be pain-free, or is it more based on her ability to function through the month? This could be done by the gynecologist, a pain specialist, and/or in collaboration with a mental health provider. This should include a discussion and time frame for taper strategies.

- Educate the client about the risks and benefits of her continued opioid use at every visit. This includes information about overdose and tolerance.

  - Provide the client with a prescription for naloxone (Narcan).

  - Review serious risks of combining any other central nervous system depressants, such as alcohol, benzodiazepines, and sleeping medications.

- Explore non-pharmacological alternatives to opioids, which might provide relief from her endometriosis pain. This could include MBSR or cognitive behavioral therapy to decrease the emotional components of pain. Elicit her thoughts on integrative approaches and, as needed, help her identify area resources.

- Where Jen is pursuing a career in medicine, share literature and articles with her regarding non-pharmacologic pain-management strategies. Help her develop a wellness regimen that she can evaluate based on outcomes of functioning, quality of life, and perception of pain.

CHAPTER 6

Co-Occurring Mental Health Problems and Opioids: Let's Get Integrated

- **Overview and Statistics**
- **I Lost My Daughter to the Disease of Addiction**
- **Metrics and Screening Tools**
- **Integrated Treatment: A Whole-Person Approach**
- **Integrated Care**
- **Case Study with Discussion and Treatment/Recovery Plan**

OVERVIEW AND STATISTICS

According to the 2016 NSDUH 3.4% of Americans (or 8.2 million) have at least one mental health and substance-use problem. This topic of co-occurring mental health and substance-use problems first received attention as large state hospitals emptied in the 1970s–1990s. These individuals, most with serious mental illness and diagnoses such as schizophrenia and schizoaffective disorder—some who'd been institutionalized for decades—struggled to integrate into communities upon discharge. Many became homeless and had legal problems. Large numbers turned to drugs and alcohol, and there was a resultant rise in diseases, such as hepatitis and HIV/AIDS. In response to this wave of people with co-occurring substance and mental health problems, large community mental health services were established, and best practices were developed that included case management, housing, vocational, medical, and other supports to help people succeed.

As we turn to the topic of opioids and co-occurring mental health issues, the demographics and diagnoses broaden. They speak to some basic facts about both. Most people with mental health problems never go for professional help. Similarly, over 95% of people who meet criteria for a substance-use disorder never seek or receive treatment. But when we come to people who have both, those numbers shift. Then, if we factor in the severity of an opioid use disorder, suddenly the person with depression, an anxiety disorder, obsessive-compulsive disorder, PTSD, and so forth is no longer able to manage on their own. This creates both challenges and opportunities for clinicians and the mental health and substance abuse industries. It also speaks

"I lost my daughter to the disease of addiction."

Heide Kapral

my story

My beautiful daughter, Amanda, died on May 5, 2014, following a heroin overdose.

She was my only child and the love of my life. She was funny, nonjudgmental, and a gifted artist. She loved nature and was incredibly loyal … till the end. Which isn't to say she didn't have issues. She had ADHD as a kid, but never abused her medications. As an adult, both her therapist and mine thought she had bipolar. We saw a psychiatrist when she was in her early teens; he thought we both had it. We saw him twice. So yes, there's mental illness and substance use on both sides of the family. She got a double whammy. Her father, David, had problems with alcohol. After she died, he had horrible guilt. He passed two years later. And I was left alone, the two most important people in my life were gone.

It was when her dad's drinking was bad that I found out about Amanda's problems. We were doing an intervention for David to get him into detox and she said, "Dad, I'll go if you go."

Why? I wondered. She said it was alcohol; it wasn't.

I think she started with the pills when she was 20 or 21. She was staying with her boyfriend and I didn't know what was going on. Plus, she and I butted heads. I thought that was due to the ADHD.

She first went to a drug program in California. The insurance company paid for her to leave the state, but not for anything in Connecticut. She stayed clean for almost a year. Then she relapsed. It was back and forth, back and forth to rehab. Sovereign in San Clemente, Orchid, Desert Hope, and Michael's House. Others too—some good, some not so good.

I learned about the heroin the night I heard gurgling sounds from her bedroom. She was blue. I started CPR and called the police. You can't imagine what that was like. They told me she had snorted heroin and almost died. They took her to the local hospital.

From there it was another rehab, another overdose, another program.

One time she used in her boyfriend's car and drove off the road right after she'd returned from rehab. She was arrested and wanted to get into another program and get on the Vivitrol. She was in withdrawal. She was desperate and told me that she wanted to kill herself. I took her to the emergency room. She recanted the suicidal stuff because she didn't want it on her medical record. But she wanted help. The nurse on duty told us to leave, "We have sicker people here." They wouldn't admit her.

Her final rehab was in California. They kicked her out for going AWOL. I flew her back. The next day, she used again and was arrested for breaking probation and DUI. It killed me, but I wouldn't post bond. They sent her to Niantic Prison for three months.

Because she wasn't sentenced and the police department didn't serve the warrant, we couldn't get her into this special program in Connecticut for women with serious substance-use problems. They had to let her go.

During her last court appearance, the state's attorney told the judge he had contacted the arresting police department three times to issue the warrant. They didn't. So even with the help of the public defender, we couldn't get her into that 45-day program.

The day I picked her up from prison I drove her to the probation office and then to a meeting. I said, "Amanda, you have a new beginning here. Don't get involved with anyone. It's important you focus on yourself."

Later, she texted me: "My sponsor and I are going out." On Sunday we went grocery shopping and planned to have lunch. She made an excuse to go back to the car. When I followed, I found her with a needle in her arm. We argued. I went to call her sponsor and when I returned, she was gone, and I discovered her so-called sponsor was someone she had met in the last rehab who had also gotten kicked out.

That night she called, "Mommy, I want to come home."

I said, "There are rules." I told her, "You need to go to methadone tomorrow." Stupid me, I gave her "sponsor" $20 for gas money to take her to the clinic. In the morning, Amanda was unresponsive. They revived her.

They don't tell you when you give them Narcan that they're going to use again. I should have known, and I didn't.

That night, she overdosed again and was brought to the hospital. She was in a coma for a week and declared brain dead. I made the decision to pull the plug. We donated her kidneys.

Shortly after she died—the day before Mother's Day—the police showed up with the warrant. That part tears at me and shows how broken our system is. If they'd served it when she was alive, my only child, the love of my life, might still be here.

She was cremated in a white dress and I scattered her ashes in the Salt River in front of the cottage where we spent our summer vacations. She loved it there.

So what gets me through? I have my grief jags. No matter what anyone says there's nothing more painful than burying a child. She was a part of me. But I believe she's in a better place. She had demons chasing her and was miserable. That last time she overdosed I think she sprinted to the other side.

And here's my advice for others with loved ones caught in addiction: It's important to educate, educate, educate. Go to support groups. Nothing against Nar-anon or Al-anon, but it's not enough. Get your own individual and family therapy. And everybody has got to be on the same page. You can't have one parent with one set of rules and another with different ones. It won't work. And remember there is always hope. There are successes.

to the importance of integration, as many people turn to drugs as a way of medicating painful emotions. To treat a person's substance-use problem without addressing the mental health issues often leaves them back where they started when the addiction first took hold.

For those in private practice, a rule of thumb is to expect 50% of your clients to have co-occurring issues. For those who work in community-based or hospital-based mental health and/or substance abuse clinics, the number rises to 70%. When we come to correctional institutions (prisons, jails) it goes as high as 90%.

Regardless of how a clinic or program is designated, an important, and ongoing, step in the assessment of anyone who walks through your door is to screen for what may not be obvious. If you don't look, you won't find it.

- The stay-at-home mom who became addicted to pain medications following an orthopedic procedure will not disclose that she spends eight hours a day cleaning due to her moderate to severe obsessive-compulsive disorder.

- The executive who presents with depression is unlikely to admit to his current oxycodone habit.

- The high school senior caught selling their Adderall, prescribed for attention deficit disorder, will not tell you they've been doing it to purchase heroin. Or that heroin is the only thing that makes their crushing anxiety manageable.

- The pregnant woman who presents with depression will likely not divulge her misuses of oxycodone for fear that she will be reported to child protective services.

Metrics and Screening Tools

This brings us to the importance of screening and screening tools (metrics). In my own practice and clinics, I select instruments that are validated, free, easy to use, and make sense for the people and populations we work with. Beyond this, certain metrics completed at intervals can be incorporated into treatment and recovery plans. This helps both the practitioner and the client see if an approach, therapy, or intervention makes a difference. From a pragmatic stance—where goals and objectives, to meet various standards, should be measurable—this is another use of metrics, as seen in the following sample treatment/recovery plan objectives:

- Charles will experience a 10% or greater decrease in depressive symptoms as measured on the Patient Health Questionnaire-9.

- Joan will report a 30% or greater decrease in PTSD symptoms using the PTSD Checklist-5.

- Using a 100-point Subjective Units of Distress Scale (SUDS), Robert will report a 20-point decrease in anxiety.

Screening tools help clarify diagnoses, but by themselves are not diagnostic. They can also provide clinicians and the people they work with a way to track progress or the lack thereof. Certain metrics can be administered over time and help determine if a therapy, medication, or wellness practice has had a positive effect. Finally, some metrics, such as the PHQ-9 for depression and the Alcohol Use Disorders Identification Test (AUDIT) for alcohol-use disorders, are considered "Meaningful Use Measures" by the Centers for Medicare & Medicaid Services (CMS) and can factor into Medicare reimbursement rates. The SBIRT model, discussed in this chapter, is reimbursable by many insurers.

What follows is a non-exhaustive list of metrics. The ones I've chosen to include, both here and in other chapters, have been published in governmental, and other, documents and are available on their websites. Some, such as the Mood Disorder Questionnaire for bipolar disorder, have been widely published and are included with permission from the authors. They are free for you to download and use with your clients.

ADHD

The Adult ADHD Self-Report Scales (ASRS-v1.1): This screening tool is owned by WHO. It's an 18-item instrument, where the first six questions are used as the screen, and the remaining are not scored, but help flesh out the client's symptoms. It's available online at: https://add.org/wp-content/uploads/2015/03/adhd-questionnaire-ASRS111.pdf

Bipolar Disorder

Bipolar spectrum disorders are among the most frequently missed and misdiagnosed conditions in behavioral health. The major reason is that most people with bipolar only seek treatment when depressed. For those with bipolar II, their hypomanic episodes may be times they feel good, happy, and energized. When someone with bipolar I has a manic episode, it's unlikely that they will self-present for treatment. If they come to a professional's attention, it's often in the setting of an emergency room or other crisis setting. Because of this it's incumbent on clinicians to screen all individuals with a mood disorder for bipolar. A wrong diagnosis can expose a person to treatment choices, such as an unopposed antidepressant, which carries the risk of a kindled manic episode, the results of which can be devastating and tragic. In the latest version of the DSM-5, a manic episode precipitated by antidepressant treatment does count toward the bipolar diagnosis.

The Mood Disorder Questionnaire: This important screening tool helps ascertain whether an individual has ever had a manic or hypomanic episode. Bipolar diagnoses are historic; this means that over the course of the person's lifetime there has been at least one full manic episode (bipolar I), or at least one episode of major depression and one hypomanic episode (bipolar II). I typically add two questions after this is completed if the screen is positive (suggestive of bipolar).

1. Do these symptoms occur only when you're high on drugs or alcohol? If the answer is "Yes, it's only when I'm doing crack cocaine" that's less of a slam-dunk for bipolar. If they say, "Yes, it can happen when I'm sober as a judge," that's a clearer indication of true mania and not an expected symptom of stimulant, or other drug, intoxication.

2. How long do these symptoms last? If they say, "Oh, a few hours," that's not typical for bipolar, and the clinician might want to consider an impulse control problem, or personality disorder, such as borderline. If they say, "Days, weeks," that's in step with criteria for a mania or hypomania.

The Mood Disorder Questionnaire (MDQ)

Instructions: Please answer each question as best you can.

1. Has there ever been a period of time when you were not your usual self and …

Place a check in each appropriate box	Yes	No
you felt so good or so hyper that other people thought you were not your normal self, or you were so hyper that you got into trouble?		
you were so irritable that you shouted at people or started fights or arguments?		
you felt much more self-confident than usual?		
you got much less sleep than usual and found you didn't really miss it?		
you were much more talkative, or spoke much faster, than usual?		
thoughts raced through your head or you couldn't slow your mind down?		
you were so easily distracted by things around you that you had trouble concentrating or staying on track?		
you had more energy than usual?		
you were much more active or did many more things than usual?		
you were much more social or outgoing than usual (for example, you telephoned friends in the middle of the night)?		
you were much more interested in sex than usual?		
you did things that were unusual for you or that other people might have thought excessive, foolish, or risky?		
spending money got you or your family into trouble?		

Copyright © 2018 Charles Atkins. *Opioid Use Disorders*. All rights reserved.

2. If you checked YES to more than one of the previous questions, have several of these ever happened during the same period of time? (circle one)

    Yes   No

3. How much of a problem did any of these cause you—like being unable to work; having family, money, or legal troubles; getting into arguments or fights? (circle one)

    No Problem   Minor Problem   Moderate Problem   Serious Problem

4. Have any of your blood relatives (i.e., children, siblings, parents, grandparents, aunts, and uncles) had manic-depressive illness or bipolar disorder? (circle one)

    Yes   No

5. Has a health professional ever told you that you have manic-depressive illness or bipolar disorder? (circle one)

    Yes   No

Copyright Robert M.A. Hirschfeld. Reprinted with permission.

Copyright © 2018 Charles Atkins. *Opioid Use Disorders*. All rights reserved.

SCORING THE MDQ

The screen is considered "positive" if:

1. There are seven or more "yes" items in question number 1

And

2. "Yes" to question number 2

And

3. "Moderate" or "Serious" to question number 3

Depression

Patient Health Questionnaire-9 (on the following page): This is a self-administered tool, where the nine refers to the nine criteria in the DSM-5 for depression. This is a useful instrument, not only as a screening tool, but to follow the client's progress in treatment. It is a CMS Meaningful Use Measure.

The Patient Health Questionnaire-9
(PHQ-9)

Over the past two weeks, how often have you been bothered by the following problems?	0 Not at all	1 Several days	2 More than half the days	3 Nearly every day
1. Little interest or pleasure in doing things.				
2. Feeling down, depressed, or hopeless.				
3. Trouble falling or staying asleep, or sleeping too much.				
4. Feeling tired or having little energy.				
5. Poor appetite or overeating.				
6. Feeling bad about yourself—or that you are a failure or have let yourself or your family down.				
7. Trouble concentrating on things, such as reading the newspaper or watching television.				
8. Moving or speaking so slowly that other people could have noticed. Or the opposite—being fidgety or restless so that you have been moving around a lot more than usual.				
9. Thoughts that you would be better off dead, or of hurting yourself.				
Add columns:				
Total:				

The PHQ-9 was developed by Drs. Robert L. Spitzer, Janet B.W. Williams, Kurt Kroenke and colleagues, with an educational grant from Pfizer, Inc. It is in the public domain.

Copyright © 2018 Charles Atkins. *Opioid Use Disorders*. All rights reserved.

Scoring: The PHQ-9 is a screening test for symptoms of depression, whether associated with major depressive disorder, bipolar depression, pervasive depressive disorder, or other conditions. By itself it is not a diagnostic instrument, but it can aid in the diagnosis of various conditions; and positive responses, especially to question 9, should be pursued.

Level of Depressive Symptoms	PHQ-9 Score
1–4	Minimal depressive symptoms
5–9	Mild depressive symptoms
10–14	Moderate depressive symptoms
15–19	Moderately severe depressive symptoms
20–27	Severe depressive symptoms

Anxiety

The Generalized Anxiety Disorder-7 (GAD-7) is an easy-to-complete, seven-item screening tool, which can be used both as a prompt to perform a more-extensive anxiety assessment, as well as to track progress over time. As seen in the following treatment/recovery plan goal: Client will display a 20% or greater decrease in anxious symptoms as measured with the GAD-7.

Generalized Anxiety Disorder (GAD-7)

Over the last 2 weeks have you been bothered by the following problems?	Not at all	Several days	Over half the days	Nearly every day
Feeling nervous, anxious, or on edge.	0	1	2	3
Not being able to stop or control worrying.	0	1	2	3
Worrying too much about different things.	0	1	2	3
Trouble relaxing.	0	1	2	3
Being so restless that it is hard to sit still.	0	1	2	3
Becoming easily annoyed or irritable.	0	1	2	3
Feeling afraid, as if something awful might happen.	0	1	2	3
Add the score for each column		+	+	+
Total Score (add your column scores) =				

If you checked off any problems, how difficult have these made it for you to do your work, take care of things at home, or get along with other people?

Not difficult at all _____

Somewhat difficult _____

Very difficult _____

Extremely difficult _____

Source: Spitzer, R.L., Kroenke, K., Williams, J.B.W., & Lowe, B. A brief measure for assessing generalized anxiety disorder. *Archives of Internal Medicine.* 2006;166:1092–1097.

Copyright © 2018 Charles Atkins. *Opioid Use Disorders.* All rights reserved.

Scoring Interpretations

Scores of 5, 10, and 15 represent cutoffs for mild, moderate, and severe anxiety, respectively. A score of 3 or more warrants a more thorough assessment of anxious and depressive symptoms.

PTSD

The PTSD Checklist for DSM-5 (PCL-5), available for free from the National Center for PTSD (Veterans Administration), is a 20-item, self-administered instrument that follows the greatly expanded DSM-5 criteria—which now include negative mood states, irritability, and aggressive behavior.

- This link is to a PDF that explains how to use and score the PCL-5: https://www.ptsd.va.gov/professional/assessment/documents/using-PCL5.pdf

- These links are to two versions of the PCL-5. One includes an expanded DSM-5 criterion A section: https://www.ptsd.va.gov/professional/assessment/documents/PCL-5_criterionA.pdf

  https://www.ptsd.va.gov/professional/assessment/documents/PCL-5_Standard.pdf

Neurocognitive Disorders (Dementias)

The Saint Louis University Mental Status Examination (SLUMS): http://medschool.slu.edu/agingsuccessfully/pdfsurveys/slumsexam_05.pdf

- A video demonstrating the administration of a SLUMS is available at: https://www.youtube.com/watch?v=jyp0ShPiUH8

- A video that explains scoring the SLUMS is available at: https://www.youtube.com/watch?v=vdQwJXgUu2o

  The Montreal Cognitive Assessment (MOCA) is available online at: http://www.mocatest.org/

Screening, Brief Intervention, and Referral to Treatment (SBIRT)

SBIRT is a public-health approach to early identification of both people who have a substance-use problem and those at greater risk for developing one. Additionally, SBIRT is reimbursable by many insurers including Medicare and Medicaid (if your state has authorized it) as a structured interview.

- Screening assesses the severity of a problem if it exists.

- Brief Intervention is an in-the-moment motivational discussion about how the person feels about the behavior and their thoughts/motivation towards changing it. Per Medicare (CMS) rules, this can be up to five sessions.

- Referral to treatment helps connect the person to appropriate resources.

- To learn more about SBIRT, including billing codes, visit: https://www.samhsa.gov/sbirt

- For the CMS guidelines regarding SBIRT, visit: https://www.cms.gov/Outreach-and-Education/Medicare-Learning-Network-MLN/MLNProducts/Downloads/SBIRT_Factsheet_ICN904084.pdf

Other Online Resources for Free Metrics

The American Psychiatric Association has a large library of metrics available through their DMS-5 website. These are downloadable as PDFs and free to use with your clients. They're arranged by diagnoses and age: https://www.psychiatry.org/psychiatrists/practice/dsm/educational-resources/assessment-measures

The Veterans Administration and the National Center for PTSD offer a range of validated metrics, as well as manuals and instructional videos: https://www.ptsd.va.gov/professional/index.asp

INTEGRATED TREATMENT: A WHOLE-PERSON APPROACH

As I've progressed in my psychiatric career, integrated care has become more of a reality, although there's still a long way to go. As we consider opioid use disorders, combined with mental health problems, a third variable must also be considered—medical issues. The medical fallout from opioid use disorders can be catastrophic, from infectious diseases secondary to intravenous drug use, to hormonal changes, to respiratory depression and death from overdose. Here, we'll examine pragmatic approaches to working with people in a holistic, compassionate, and competent fashion.

To begin, there is no single face of a person with co-occurring issues. The combinations are infinite, though if we restrict the discussion to opioids, that list is whittled down. However, most people don't misuse a certain substance or have a single crisp DSM-5 diagnosis. I often tell clients, clinicians, and family when discussing diagnoses, "These are man-made boxes that are best-fit approximations for someone's symptoms and their history. They help us think about what therapies and medications might help, but they're limited." In behavioral science we lag behind the rest of medicine regarding objective findings. We can test for diabetes, do a culture or assay for an infection to find out what the bacteria or virus is, or see a tumor on an MRI. At present, there is little of this kind of diagnostic clarity in our field.

Our clients with co-occurring disorders can be complex and present challenges to keep the treatment and recovery ship on course. Which brings me to the Thanksgiving metaphor. It goes like this. My mother is a world-class Thanksgiving hostess. It's not a holiday if there aren't 40 or more family and relatives crammed into the house where I grew up in Massachusetts. And everyone has special dietary needs. Indeed, some family members bring their entire feast in separate coolers.

Here's the connection to co-occurring — to pull off a complex meal, where every person at the table needs attention, it's crucial to attend to the saucepan of cranberry sauce set to boil, while minding the turkey, which, if it goes too long, will be dry as dust. The gravy must not be forgotten, nor the side dishes; and how disappointing if there's not a broad assortment of desserts, pies, cakes, and cookies at the end. This is how I work with people who have complex needs. You have important things that must be attended to immediately; and then you have other issues, which have importance, but can wait or be worked on over time. Sort of like front burners, back burners, ovens, and dishes that others bring to the table.

Let's break it down. These are what I consider the front-burner issues that must be addressed at the start of treatment. The order of importance is dependent on the individual, but all should be managed.

Establish a trusting clinical relationship. Can this person who has come to you for help know that they've been heard and that you can be trusted? Without this, it's unlikely they'll return. Studies that examine what makes one therapy more effective than another, show that it's the relationship that matters the most. Does your client like you and trust you, and do you feel the same about them?

Establish goals. For someone with an opioid use disorder this will include what they do, or don't, want regarding MAT. Open-ended questions work well: "What would you like to work on?" "What brought you in today?" "Tell me what's been stressing you out?"

Their opioid use may be the issue that got them to come through the door to seek treatment. At times, goals will get modified based on outside factors, which neither you nor the client can control. This might include a court stipulation for treatment, child-protective services, probation, and the realities of what is, and is not, available in the community. Even so, when there are outside forces at play, these can be folded into the client's goals. "I know you're not crazy about an inpatient detox, but the judge says it's that or jail. And you've told me you don't want to go to jail. So, let's figure out how you can make the best of it. You know, lemonade from lemons." As you help your client develop her goals, it may be useful to identify what's a goal of treatment, and what are life goals? These may be the same, they may be different, but either can serve as the rudder that steers things forward.

Active withdrawal, or intoxication. If a client is in withdrawal or nodding off, it's difficult, if not impossible, to complete a diagnostic evaluation. People in withdrawal can look as though they are depressed, suffering from an anxiety disorder, or any other number of emotional and behavioral presentations that are directly related to withdrawal.

High risk for relapse and overdose. Is this someone who has just been through a detox from opioids or someone recently released from incarceration? These are two scenarios where a person has lost their tolerance to opioids and is at high risk for relapse and fatal overdose. Rapid, ideally same day, initiation of MAT needs to be explored.

Suicidal or homicidal thoughts or actions. What is this person's current level of risk for self-harm or hurting someone else? What is their history of suicide attempts and of violence? If they've had overdoses, were any intentional? In conducting a risk assessment it's useful to divide potential risk factors into those that are static and cannot be changed, and those that are dynamic and can be altered and may be a focus of treatment or intervention. Certain risk factors, such as a history of mental health and substance-use disorders, can be considered both static—what's happened in the past—and dynamic—current signs and symptoms.

Static Risk Factors (can't be changed)	Dynamic Risk Factors (changeable)
Age.	Active substance use.
Gender. Men of all ages and races carry a higher risk for suicide than women of the same age and race. Older white males have the single greatest risk level.	Mood state (depression, anxiety, panic). Hopelessness. (By itself, hopelessness—the inability to see a positive future—is a risk for suicide.) Feelings of isolation and loneliness.
History of suicide attempts. The more serious the attempt, the greater the continued risk.	Current thoughts of suicide or of harming others. Are these more than thoughts? Have they prepared the means and practiced, such as made a noose or purchased a gun?
History of violence to others. The more serious the act, the greater the continued risk.	Delusions, including paranoia. Paranoia, especially when directed toward another person, is a serious risk factor.
History of mental health and substance-use disorders.	Access to lethal means including firearms and lethal doses of drugs.
Family history of suicide.	Active medical issues.
Recent loss (work, relationship, housing, other).	Recent loss (work, relationship, housing, other).
High incidence of ACES (adverse childhood experiences).	Impulsivity.

In addition to static and dynamic risks for dangerousness, it's useful to assess the protective factors the person has that stops them from committing harm. Common ones include:

- Religious beliefs and/or spirituality: "Suicide is a sin and you go to hell." "God has a plan for me. I can't see it right now, but I know it's there."

- Concern for how it would impact others: "I'd never do that to my children."

- Future orientation: "I know things are bad, but I'll get through this."

- Safety plans: "While I feel this bad I'll stay with my folks."

Other altered and potentially dangerous mental states. This can include delirium, dementia (neurocognitive disorders), or active psychosis.

Dangerous patterns of substance use. Is the client purchasing street drugs that contain fentanyl? Are they taking opioids combined with alcohol, benzodiazepines, and other central nervous system depressants? Are they getting opioids and other scheduled drugs from multiple providers? Are they taking more than 90MME/day of opioids? All the above greatly increase the risk for a fatal overdose, whether intentional or accidental.

Homelessness. If a person's basic needs of adequate clothing, food, and shelter are not met, treatment is problematic. As opioid use disorders progress, it's common for people to experience disruptions and loss of jobs, housing, possessions, and important relationships. Does this person have stable housing? Have they moved back home into a parent's basement or garage? Do they live out of their car or on the street?

Domestic violence (DV). People with opioid use disorders are at increased risk for violence of all kinds. Is the home setting and primary relationship a safe one? Is there domestic violence? Reasons why women and men remain in physically, emotionally, and sexually abusive relationships are varied (money, children, drugs, love). If a client reports DV, it warrants a careful and nonjudgmental discussion. Resources regarding shelters, with numbers to call, and a discussion of safety plans should be reviewed.

Active legal issues. As all aspects of non-medical opioid use are illegal, people with opioid use disorders often experience arrest and incarceration. For many, dealing drugs becomes a way to both support their own habit and to make money. Shoplifting, robbery, forgery, prostitution, and other crimes may be needed to support an insatiable habit.

For a host of reasons, including shame, negative self-judgments, and fear of being reported, people may not be candid about active legal problems, especially in the beginning of a therapeutic or helping relationship. Alternatively, some may be mandated to treatment through a drug court, jail diversion program, probation, or as a condition of their parole. Many states have searchable databases connected to their judicial and correctional websites. Unlike protected health data, these records are public information, and can be a useful source of both current and past legal involvement.

Critical and unattended medical problems. At the time of intake, it's important to get a feel for any active medical issues.

Level of motivation. To address, and hopefully change, whatever the presenting issue(s) are.

Barriers to treatment (non-exhaustive list).

- Lack of insurance, or other resources, that cover the service(s) they require.

- Insurance with high deductible and/or co-pays that the person cannot afford.

- Transportation.

- Childcare.

- Lack of a specific resource in the community.

    - A pregnant woman with small children who requires a residential program but will only go if her other children can be with her.

    - Inadequate, or restricted, access to medication-assisted treatment.

- Lack of integrated programs that work with both mental health and substance-use issues.

- Many substance-use programs are unable, and unequipped, to work with serious and active emotional and/or behavioral symptoms.

- Many behavioral health programs will not accept individuals with active and severe substance-use problems.

- Programs with rules that make attendance problematic, such as:

  - A MAT program that insists a client get all their treatment with them, when they have an existing relationship with an outside therapist.

  - Programs that can't accommodate the hours of a working person.

INTEGRATED CARE

As we'll see in the case study exercise at the end of this chapter, things not on a front burner must be addressed. Which moves us into the discussion of integrated care. This can be thought about in a few broad concepts. The first big question is how integrated is a program or practice? This is something that clinicians and people seeking services, for themselves or a loved one with co-occurring disorders, need to consider. The lack, or absence, of fully-integrated programs is a common barrier for people with co-occurring issues, especially when both are severe. It can lead to an unfortunate sort of gamesmanship where clinicians know that if they want to help a client get a spot in a certain detox or residential program, they need to downplay the severity of psychiatric symptoms and past psychiatric history. Or, on the flip side, to get a bed on a psychiatric unit, people know that they have to say they're suicidal. This benefits no one and carries the added risk of a client being admitted to a program, only to be discharged, or t ransferred to a hospital, when the provider discovers that they are unable to meet this person's needs.

On a positive note, programs that embrace an integrated philosophy and practice move closer to a whole-person approach. As many people with emotional and behavioral issues turn to opioids—and other drugs and alcohol—to medicate away depression, anxiety, and other negative emotions and mood states, it's important to address both the substance use and the emotional/behavioral issues.

From a practical perspective, providing all aspects of care decreases the risk of miscommunication, or lack of communication, between the person in treatment and their providers. For people with opioid use disorders, especially those in early recovery, this is crucial as it increases the likelihood of catching high-risk symptoms and behaviors—such as increased drug cravings, or a relapse—in a timely fashion.

People with opioid use disorders often present for help in crisis. They may be in withdrawal and/or have just been revived with naloxone, or have some other urgent matter that propels them to seek treatment. They want it now. And if it's not immediate, worsening withdrawal symptoms and drug craving will overtake the moment. Because of this, clinicians need to educate themselves about what's available in their state and community. This can be a challenge, and lack of immediate access is an often-cited barrier to treatment.

- "They don't take my insurance."

- "They're not taking new patients."

- "They don't have beds."

- "They have a waiting list."

- "They won't take my son because he has a history of a suicide attempt."

- "I have to show up every day and wait in line to see if they have a bed."

- "I have no way to get there."

There's tremendous variability from state to state, and even within states, as to what is available at all levels of care, from inpatient detox to intensive outpatient programs, and outpatient clinics and offices. Approaches that may help include:

- Infoline 211 may be a resource.

- SAMHSA's Behavioral Health Treatment Locator: https://findtreatment.samhsa.gov/

- For those with private insurance, call the carrier and ask who's on their provider list for the services you want.

- Many state departments of mental health, public health, and/or substance use maintain lists of providers and their scope of services. In some states these are freestanding agencies, in others they may be nested under the Department of Public Health and/ or Human Services. Some states also have 1-800 lines that can assist people in finding resources.

    - Some states maintain lists of open beds, along with information as to the level of integrated care.

- Local crisis centers, typically funded by departments of mental health, can also be a good source of information. At the very least, they will be familiar with what is available in the immediate area.

- Consumer organizations. Increasingly, peer-based organizations have created and maintain online resources. These can be especially useful as there may also be testimonials about the quality of care, but watch for bias, and false information due to commercial interests.

- Area hospitals that have dedicated psychiatric emergency rooms.

- Peer groups and resources for both the individual with the opioid use disorder and their family. Organizations such as Nar-anon, Al-anon, and others, will have members familiar, from personal experience, with what is available and what they found useful.

- For opioid treatment programs (OTPs) that provide methadone, and possibly other forms of MAT, the following searchable directory maintained by SAMHSA gives addresses and contact information: https://dpt2.samhsa.gov/treatment/directory.aspx

- A list of prescribers approved to prescribe buprenorphine (Suboxone, Zubsolv, etc.) for opioid use disorders can be found at: https://www.samhsa.gov/medication-assisted-treatment/physician-program-data/treatment-physician-locator?page=1. However, not all practitioners who can prescribe buprenorphine do so.

- Online resources such as intherooms.com, which maintains an extensive directory of resources, as well as a rich array of online groups, and themighty.com, which provides a rich blog community of people facing a broad range of health challenges.

Fully Integrated/Co-Occurring Enhanced: In programs that earn the co-occurring-enhanced designation, there's a commitment to address and provide treatment for both the substance use and mental health issues. For a person with an opioid use disorder, this includes the availability of MAT and an array of psychosocial supports that address the use disorder. Beyond this, fully integrated programs offer clinical services that address the mental health issues. Examples of fully integrated programs can be found across the level-of-care spectrum, from inpatient medically supervised detox, to residential options, to partial hospital, intensive outpatient and outpatient settings.

An added, and positive, development to the above are Behavioral Health Homes (BHHs). These take the integration of behavioral health and substance use and fold in medical care and wellness. Agencies, such as the one I work for, that have the Joint Commission BHH designation, attach nurses and case managers/clinical navigators to clients, to help ensure that medical needs are addressed. Some BHHs provide primary care on-site, and others utilize community providers and clinics, including Federally Qualified Healthcare Clinics (FQHCs). The BHH model is well suited for clients with higher behavioral health, medical, and substance-use needs. For these individuals, access to case managers, housing specialists, peer supports, and a combined medical and psychiatric support team, can go a long way toward improving outcomes and satisfaction across all domains.

While ideal, fully integrated programs are not widely available. One often cited reason is that these services may be costlier to provide than non-integrated care, and reimbursement rates often don't take that into account.

Partially Integrated/Co-Occurring Informed: This term refers to programs, agencies, and practices that identify as being either behavioral health or substance-use based. However, they assess for both, and to varying degrees either treat both, or refer out for those services/needs they do not provide. Examples include:

- Methadone programs (OTPs), which by statute must provide some behavioral health assessment and treatment, but this can be limited. An individual, such as a person with a psychotic disorder like schizophrenia, might need to receive their behavioral health treatment with another provider.

- Residential substance abuse programs that provide limited on-site behavioral health care.

- Mental health programs that assess for substance-use disorders, but don't offer MAT and other targeted interventions for opioid and other substance-use disorders.

Not Integrated/Parallel Treatment: Parallel treatment is where an individual gets their behavioral health services from one provider, and substance treatment from another. Examples include:

- Behavioral health clinics that do not provide substance-abuse services, including MAT.

- Individual therapists with scopes of practice that restrict what they can address. In some states it can be prescriptive that certain professionals/licensures can only address behavioral health or substance use, but not both.

- Substance-use programs that do not address mental health needs.

- Methadone programs (OTPs) with minimal behavioral health services.

Treating Co-Occurring Disorders: A challenge when trying to determine what therapies and strategies, including medication, might be effective for someone with co-occurring disorders is that there is a paucity of good studies to guide us. Pharmaceutical companies who want to bring a new antidepressant to market don't want to study it in people who use opioids. Likewise, a researcher who wants to see if therapy X will help someone cut down on their substance use, won't include test subjects who have additional factors such as depression, schizophrenia, or borderline personality disorder.

Here are some guiding principles as we think about what works:

- If you manage the substance-use disorder, the co-occurring behavioral health problem(s) are likely to improve some.

- If behavioral symptoms of depression, psychosis, anxiety, and so forth are managed, substance-use behaviors tend to decrease.

- Look at therapeutic strategies that have been studied and found to be effective with both substance use and mental health/behavioral problems. These include:

  - Cognitive behavioral approaches

  - Peer supports

  - Certain medications

  - Mindfulness

  - Dialectic behavior therapy

  - Certain trauma treatments

  - Wellness and integrative strategies—everything from exercise, sleep hygiene, prayer, meditation, nutrition, mind-body techniques, and so forth. This is a broad whole-person approach, which focuses on the establishment of healthy routines in all aspects of a person's life. These tend to carry limited downside risks and can be tremendously beneficial.

- Family work. This ranges from crucial education, to professional-led multi-family strategies, family-to-family groups (peer-based), individual family therapy, and specific interventions geared toward adolescents and adults.

$\boxed{\text{Case Study}}$

Anxiety and Depression

Evie is a 19-year-old mother of one 4-year-old (Lilly). She is referred by child protective services for a psychiatric and substance-use evaluation.

She complains of intense anxiety and depression, 9 on a 10-point scale. She admits to frequently wishing she were dead and admits to both intentional and unintentional overdoses in the past. She denies an active plan to kill herself. Her sleep is poor, both in initiation and maintenance. She has little appetite and has lost 15 pounds—not intentionally—over the past two months.

Evie expresses a strong desire to be substance-free, but admits that for the past two years she has been using opioids. It started with pain medications she stole from her terminally ill grandmother and progressed to her current use of heroin (10 bags/day or the equivalent in oxycodone pills). She has never used needles, but says, "It's just a matter of time."

She currently lives in the basement of her mother's house, which allows her access to her child. However, both her Department of Children and Families worker and her mother, who has custody of Lilly, have told her that she will have to move out if she continues to use drugs.

Past Psychiatric History

Evie states, "I've been depressed my entire life." Her first formal treatment was at age 10, following a suicide attempt (OD). She was briefly hospitalized and put on an antidepressant and a tranquilizer, which she stopped immediately after leaving the hospital because "I didn't like the way they made me feel." She reports self-injurious behavior, starting around age 12—cutting with razors on her arms and inner thighs.

Evie has had eight inpatient hospitalizations, all either following suicide attempts or with suicidal thoughts. She has tried numerous medications but admits that she rarely stays on anything long enough to know if it's helpful. She also doesn't like to mix the medication with street drugs. She likes the way benzodiazepines decrease her anxiety but reports that she abuses them and had a difficult withdrawal from alprazolam (Xanax®).

Substance-Use History

Evie first smoked pot at age 10 with her mother, and she first used prescription pain pills she took from her grandmother. She admits to a daily opioid habit for at least two years. She first tried heroin at 14. "It's so much cheaper than the pills." She's tried cocaine, but states that she doesn't like the way it makes her feel.

She smokes cannabis daily because, "It's the only thing that calms me down." She denies use of alcohol.

She has decreased her cigarette intake from two packs per day to one, and has smoked since age 14.

Family Psychiatric History

Evie's mother is in recovery, but has an extensive history of cannabis and prescription-pain-medication abuse. She is currently treated for anxiety and depression. Evie's father died of a heroin overdose when she was five. Her older brother has bipolar and substance problems and is out of the home.

Medical History

Evie has no known allergies. She delivered her daughter at seven months. Lilly required four weeks of treatment in a neonatal intensive care unit, secondary to prematurity, and for neonatal abstinence syndrome (opioid withdrawal). Evie has not been seen medically in three years.

Social and Developmental History

Evie was born three weeks prematurely to a 17-year-old opioid-dependent mother. She was exposed in utero to cannabis, nicotine, and alcohol. All developmental milestones were achieved in the expected time frames. Patient reports her mother had a series of boyfriends and speculates that she might have been prostituting. She has little memory of her childhood but believes her first sexual molestation occurred when she was under 11.

At 12, she was raped by three men in the neighborhood. Following this she became suicidal and was hospitalized. She pressed charges, and the men were convicted. Around that time her mother entered a methadone program and has been in recovery since.

Evie became pregnant at 14 and dropped out of school. She has had two arrests for possession and larceny. She is not currently in school but reports that it is her goal to complete high school.

She has never divulged the name of Lilly's biologic father. "He's a lot older than me. If I ever tell, he'll get locked up."

Evie voluntarily gave custody of Lilly to her mother, but adds, "Someday I'll get my shit together and be able to take care of her."

DISCUSSION

When working with people who have complex co-occurring substance use and mental health problems, it's important to identify high-risk and high-importance items that must be addressed immediately, versus those that are important, but can wait.

What are the goals? What does she want (not what others want for her)?

In Evie's case, she provides at least three important goals:

- To be substance-free.

- To be able to regain custody of her daughter.

- To get her high school diploma or GED.

How will you create a working alliance with this person?

Focus on her goals and validate them. Be genuine. Listen carefully and observe judgmental thoughts, but do not voice them. "Evie, these are great goals. Let's see what we can do to help you get there."

Are there crises that must be attended to immediately? Such as active suicidality, homicidality, serious legal problems, threat of child removal, or severe and unaddressed health issues?

Evie presents with several high-risk behaviors:

- Opioid use with progressing tolerance and increased drug consumption.

- A history of suicide attempts. What is her current level of risk? This needs to be assessed.

- Her current consumption of benzodiazepines (alprazolam/Xanax) is unknown. Benzodiazepines mixed with opioids increases her risk for fatal overdose. Furthermore, she describes a "difficult withdrawal" from alprazolam (Xanax). More information needs to be obtained. Is she currently using benzodiazepines? The answer may impact recommendations around level of care. Will she require, and be willing to undergo, an inpatient detox from the alprazolam?

  - Ask about her current use of benzodiazepines.

  - Get a drug test.

  - Query the prescription monitoring program to see if she's been prescribed any.

  - Obtain records pertaining to prior hospitalizations, especially the one where she described a difficult withdrawal.

What diagnoses will you use and in what order? This has real-world implications as whatever diagnosis gets listed first is the one for which you will bill the current episode of care.

- For Evie, where the initial recommendation will include some form of MAT, the opioid use disorder diagnosis will go first. A list of diagnoses might look as follows:

Diagnosis	ICD-10 Code
Opioid use disorder, severe	F11.20
Post-traumatic stress disorder	F43.10
Sedative hypnotic-use disorder, severe (benzodiazepines)	F13.20
Tobacco-use disorder, severe	F17.200
Cannabis-use disorder, moderate	F12.20
Parent-child relational problems	Z62.820

What is/are appropriate levels of care?

- Based on a clarification of her current benzodiazepine use, and active suicidality, as well as her willingness for treatment, Evie's initial treatment/recovery plan might include an inpatient detoxification from benzodiazepines, while simultaneously getting her started on either methadone or buprenorphine. The challenge will be to find a program willing and able to do this. Alternatively, if she is not actively using benzodiazepines and is not imminently suicidal, an outpatient co-occurring focused partial hospital program (PHP) or intensive outpatient program (IOP) that can provide MAT makes sense.

- Also to consider will be other agencies involved in her life and how these can impact, for better or worse, her goals. For instance, she clearly wants to regain custody of her child. Is there an active child protective services (CPS) case? If yes, would they be willing/able to consider a mother/child program? Not every state has these, but where they are available, they can provide a broad array of supports to mothers with young children, including residential options. If such a program were offered, this might be the carrot to help jump-start a path to recovery.

Clearly, many other issues need to be addressed, from problematic housing to severe PTSD symptoms, and so forth, but the previous discussion separates out the most pressing issues. If we get back a urine toxicology that is negative for benzodiazepines, and she's not imminently suicidal, an initial treatment/recovery plan might look as follows.

Treatment/Recovery Plan

Patient's Name: Evie Greene   **Date:** 9/2/2018
Date of Birth: 6/4/1999
Medical Record #: 000-00-0000

Level of Care: Co-occurring Enhanced PHP followed by IOP

Diagnosis	ICD-10 Code
Opioid use disorder, severe	F11.20
Post-traumatic stress disorder	F43.10
Sedative hypnotic-use disorder, severe (benzodiazepines)	F13.20
Tobacco-use disorder, severe	F17.200
Cannabis-use disorder, moderate	F12.20
Parent-child relational problems	Z62.820

The Individual's Stated Goal(s): "To not use drugs. To get back custody of Lilly. To get my high school diploma."

1. **Problem/Need Statement:** Active and dangerous polydrug use, as evidenced by 10 bag/day heroin, with history of concomitant benzodiazepine use, history of alprazolam withdrawal, daily cannabis consumption, and one pack/day of cigarettes.

Long-Term Goal: To be abstinent from illicit opioids and benzodiazepines.

Short-Term Goals/Objectives/Target Date:
1) Complete intake to include necessary lab work and mental health evaluation. 9/2/2018
2) Provide psychoeducation around buprenorphine and other forms of MAT. 9/2/2018
3) Complete pre-MAT checklist. 9/3/18
4) Begin MAT with buprenorphine. 9/3/2018

Copyright © 2018 Charles Atkins. *Opioid Use Disorders*. All rights reserved.

2. Problem/Need Statement: Active and severe symptoms related to history of and recurrent trauma, including rape. History of multiple hospitalizations, suicide attempts, and severe negative emotional state including depression and anxiety. Frequent nightmares and flashbacks. Continues to reside in a house with frequent reminders of past trauma and problematic relationship with her mother who has custody of her daughter.

Long-Term Goal: To have at least a 50% decrease in symptoms related to PTSD.

Short-Term Goals/Objectives/Target Date:
1) Complete psychiatric evaluation to include a PTSD Checklist 5, to better quantify symptomatology. 9/5/2018
2) Begin individual and group psychotherapy to include *Seeking Safety*, and dialectic behavior therapy skills training group to enhance emotional regulation and distress tolerance. 9/5/2018 and ongoing
3) Work with client on housing/educational/and parenting goals. 9/5/2018 and ongoing
4) Engage with client's child protective service worker to clarify what additional services might be available to support her goal of reunification with her daughter, Lilly.

3. Problem/Need Statement: Need for medical evaluation.

Long-Term Goal: Client will obtain ongoing medical follow-up.

Short-Term Goals/Objectives/Target Date:
1) Pre-MAT physical with labs to include urine toxicology, hepatitis and HIV screens, and pregnancy test. 9/2/2018
2) Provide client with referrals to area PCPs who accept her insurance. 9/3/2018

Interventions					
Treatment Modality	**Specific Type**	**Frequency**	**Duration**	**Problem Number(s)**	**Responsible Person(s)**
Psychiatric Evaluation	Individual	Once	One hour	1,2,3	Dr. Fitzgerald
Nursing Evaluation	Individual	Once, and as needed	One and a half hours	1,2,3	Jeanne Gray, RN
Individual Co-Occurring Focused Therapy	Individual	Once/week	One hour	1,2,3	Melanie Wright, LCSW

Copyright © 2018 Charles Atkins. *Opioid Use Disorders*. All rights reserved.

Seeking Safety	Group	Three/week	One hour	1,2	Jane Ross, MSW
DBT Skills Training Group	Group	Three/week	One hour	1,2,3	Melanie Wright, LCSW
Relapse Prevention	Group	Three/week	One hour	1	Kelvin Harris, MS
Medication Management	Individual	Once/week and as needed	20 minutes	1,2	Dr. Fitzgerald

Identification of Strengths: Is able to advocate for herself. Has a clear sense of what she wants and expresses a willingness to make changes.

Peer/Family/Community Supports to Assist: Unclear at present. Describes a difficult relationship with her mother, but lives with her to have access to her daughter. Might want to explore resources through protective services, such as parenting classes that might assist with stated goals. Will explore willingness and help client engage with a local peer recovery community.

Barriers to Treatment: None reported.

Staff/Client Identified Education/Teaching Needs: Help client with identifying how her goals and problematic substance use are connected. Provide education and treatment around PTSD.

Assessment of Discharge Needs/Discharge Planning: To be stable on buprenorphine, with no cravings for illicit opioids. To be free from active suicidal thinking. To be connected with an appropriate level of care to support her ongoing recovery.

Completion of this Treatment/Recovery Plan was a collaborative effort between the client and the treatment team:

SIGNATURES		Date/Time:
Client:	Evie Greene	9/2/2018
Physician:	Granada Fitzgerald, MD	9/2/2018
Treatment Plan Completed By:	Melanie Wright, LCSW	9/2/2018
Primary Clinician:	Melanie Wright, LCSW	9/2/2018
Other Team Members	Kelvin Harris, MS	9/2/2018
	Jeanne Gray, RN	9/2/2018

Copyright © 2018 Charles Atkins. *Opioid Use Disorders.* All rights reserved.

Medication-Assisted Treatment (MAT) for Opioid Use Disorders and Overdose Reversals: What You Need to Know

- **Overview**
- **Establishing Goals for MAT**
- **Informed Consent for MAT**
- **Pre-MAT Assessment**
- **Prescription Drug Monitoring Programs (PDMPs)**
- **Duration of Treatment with MAT**
- **Buprenorphine**
- **Methadone**
- **Naltrexone and Naltrexone XR**
- **Switching from One Form of MAT to Another**
- **Drug Testing**
- **Overdose Reversals with Naloxone (Narcan)**
- **Benzodiazepines, Sedative Hypnotics, and Alcohol in MAT**
- **Diversion**

OVERVIEW

This chapter provides an overview of the three FDA-approved medications for the treatment of opioid use disorders: methadone, buprenorphine, and naltrexone. Collectively these are referred to as MAT. We'll review the pros and cons of each, the assessment process, and guidelines for management and treatment. We'll then discuss the life-saving overdose reversal medication, naloxone, most common brand name—Narcan.

Without doubt, MAT can provide people caught in the life-destroying cycle of opioid use disorders with hope and paths to recovery. These are evidence-based treatments and represent the current standard of care. People on methadone and buprenorphine show higher rates of treatment retention and decreased illicit drug use, especially when medications are of an adequate dose. For pregnant women with opioid use disorders (discussed at length in Chapter 12) both methadone and buprenorphine are associated with improved maternal and newborn outcomes. While less well studied, long-acting injectable naloxone provides an alternative path for motivated individuals wishing to remain opioid free.

These are not panaceas or cures. Relapses do occur, and these medications are best viewed as important tools in recovery. While not perfect, they unequivocally provide superior outcomes compared to treatment without MAT. With the current added epidemic of fentanyl-laced drugs on the street, there are new concerns that some of the protective opioid-blocking factors of these medications, buprenorphine and naltrexone, can be diminished or overridden altogether.

ESTABLISHING GOALS FOR MAT

What does the client know about MAT? Have they been on some form(s) of it before? Both methadone and buprenorphine have street value and diversion potential (share with friends and family or sell). As a result, many people have purchased or been given these medications illicitly. This may be why they've decided to come to a practitioner as they know the medication can help, especially to break the cycle of use and withdrawal.

Ask questions and find out what they know, or think they know, about the various medications. There can be tremendous confusion and twisting of the facts relating to MAT. Occasionally, someone will tell you they tried buprenorphine and it didn't work for them. What might have occurred is they either swallowed the pill or strip—it must be dissolved under the tongue or in the cheek—or it made them go into withdrawal. The latter can happen if the medication is taken too soon after using another opioid.

This is a wonderful opportunity to begin the discussion of the pros and cons of all three agents, and to correct misconceptions. For clinicians, it's prudent to not assume we have all the facts and to let our clients teach us about their experiences and those of their friends with these medications and other substances bought, sold, and traded in the community.

Provide both written and verbal information about all three medications—methadone, buprenorphine, and naltrexone—even if you, or your clinic, do not provide them all. A signed patient agreement has also been included and can serve as an opportunity to discuss your practice's/clinic's rules, high-risk scenarios, and approaches to such issues as relapse and diversion of medication.

Once the client has the information they need, they'll be better able to make an informed choice about what medication, or no medication, might be best for them at this point in their lives and their recovery. Some key issues that will steer their choice include:

• Availability: Are all forms of MAT available in your community?

• Does their insurance, including Medicaid and/or Medicare, cover the medication? There's tremendous variability in what different state Medicaid/Title-19 programs will pay for as it relates to MAT. This includes dose limits, duration of treatment, and whether a medication is even included in the Medicaid formulary. So too, private insurance may offer barriers to some forms of MAT in the forms of pre-authorizations or high co-pays.

- Transportation. Methadone will require daily travel to the clinic for at least the early months of treatment.

- Preference and prior history with MAT.

- Setting and frequency.

  - Is the client able to commit to daily attendance at an OTP for methadone (some also offer buprenorphine)?

  - Do they have active co-occurring mental health issues that might be better addressed in an intensive outpatient or partial hospital setting?

  - Are there additional high-risk factors, such as active alcohol or benzodiazepine use, which might require an inpatient detox component?

- Outside influences: Is the client mandated to treatment? Such as:

  - Medical professionals under public health oversight.

  - MAT as a condition of probation or parole.

  - MAT in conjunction with an active child protective services case.

INFORMED CONSENT FOR MEDICATION-ASSISTED TREATMENT

It's important before starting any form of MAT that a person has the information they need to make an informed decision. The following chart goes through frequently asked questions and concerns a person might have about MAT. Ask them, "Is there anything else you'd like to know?" And for the two opioid-replacement therapies (methadone and buprenorphine), it's important that they understand they will be on an opioid and need to take it in an ongoing fashion to prevent withdrawal.

Compare and Contrast: Methadone, Buprenorphine, Naltrexone

	Methadone	Buprenorphine	Naltrexone XR
Tradename(s)	Methadose™ Dolophine Methadone Diskets Methadose Sugar-free	Suboxone, Zubsolv, Bunavail Sublocade (monthly injectable) Probuphine® (implants)	Vivitrol (long-acting injectable) Revia (oral)
What's it used for?	Treatment of opioid-use disorders	Treatment of opioid use disorders	Treatment of opioid and alcohol-use disorders
Is this an opioid-replacement therapy?	Yes	Yes	No, this is to help with relapse prevention.
How do I take it? and How often do I take it?	By mouth. Daily. Usually liquid, may be a powder or diskette.	* Film or tablet dissolved under the tongue or in the cheek. Once or twice a day. * Monthly injection (Sublocade). * Implant—every six months (Probuphine).	Monthly intramuscular injection (IM) in the gluteus muscle. May receive a test dose before starting to ensure there are no withdrawal symptoms.
Who can prescribe it for opioid use disorders?	SAMHSA-approved and state-licensed OTPs.	Physicians, physician assistants (PAs) and advance practice nurses/nurse practitioners who have undergone special training and received permission from the DEA. There may be additional state regulations.	Any medical provider licensed to prescribe medication in your state.

Will it stop/prevent withdrawal (jonesing, dope sickness, etc.)?	Yes	Yes	No. Should only be used when someone is fully detoxed.
If I stop this medication, without a taper, will I have withdrawal?	Yes, should be tapered.	Yes, should be tapered.	No
Attendance frequency	Daily clinic attendance, possibly with weekend take-home doses. Over time, clients may be given greater numbers of take-home doses.	Variable. If provided in an office-based setting, likely weekly to start, and when stable, monthly. May also be part of a partial hospital or intensive outpatient program where attendance is multiple times/ week for several weeks.	Variable, based on program requirements. The injection is monthly and requires coordination between the client, a pharmacy, and the administering clinician (typically a nurse).
Decreases or stops cravings/urges to use	Yes	Yes	Yes, but not as much as the replacement therapies.
How long will I be on this medication?	No set length. To be determined by you and your treatment team.	No set length. To be determined by you and your treatment team.	No set length. To be determined by you and your treatment team.
If I use another opioid on top of this medication, what can happen?	Additive effect, up to and including overdose, coma, respiratory arrest, and death.	Some blocking properties, but overdose deaths have been reported when combined with other opioids, alcohol, benzodiazepines, prescription sleeping medications, and other sedating substances.	Naltrexone is a strong opioid blocker. But dangerous when high-potency opioids, such as fentanyl, are taken in a deliberate attempt to override its effects. Can result in overdose and death.

Compare and Contrast: Methadone, Buprenorphine, Naltrexone

	Methadone	Buprenorphine	Naltrexone XR
Dangerous combinations	Do not combine with alcohol or other sedating medications, including benzodiazepines and prescription sleeping medications. Avoid combinations with other medications that can increase its cardiac risks.	Do not combine with alcohol or other sedating medications, including benzodiazepines and prescription sleeping medications.	Only if attempts are made to deliberately override the blocking properties.
Common side effects (>10%)	Constipation, dry mouth, blurry vision, urinary retention and hesitancy, sedation.	Constipation, dry mouth, blurry vision, urinary retention and hesitancy, sedation.	Nausea, sleep disturbance, anxiety, headache, joint pain.
What other risks are associated with this medication?	Allergic reaction. Potential cardiac risk, especially when combined with other medications that can cause heart problems (QT prolongation). Suppression of testosterone. Respiratory depression. Overdose.	Allergic reaction. Reaction site swelling or redness for both the injectable and implant forms. Acute withdrawal if client is taking another opioid agonist.	Allergic reaction. Swelling or redness at the injection site. Acute opioid withdrawal if the client has not been completely detoxed. Risk of liver damage; may need to be avoided in people with active liver disease.

Pre-MAT Assessment

Well-run office- and clinic-based buprenorphine practices and OTPs establish clear guidelines with the client before treatment begins. While treatment is individualized, this must be balanced with consistent and safe practice. It's natural for people receiving services from the same practice or clinic to compare notes. If there are large discrepancies in how treatment is provided, this can create problems, "Why does Joe get a month's worth of medication and I only get four days at a time?"

Prior to induction with MAT, a comprehensive assessment is begun (not all components may be completed at the time of induction). This can be performed by a single practitioner, or done in a team format (nurse, prescriber, intake clinician, counselor). While assessment is ongoing, standard components include:

- Chief complaint: Why is this person here today? What is/are their stated goal(s) for treatment?

- Medical history, including hospitalizations, and current chronic and acute medical problems. Is there an ongoing pain issue for which the person was, or is, prescribed opioids? A complete medication list is obtained. Are there urgent/emergent medical issues that will need to be addressed early in treatment? What form(s) of contraception does the client use if they are sexually active?

  - For female clients: Do they have a gynecologist?

  - Last dental exam and do they have a dentist?

  - A complete list of all current medications, including over-the-counter, herbal, nutritional, and vitamins.

  - Any known allergies or adverse reactions to medications?

- Alcohol and drug history, to include past and current use of tobacco/nicotine. When did they first use? What have they used? How often? How much? What is their history of treatments (to include inpatient, residential, and outpatient settings)?

  - A detailed history of opioid use needs to be obtained. This will form the basis for the opioid use disorder diagnosis. When did they start and how has it progressed? How do they use (pills, snorting, skin popping, intravenous, smoking)? How much? When did they last use? What problems has their opioid use caused? What prior treatments have they had?

- Psychiatric history: Have there been diagnoses made of co-occurring disorders? Have there been either outpatient or inpatient treatments? Is there a history of dangerousness to self or others?

- Family history: This will include medical, substance, and psychiatric dimensions.

  - "Dad was a big pot head and had hypertension."

  - Mother had diabetes and was treated for depression and anxiety.

- Legal history: Have there been arrests, convictions, and/or incarcerations? What is the client's current legal status? In most states there are searchable databases through corrections or the Department of Justice, where this can be looked up and verified.

- Social history: Educational level, work history, current living situation, hobbies and interests. Are they living in a safe and substance-free environment, or are there factors (such as homelessness) or a significant other or family members using drugs and/or alcohol in the home? What other stresses or resiliency factors can the client cite? What is their history of early trauma?

- Mental status examination (MSE): While every assessment should include an MSE, if the client is either intoxicated or in withdrawal at the initial intake, this may need to be followed up with a thorough psychiatric diagnostic evaluation after the induction is complete. The symptoms of these two states can cloud the diagnostic picture (i.e., anxiety and irritability due to withdrawal, or sedation and lack of focus and concentration from opioid intoxication). Regardless, an assessment of risk of harm to self or others should be done at the outset.

- Physical examination: This may be a focused exam with attention to those medical conditions for which people with opioid use disorders carry a higher risk—especially if they've used intravenous drugs. It may be completed by the person who will prescribe the medication, or it may be obtained from another provider.

- Blood work and other tests, to include liver enzymes and screens for hepatitis B and C, and HIV, are recommended. A pregnancy test for women of reproductive age is standard. You might also include tests for medical conditions the client has reported (such as an electrocardiogram, especially if methadone is being considered, electrolytes, blood sugar, and lipids), a test for tuberculosis, and for sexually transmitted diseases.

- A drug test should be obtained and checked.

- The PDMPs should be checked.

PRESCRIPTION DRUG MONITORING PROGRAMS (PDMPS)

All states, Missouri being the last, now have PDMPs which can be checked by prescribers (MDs/DOs, nurse practitioners, physician assistants, veterinarians, dentists, and others). The PDMPs contain information on all controlled substance prescriptions a person has filled, with the notable and unfortunate exception of methadone prescribed through opiate treatment programs. Medications found on the PDMP will include prescription pain medications, benzodiazepines, stimulants (such as those prescribed for ADHD), medical marijuana for those states that have made it legal, and prescription sleeping medications. Many states now share data on their PDMPs, so if a client is seeing prescribers in adjoining states, this will show up.

Regulations on when, how, and who can query the database vary by state. In some, prescribers can deputize other members of their team, such as a nurse, social worker, or psychologist, to check the database for them. Some states have made checking the PDMP a mandatory step prior to prescribing any controlled substance. Some have also made signing up for, and using, the database a condition for license renewal.

Important information can be gleaned from the databases. This includes:

- How many different prescribers have written prescriptions for this client?

- Are the prescriptions consistently filled early?

- How many pharmacies does this person use?

- Have there been frequent emergency room visits where the person gets prescriptions written?

- Is the client prescribed medications, such as benzodiazepines or other sedating controlled substances, which make the use of replacement therapies—methadone and buprenorphine—more dangerous?

The PDMP should be checked prior to initiating MAT, especially for methadone and buprenorphine, and then throughout treatment (some states will have guidelines/mandates on the frequency, but at least quarterly). I do it at most visits.

Other Things to Consider at Intake Include

- Releases for records from prior treaters and facilities.

- Releases for other providers, such as their primary care provider, gynecologist and other specialists, and therapist.

- Releases for other key individuals or agencies the client wants involved with their treatment.

  - Family members, parent(s), significant other/spouse the client wants involved.

  - If the client is on probation, this could be their probation officer.

  - Child protective services.

DURATION OF TREATMENT WITH MAT

Due to the relapsing and remitting nature of opioid use disorders, there should be an open-ended approach to treatment duration. Studies have shown that clients who discontinue replacement therapies—methadone and buprenorphine—have higher rates of relapse than those who do not. Short-term detoxification from opioids carries both high rates of relapse and fatalities from overdose deaths in clients who have lost some, or all, of their tolerance. So too, a client who has been fully detoxed and been on naltrexone injections will no longer have tolerance to opioids.

Treatment duration should be a collaborative and ongoing discussion. What are this person's goals as they relate to MAT? If they want to taper off a replacement therapy, a backup plan should be in place in case of a relapse or increased urges to use. If they want to remain on MAT indefinitely, that should be supported.

BUPRENORPHINE

Buprenorphine (Suboxone, Zubsolv, and others), often shortened to "bup" or "bupe," is a partial mu-agonist and partial opioid blocker. It can be prescribed as maintenance therapy and to manage withdrawal. Its strengths include decreasing and eliminating drug cravings and preventing/stopping withdrawal. It has some blocking ability at the opioid receptor, but can be overwhelmed by opioids with a stronger affinity for the receptor, such as hydromorphone (Dilaudid) and fentanyl.

Sublingual buprenorphine is typically combined with the opioid antagonist naloxone (Narcan). When taken as prescribed (under the tongue), the naloxone has minimal effect. However, should the medication be snorted or injected, the naloxone becomes active (bioavailable) and produces withdrawal symptoms. This strategy was conceived to decrease misuse and diversion. However, buprenorphine has significant street value and practitioners need to develop strategies to detect and decrease its misuse and diversion. Buprenorphine is also available as a long-acting injectable—Sublocade—(monthly) and an implant—Probuphine—(every six months). The formulation without naloxone is typically used only in those who are pregnant.

Buprenorphine Induction

Perhaps the most important aspect of buprenorphine initiation is for the client to be in mild to moderate withdrawal. For clinics/practices that provide same-day initiation, you need to inform and educate the client prior to his appointment to arrive, "as dope sick as you can stand. If you've used and you take the medication, it can make you dope sick."

Practices that do an intake on day one and induction on day two should instruct the client to use no opioids until they start the medication in the morning. An exception to the above, where you might do the induction on day one, would be a client who clearly has a moderate or severe opioid use disorder but is not currently on opioids and is at risk for a relapse and fatal overdose due to loss of tolerance and high-potency illicit opioids. This could include someone coming out of jail/prison, or someone following a detox from opioids.

The level of withdrawal is most typically assessed using the COWS, the Objective Opioid Withdrawal Scale (OOWS), and possibly the SOWS, or other instrument. The first two are completed by the clinician, and the SOWS is a 16-item self-report metric. All three are available for free download at: https://www.ncbi.nlm.nih.gov/books/NBK143183/

The final dose of buprenorphine is specific to the client. The goals are to eliminate both drug cravings and withdrawal symptoms. Average doses range between 8–16mg of buprenorphine/day. In some instances, higher doses may be required, but will necessitate greater vigilance to monitor for misuse and/or diversion.

As clinicians have become more comfortable in the use of buprenorphine, they may, with certain clients, provide instructions for in-home inductions. Here, the client is provided instructions and parameters on how to start the medication. This is coupled with a timely (within a week or two, sooner if needed) follow-up visit.

Clinical Opiate Withdrawal Scale (COWS)

For each item, write in the number that best describes the patient's signs or symptom. Rate on just the apparent relationship to opiate withdrawal. For example, if heart rate is increased because the patient was jogging just prior to assessment, the increased pulse rate would not add to the score.

Patient's Name: _____ Date: _____
Buprenorphine induction:
Enter scores at time zero, 30 min after first dose, 2 hr after first dose, etc.

Times: _____ _____ _____ _____

Resting Pulse Rate (*Record beats per minute. Measured after patient is sitting or lying for one minute.*) 0 pulse rate 80 or below 1 pulse rate 81–100 2 pulse rate 101–120 4 pulse rate greater than 120				
Sweating (*Over past ½ hour, not accounted for by room temperature or patient activity.*) 0 no report of chills or flushing 1 subjective report of chills or flushing 2 flushed or observable moistness on face 3 beads of sweat on brow or face 4 sweat streaming off face				
Restlessness (*Observation during assessment.*) 0 able to sit still 1 reports difficulty sitting still, but is able to do so 3 frequent shifting or extraneous movements of legs/arms 5 unable to sit still for more than a few seconds				

Copyright © 2018 Charles Atkins. *Opioid Use Disorders*. All rights reserved.

Times: _____ _____ _____ _____

Pupil Size 0 pupils pinned or normal size for room light 1 pupils possibly larger than normal for room light 2 pupils moderately dilated 5 pupils so dilated that only the rim of the iris is visible				
Bone or Joint Aches (*If patient was having pain previously, only the additional component attributed to opioid withdrawal is scored.*) 0 not present 1 mild diffuse discomfort 2 patient reports severe diffuse aching of joints/muscles 4 patient is rubbing joints or muscles and is unable to sit still because of discomfort				
Runny Nose or Tearing (*Not accounted for by cold symptoms or allergies.*) 0 not present 1 nasal stuffiness or unusually moist eyes 2 nose is running or tearing 4 nose constantly runs or tears streaming down cheeks				
GI Upset (*Over last ½ hour.*) 0 no GI symptoms 1 stomach cramps 2 nausea or loose stool 3 vomiting or diarrhea 5 multiple episodes of diarrhea or vomiting				

Copyright © 2018 Charles Atkins. *Opioid Use Disorders.* All rights reserved.

Times: _____ _____ _____ _____

Tremor *(Observation of outstretched hands.)* 0 no tremor 1 tremor can be felt, but not observed 2 slight tremor is observable 4 gross tremor or muscle twitching				
Yawning *(Observation during assessment.)* 0 no yawning 1 yawning once or twice during assessment 2 yawning three or more times during assessment 4 yawning several times/minute				
Anxiety or Irritability 0 none 1 patient reports increasing irritability or anxiousness 2 patient is obviously irritable or anxious 4 patient is so irritable or anxious that participation in the assessment is difficult				
Gooseflesh Skin 0 skin is smooth 3 piloerections of skin can be felt or hairs standing up on arms 5 prominent piloerections				
Total scores with observer's initials				

Copyright © 2018 Charles Atkins. *Opioid Use Disorders*. All rights reserved.

Score:
5–12 = mild
13–24 = moderate
25–36 = moderately severe
more than 36 = severe withdrawal

Documents, Policies, and Procedures to Consider

- Buprenorphine checklist: This is completed prior to/during initiation/induction of the medication.

- Buprenorphine treatment agreement/contract: This is where you can discuss program guidelines and client and provider responsibilities.

- Urine/drug testing guidelines.

Buprenorphine Checklist
(Induction)

Date		Comments
☐	Diagnosis of opioid use disorder, moderate or severe, has been documented.	
☐	Informed consent provided, including alternative forms of MAT.	
☐	Patient agreement/contract reviewed and signed.	
☐	Physical examination completed.	
☐	Blood work and other tests completed.	
☐	Pregnancy test for women of child-bearing age.	
☐	Drug test has been provided and checked.	
☐	PDMP has been checked.	
☐	Insurance/program eligibility has been verified.	
☐	Supportive/therapeutic services have been recommended and are in place.	
☐	Induction dose provided, and complete induction reviewed with client.	
☐	Prescription limited to amount needed until follow-up appointment.	
☐	Prescription for naloxone (Narcan) or overdose kit provided.	
☐	Follow-up appointment provided.	

Copyright © 2018 Charles Atkins. *Opioid Use Disorders*. All rights reserved.

Buprenorphine Treatment Agreement/Contract

As a participant in buprenorphine treatment for opioid use disorders, I accept this treatment agreement/contract as follows:

- I agree to keep and be on time for my scheduled appointments with the doctor/prescriber, and to keep all other clinic/office appointments.
- I agree to conduct myself in an appropriate manner in the office/clinic.
- I agree not to arrive under the influence of drugs and/or alcohol.
- I agree not to sell, share, or give any of my medication to another individual. I understand that such mishandling of my medication is a serious violation of this agreement and could result in my treatment being terminated.
- I agree not to deal, steal, or conduct any other illegal or disruptive actions in the office/clinic.
- I agree that my medication (or prescription) can be given to me only at my regular visits. A missed visit could result in my not being able to get medication until I am next seen.
- I agree that the medication I receive is my responsibility and that I will keep it in a safe and secure place.
- I agree that lost medication will not be replaced.
- I agree not to obtain medication from any physicians, pharmacies, or other sources without informing my treating physician/prescriber.
- I agree that I may be called in for a medication count and will show up within 24 hours with all of my buprenorphine, and any other requested medications.
- I understand that mixing buprenorphine with alcohol or other sedating medications, especially benzodiazepines such as Valium®, Xanax, and Klonopin®, can be dangerous and even deadly.
- I agree to take my medication as the doctor/prescriber has instructed and not to alter the way I take my medication without consulting with him/her.
- I agree to provide a urine toxicology or other screen when asked.
- I agree to inform my physician/prescriber immediately if I become pregnant.
- I understand that medication alone is not sufficient treatment for my disease. I agree to participate in the patient education, relapse prevention, and other clinical programs as provided to assist with my treatment and recovery.
- Other: _____

Printed Name: _____ Signature: _____

Date: _____

Copyright © 2018 Charles Atkins. *Opioid Use Disorders*. All rights reserved.

METHADONE

Methadone is a pure mu-agonist opioid. It's used for the treatment of opioid use disorders—both for maintenance and to manage withdrawal. It was first synthesized in Germany in 1939 and was brought to America in 1947 for the treatment of narcotic dependence. It can only be provided for the treatment of opioid use disorders by SAMHSA-approved and state-licensed OTPs. A searchable list of these can be found at: http://dpt2.samhsa.gov/treatment/directory.aspx

Methadone is an ideal choice for individuals who will benefit from daily dosing and frequent contact with providers. It may be an option for clients who have found that buprenorphine and/or naltrexone did not adequately address their symptoms and urges to use.

OTPs have been in existence in the United States since the 1960s and there is extensive literature to support the efficacy of methadone to reduce cravings and relapses with illicit opioids and other drugs. As with buprenorphine, pregnant women with opioid use disorders have improved outcomes when they are maintained on replacement therapy.

In the informed consent process (see comparison chart earlier in this chapter) clients should be made aware of potential cardiac concerns, and medications that might worsen these. Also, there are many drug-to-drug interactions that are possible with methadone, based on its metabolism by a specific liver enzyme (cytochrome p450 A4). Co-administration of these medications, which include several psychiatric medications such as quetiapine (Seroquel) and sertraline (Zoloft®), and also grapefruit and grapefruit juice, can cause elevations in blood methadone levels. This increases the risk of side effects and adverse reactions including sedation, respiratory depression, coma, and death.

Methadone Induction and Dosing

Federal guidelines state that an initial dose of methadone cannot exceed 40mg. Standard first-day doses range from 10–30mg. This is then titrated upward. The first two weeks of treatment carry a higher risk for overdose.

Dosing is based on the client. There can be a significant range. Studies show that less than 60mg/day is associated with higher rates of relapse. Average doses range between 60–120mg/day, though some individuals will require higher or lower amounts.

NALTREXONE AND NALTREXONE XR

Naltrexone is a long-acting opioid antagonist and is used for relapse prevention in people with opioid use disorders once they are fully detoxed. It also has an indication in alcohol-use disorders, where it decreases the rewarding effects of alcohol.

Naltrexone should not be used with clients currently on an opioid agonist, as it will precipitate withdrawal. It comes in two forms: oral/daily and a long-acting intramuscular injectable/monthly. The injection is given into the gluteal muscle (buttocks), and the site should be rotated monthly.

The biggest challenge to using naltrexone XR is a logistic one. This involves ensuring that the medication, which requires refrigeration, the patient, and the person giving the injection—typically a nurse—are all together monthly. Strategies that may help include having all clients on naltrexone XR be in the same group, or having regularly scheduled clinic hours when the injections are to be given.

People most likely to benefit from naltrexone must be completely detoxed from opioids and express a high-level of motivation to remain off them. Good candidates for naltrexone include:

- People with a strong desire to be off all opioids, including replacement therapies.

- People who have been completely detoxed from opioids and want to be on a long-acting blocker. If someone has been on an inpatient detox/rehab unit/program, it's recommended that they receive their first injection prior to discharge.

- People who are incarcerated and have a history of an opioid use disorder. Where the risk of relapse and fatal overdose is so high in this group, a first shot of naltrexone XR is recommended prior to their release date. This must be coupled with an outpatient clinic/treater that will follow them closely.

- People mandated to treatment—such as healthcare, law enforcement, and legal professionals—whose ability to retain or get back their license or job is dependent on remaining substance free.

- People on probation or referred from a drug-court or court-diversion program who have been court-mandated to treatment.

Prior to its use, informed consent should be obtained, and clients made aware of the risks, which include:

- Liver damage: Prior to initiating naltrexone, and periodically thereafter, liver function tests should be obtained. It should not be used in people with liver failure or acute hepatitis.

- For those on the injectable form, there can be injection-site reactions, which can range from mild pain, redness, and swelling, to reports of more severe outcomes.

- Clients with a history of mood and other disorders may experience a worsening of symptoms, including suicidality (though studies are inconsistent with this finding).

Naltrexone Induction and Dosing

Prior to starting naltrexone, the client must be completely detoxed from opioids. For short-acting medications and heroin, this is about six days; for longer-acting medications such as methadone, buprenorphine, and extended-release opioids, this can be between one to two weeks. A naloxone challenge, where an injectable dose 0.4–0.8mg is given to see if it precipitates withdrawal, may be done prior to starting. Or the person could begin with the oral form of naltrexone for 7–10 days. So too, a quick-read drug test should be negative for opioids.

Standard doses of naltrexone are 50mg daily for the oral form. This can also be given in three oral doses/week of 100mg, 100mg, and 150mg. The injectable form is given monthly in the gluteal muscle of 380mg/injection.

SWITCHING FROM ONE FORM OF MAT TO ANOTHER

There are several reasons why a person might wish to switch from one form of MAT to another. These include:

- Intolerable side effects or an allergy

- Inadequate treatment response

- Wanting to try something different

- Wanting to switch from a replacement therapy to a blocker

- Pregnancy

- Need for a higher level of oversight and frequency of contact

- Availability

There are a few guidelines to keep in mind when switching.

- Switching from methadone to buprenorphine: Here, clients should be tapered down to no more than 30mg. Because methadone is long-acting, and buprenorphine is a partial antagonist, clients should be advised that they may experience some symptoms of a precipitated withdrawal. If they can taper lower than 30mg, this risk is diminished but must be balanced against the risk of relapse prior to the transition. Strategies that can help include:

  - Maximize the length of time from the last dose of methadone to the first dose of buprenorphine.

  - Consider a slower induction of buprenorphine, with careful attention to the development of withdrawal symptoms.

  - Follow-up contact with the client later in the day to assess their symptoms.

- Switching from buprenorphine to methadone: There are few reports of adverse outcomes. Clients should be advised that there may be an initial additive effect (sedation) or conversely some symptoms of withdrawal. Where initial methadone doses are low, this should be minimal.

- Switching to naltrexone from either buprenorphine or methadone: The person needs to be off methadone or buprenorphine entirely. This can take between one to two weeks.

  - Begin with 7–10 days of oral naltrexone, or a naloxone challenge, described earlier in this chapter, as well as a negative drug test for opioids, including methadone and buprenorphine.

DRUG TESTING

Drug testing, and other strategies to obtain objective data around substances the client might, or might not, be using is an important aspect of treatment. For clients treated with methadone at OTPs, there are federal guidelines that require at least eight tests per year. Drug tests provide information about substances the person takes, both as part of treatment and those they use illicitly.

- If they are prescribed methadone or buprenorphine, you expect that to be positive. A negative reading could be a sign of misuse or diversion.

  - For clients on buprenorphine, it is helpful to obtain levels of both buprenorphine and its active metabolite, norbuprenorphine. For clients on maintenance therapy, the levels of metabolite (norbuprenorphine) should be higher than the parent drug (buprenorphine). Occasionally a client might spike/adulterate a urine sample with buprenorphine if they've not taken the medication. This will provide a positive reading for buprenorphine and a negative for norbuprenorphine.

- If the client is on a psychostimulant for ADHD, you expect that to be positive. A negative reading might indicate they are not taking the medication and raises concerns of diversion.

Drug tests can be likened to obtaining blood sugar readings for a client with diabetes. However, it can also be viewed as intrusive—especially where observed urines need to be obtained. In addition, clinicians need to be aware of limitations with drug tests, which include:

- False positive and false negative readings. Every test, especially quick-read cups and strips, carry a rate of false positive and negative results. If there is a dispute, or uncertainty, it's best to send to a lab for confirmation.

  - Other substances, possibly prescribed or over-the-counter medications, can cause false positive readings.

- Substances the client has ingested are not included in the screen you use.

  - Quick-read cups currently do not include fentanyl.

  - Clonazepam (Klonopin) may not be detected as a benzodiazepine.

  - Synthetic cannabinoids (K2, Spice) will not be detected.

  - Bath salts and other psychostimulants will not be detected.

- Falsification of the test.

  - Client uses someone else's urine.

  - Client puts something into the urine or takes something that will skew the result.

  - The sample is too dilute.

$\fbox{Guidelines}$

Drug Testing in the Treatment of Opioid Use Disorders

Drug testing, the collecting of biological samples (urine, blood, saliva, sweat, hair, other), is a crucial therapeutic tool in the identification, assessment, recovery, and ongoing treatment of individuals with opioid use disorders (as well as other substance-use disorders). The results of a drug test, as with any medical test, must be evaluated alongside other pertinent clinical, self-report, and historical data.

- An agency's/program's procedures regarding drug testing should be reviewed, and provided verbally and in writing to clients, upon intake.
  - If drug tests are to be used as part of a contingency plan, this must be clear to the client.
    - o Example: A certain number of consecutive negative drug screens could equate to an increased amount of take-home medication or decrease in visit frequency.
    - o Example: A specific positive result, such as a non-prescribed benzodiazepine in a client on methadone or buprenorphine, might increase the intensity of services or signal the need for a higher level of care.
  - Staff need to be trained that drug tests are a therapeutic tool to guide assessment and treatment for clients with opioid use disorders. They should never be used as a "gotcha." Drug tests simply report whether substances are present or absent.
  - Drug tests are confidential. Exceptions to this must be client/program specific and accompanied by necessary releases and permissions.
- Drug-test refusals and discrepancies between self-report and a drug test are clinical matters to be explored.
- If in-office "quick-read" (presumptive/qualitative/point-of-care) tests are used, there should be accompanying guidelines as to when more definitive/quantitative confirmatory tests through a certified laboratory/vendor will be used. Such as:
  - When there is a discrepancy or dispute between results and self-report.
  - When additional substances need to be screened, such as fentanyl(s), or clonazepam.
  - When quantification of drug levels is desired.

Copyright © 2018 Charles Atkins. *Opioid Use Disorders*. All rights reserved.

- When results are unclear.
- When there are concerns over a possible false positive or false negative result.
- Other.

• Frequency and timing of drug tests. Random versus scheduled drug tests are preferred, though they may not always be feasible/possible. Frequency takes into account: the level of care, client's progress, program/clinic expectations, cost, regulatory requirements, client choice, and other factors.

  - In general, testing will be more frequent (weekly or more often) at the beginning of treatment, or following a relapse, and then decrease in frequency.
  - For those in maintenance treatment, a monthly drug screen is within the standard of care.

• If urine drug testing is to be supervised, programs will have a written policy or procedure that addresses: client dignity, privacy, and staff training.

• If it is believed that a sample has been tampered with, a repeat is recommended.

• Results of drug tests should be communicated to clients in a timely fashion.

• Language used by all staff communicates the therapeutic function of drug testing. Results are reported as being positive or negative and never "dirty" or "clean."

Copyright © 2018 Charles Atkins. *Opioid Use Disorders*. All rights reserved.

OVERDOSE REVERSALS WITH NALOXONE (NARCAN)

Naloxone, most common trade name Narcan, is an opioid antagonist that can reverse an opioid overdose. It's a life-saving medication that comes in several forms, both injectable and intranasal. The selection of one over another will be determined by ease of use, cost, and availability. Most insurance covers naloxone, and some states have made it available without a written prescription.

For family members and people who use opioids, and other street drugs that may be laced with fentanyl or heroin, naloxone in the home is essential. Clinicians need to educate clients, their families, and involved others about naloxone. In my experience, a written prescription for a double-dose overdose kit (these should always have at least two doses) often goes unfilled. Strategies to get around this include:

- Have the pharmacy deliver an overdose kit to either the client's home or to the program they attend. As many programs cannot, by policy and statute, store medication, the pharmacist will hand it to the individual in treatment.

- Programs with embedded pharmacies, or those that can dispense medications, can have kits made up and distribute them.

- Hold distribution events. Where most insurance will cover naloxone, a distribution event can both educate members of the community about opioids and naloxone, while simultaneously handing out overdose kits.

- Some states/facilities have instituted programs where people who leave prison or detox/rehab facilities are provided a kit.

How to Recognize an Overdose and Administer Naloxone (Narcan)

When someone has overdosed with opioids they will initially appear sedated, then become unconscious, unresponsive, and eventually stop breathing. If the overdose is not reversed, death occurs in a matter of minutes as the lungs collapse and fill with fluid.

As the person overdoses, their breathing can become loud, they may snore, or gurgle. As breath stops, their lips and fingers may turn blue, gray, or purplish.

Steps to Take in an Overdose

Try to arouse the person. Shake them by the shoulders and rub your knuckles along the center (sternum) of their chest. "Hey Joe, wake up!"

- Administer the first does of naloxone (Narcan).

- If you're with someone else, have them call 911. If you're alone, call 911 after the first dose. Do not leave the person alone and continue to try and wake them up. Keep the line open with 911. Hang up only when they tell you to do so.

- If they have stopped breathing, administer rescue breaths; and if there's no pulse, and you know how to do it, administer CPR.

- After two or three minutes, if they have not awakened, give the second dose. If you're using an intranasal form of naloxone, use the other nostril.

- As the person wakes up, roll them onto their side into the rescue position. This is in case they vomit, so the gastric contents won't go back into their lungs and create an aspiration pneumonia or make them choke.

- Stay with them until help arrives. Keep them awake. If they again become unconscious, administer another dose of naloxone.

As someone is revived, be aware they will experience typical symptoms of withdrawal, which can be severe. The individual should be encouraged to go with medical personnel to the nearest emergency room. Ideally, this may be a time to try and help someone engage in treatment, such as a replacement therapy. Some hospitals have introduced programs that rapidly connect people with treatment following an overdose. Some will even start a first dose of buprenorphine in the emergency room with next-day follow-up at a local clinic or practice. And others have brought in recovery coaches/navigators/peers (people in recovery) to meet with the client and help get them connected to services.

Many people with opioid use disorders will be unable to tolerate hours of withdrawal in an emergency room or they may refuse to go at all. Often, following a reversal, the person returns to the dealer who sold them their near-death dose and buys more. A recent study from Boston showed that about 10% of people who have been revived from an overdose are dead within a year.

Benzodiazepines, Sedative Hypnotics, and Alcohol in MAT

The majority of opioid-related overdose deaths include the co-administration of other sedating substances, such as benzodiazepines (alprazolam/Xanax, clonazepam/Klonopin, diazepam/Valium, lorazepam/Ativan and many others, including ones obtained from other countries via the internet). Any substance that causes sedation, including nonscheduled medications such as gabapentin (Neurontin), can be linked to a worsening of respiratory depression. Even when clients are educated about these risks, they often continue to seek benzos and other sedative hypnotics, such as the prescription sleeping medications zolpidem/Ambien®, eszopiclone/Lunesta®, and zaleplon/Sonata®.

Reasons clients cite for wanting to take these include:

- Unrelieved anxiety or depressive symptoms.

- The euphoric effects obtained from combining these medications with methadone or buprenorphine. People further into their recovery will candidly discuss how benzodiazepines with methadone provides a taste of the euphoria they first experienced with opioids.

- Insomnia.

Clinicians, clinics, and other facilities need to consider how they will manage issues related to people who continue to seek and obtain these substances, which significantly increase the risk for fatal overdose.

- For individuals with complaints of depression and/or anxiety, what other strategies—including non-sedating pharmacological ones and non-pharmacologic therapies and other interventions—have been tried?

- For those who are on benzodiazepines, is there an ability to taper them off? This might require an inpatient detox prior to, or simultaneous to, initiating MAT. Or if they insist on remaining on the benzodiazepine(s), would the non-agonist (non-opioid) option of naltrexone be a safer choice over methadone or buprenorphine?

- For complaints of insomnia, there are several approaches to take. First, be aware that many individuals on opioids complain of insomnia. This may be a sign of opioid-induced apnea or other form of sleep-disordered breathing. Ask their bed partner, if they have one, about snoring and frequent awakening throughout the night. As both methadone and buprenorphine are opioids, the prescriber might want to consider a sleep study to rule out apnea, which is a common finding in people on replacement therapies.

- Sleep hygiene. Work with individuals around maximizing healthy habits and routines around sleep.

  - Avoid doing anything in bed other than sleeping or having sex. Do not read, play video games, or watch television in bed. This is a behavioral intervention that retrains the brain to equate the bed with sleep, and not with other activities.

  - Make sure that everything in the sleep environment is comfortable, from the mattress, to the pillows, to the noise level, light and so forth.

  - Consider techniques to help promote sleep including progressive muscle relaxation training, such as can be found on the following free app (CBT-I Coach) from Stanford University and the Veterans Administration:

    o https://mobile.va.gov/app/cbt-i-coach

  - Establish routines around sleep, including a regular bedtime and wake-up time. This helps to reestablish a set circadian cycle. The brain and body begin to associate times of the day with going to sleep and waking up.

- Download a white-noise app or find a soothing background sound that facilitates sleep onset and maintenance.

- Have clients keep a sleep diary, which can be brought into sessions to review what has been, and has not been, effective. This also helps quantify the problem in terms of numbers of hours slept, and patterns that may be making things better or worse.

- Educate clients that a sleep hygiene plan takes at least two weeks of following it to see if it's effective.

Finally, establish clear rules with clients around your program's or practice's rules and expectation around benzodiazepines and other sedating substances. The following document, or one like it, which is specific to benzodiazepines can be used both as signage in a clinic waiting area, or as part of an informed consent.

Use of Benzodiazepines for the Treatment of Anxiety and Insomnia

Benzodiazepines are medications that are sometimes used to treat anxiety and insomnia. **They are best avoided all together with people on methadone or buprenorphine/Suboxone/Zubsolv/Sublocade.**

They include:

- Ativan (lorazepam)
- Klonopin (clonazepam)
- Valium (diazepam)
- Xanax (alprazolam)

While these medications can be effective for short-term use, they can have serious side effects and health risks when used for longer periods. They have been shown to increase the risk of death by accidental overdose, as well as falls, memory impairment, and confusion.

Benzodiazepines are habit-forming. Once a person has been on them for more than a few weeks, stopping abruptly can cause serious withdrawal including worsening anxiety, trouble sleeping, shakiness, seizures, hallucinations, and in extreme cases, death.

In combination with other sedating medications/drugs, such as oxycodone, methadone, heroin, fentanyl, and other opioids, including buprenorphine/Suboxone, benzodiazepines increase the risk of fatal overdose.

Because of the above we have put extra safety precautions in place.

1. Your psychiatrist, nurse practitioner, or physician's assistant, will conduct a thorough evaluation to determine your diagnosis. This includes:
   a. Questions about how you feel now, and about symptoms and treatment(s) you have had in the past.
   b. Your medical history and any current or past use of alcohol, medications, and street drugs. We may ask you for a urine screen, and we collect information from the state database about your medication history. We will ask for your consent to contact previous providers and family

Copyright © 2018 Charles Atkins. *Opioid Use Disorders*. All rights reserved.

members for additional information. For your safety, it is important that you provide us with thorough and honest information.

2. Your prescriber may suggest treatment with alternative medication or may recommend effective non-medication therapies and lifestyle changes.

3. If the decision is made to prescribe a benzodiazepine, we will aim for the lowest effective dose and will regularly assess the need for continued treatment. Urine drug screens, checking the state medication database, and ongoing collaboration with other providers will be maintained.

4. To receive ongoing prescriptions, follow-up appointments will need to be kept. An in-person appointment is necessary to assess the safety, effectiveness, and overall appropriateness of treatment.

5. At any point in treatment, we may discuss the need to lower your dose and/or taper you off the medication while providing alternative mode(s) of treatment.

Copyright © 2018 Charles Atkins. *Opioid Use Disorders*. All rights reserved.

DIVERSION

Both buprenorphine and methadone carry a high potential for misuse and diversion. As mentioned throughout this, and other chapters, a variety of strategies can help decrease diversion. These include:

1. Clearly written patient guidelines that specifically address the consequences for misuse and diversion.

2. Query the Prescription Drug Monitoring Program (PDMP) before initiating MAT and periodically thereafter.

3. Careful, and frequent, drug testing.

4. Listen and respond when clients report that medication is being diverted.

5. Pill/strip/bottle counts. This is where a client needs to present to the clinic/office within a prescribed time frame with all their medications, so they can be counted. To decrease the risk of a certain patient feeling singled out, some clinics have random pill counts, so that everyone knows this could happen to anyone at any time.

6. Be consistent and follow the rules you've established for your clinic/practice.

CHAPTER 8

The Medical Fallout: It's Not Just Overdoses

- **Overview**
- **Facts and Figures**
- **Opioid Side Effects and Adverse Reactions**
- **Interview with Harm Reductionist Mark Jenkins**
- **Intravenous Drug Use**
- **How to Decrease Harms Associated with Intravenous Drug Use**

OVERVIEW

This chapter reviews what's known about the short-term and long-term effects of opioids, both prescribed and illicit, on physical health and well-being. We'll look at specific concerns relative to intravenous drug use and ways to decrease the risks of transmission of blood-borne pathogens, such as HIV and hepatitis B and C.

FACTS AND FIGURES

- Estimates of people infected with the hepatitis B virus in the United States range from 850,000–2.2 million. Major risks include blood-borne and sexual transmission.

- Rates of newly infected individuals with hepatitis C, largely through intravenous transmission, increased more than 2.9 times between 2010–2015.

  - The CDC estimates that there are 3.5 million Americans currently infected with hepatitis C.

OPIOID SIDE EFFECTS AND ADVERSE REACTIONS

Because we have opioid receptors throughout the body, effects of opioids go far beyond those associated with pain management, and the euphoria pursued by those who misuse them. What follows is a systematic review of side effects and adverse reactions seen with opioids.

"I no longer dreamt when I slept—there was just darkness."

Mark Jenkins
Greater Hartford Harm Reduction Coalition

my story

My story is not a secret. My drugs of choice were cocaine and alcohol, but I've tried them all. I've been to jail in six different states, had 35 detoxes, five psych hospitalizations, and 17 inpatient rehabs, the last at Lebanon Pines in April 1997. I remember sitting around that table of clinicians and knowing what they wanted to hear, but I was out of answers. I had reached a point where I no longer dreamt when I slept— there was just darkness.

Something happened there. Somebody gave me a little piece of a spider plant. I put it in water, and it grew roots. A week later I put it in a Styrofoam cup with some soil and began to look at that plant as a reflection of myself. As long as I kept that plant healthy, I thought the same could apply to me. Immediate change was necessary. It became a life-or-death situation. I didn't know if I had another shot or if I even wanted one. I was doing increasingly dangerous things to get high—I committed crimes.

Although I didn't know how to stay clean, I did know about relapse. I couldn't keep anyone's secrets anymore. If you got high in Building 2 and I knew about it, you had to go. I've seen it happen in programs time and time again. Someone would sneak and get high, others would cover for them, and before you knew it, everyone was high.

I took my little plant on walks through Lebanon Pines. I nurtured it, and it grew. When I left the Pines, I took it to a sober-living house and then to my first apartment. It outgrew five different containers, and the baby spiders went into more than half a dozen homes. Like recovery, they could be shared.

I stayed close to positive people, and I volunteered and was eventually hired as an AIDS risk reduction outreach worker (ARROW) and got a part-time job with a transitional HIV program.

I was introduced to some people who were doing harm reduction, but I wasn't buying. I went back to college and went to lots of trainings, all in my first year clean. I wasn't content with just being clean; I knew there was more. I fell in love with frontline work, meeting people where they were in their own environments and in their own time—no clocking in and no clocking out.

In time I moved back in with my family, and everything I had lost because of my drug use was given back to me. But the work is in my blood. They say that from those to whom much has been given, much is required. I've been spared a lot of circumstances where the outcome should have been death for me, yet today I'm wearing a shirt that bears the name of an organization that I founded.

Now, I am a harm reductionist to the root of my being. I'm a fan of abstinence. It's something to aim for, but I understand that it doesn't work for everybody and it may not be the goal for every individual. It's my job to help participants remove barriers to getting clean but still support their use. I help people reduce the negative behaviors associated with active use by providing access to clean and sterile supplies such as syringes, cookers, water, condoms, alcohol wipes, and Narcan.

We need safe injection facilities (SIFs) so people stop dying behind bathroom and bedroom doors. They need to be in urban centers, and they need to be welcoming and nonjudgmental. If someone is in "the moment," and ready for treatment, we help make those services available. And if they're not ready, we support that too. Just tell me when you want it, and we can talk.

If an individual is alive, there is opportunity. Participants grow to trust us, and they refer others within their social circles.

I understand and protect the confidentiality of one-on-one discussions. That's the secret of my longevity on the front line—love for the work and the people we serve. This isn't a nine-to-five problem, and we understand the importance of "the moment." The lifeblood of harm-reduction practice is to meet folks where they are at, in their own time, place, language, and lived experience.

my story

Respiratory System

- Opioids all can lead to respiratory depression, which in overdoses is the proximal cause of death. Opioids depress respiration three ways:

    - Decrease the rate of respiration.

    - Decrease urges to breathe when carbon dioxide (CO_2) levels are high.

    - Depress chemical sensors in the carotid artery and aorta when oxygen levels are low.

- For people with preexisting lung problems, such as COPD (emphysema and bronchitis) and asthma, opioids increase the risk for respiratory depression. Morphine can worsen or precipitate asthma attacks through the release of histamine.

- Opioids should be avoided in people with sleep apnea, who are already prone to diminished levels of oxygen and higher levels of carbon dioxide.

- The respiratory depressant effects of opioids are magnified when combined with other sedating medications, drugs of misuse, or alcohol, and even the anticonvulsant gabapentin (Neurontin), which has been present in the toxicology reports of hundreds of fatal overdoses.

Gastrointestinal

- Constipation: This common side effect, found in 40–90% of people on opioids, can range from mild to severe. Clinicians/clinics that provide buprenorphine and methadone need to educate clients about this side effect and to regularly ask about it. Symptoms of a problem include: bloating, abdominal pain, nausea, vomiting, no passage of stool in more than two days, and changes in bowel pattern.

    Constipation, if severe and unchecked, can progress to bowel obstruction, perforation, peritonitis, and death. It's common for individuals on replacement therapies to take stool softeners daily. If laxatives are also required, the individual should be educated as to which ones are okay—bulk/fiber laxatives—and which ones to avoid—laxatives containing phenolphthalein. The major causes of constipation have to do with opioids' effects throughout the GI system, which slow the passage of food, and increase the reabsorption of water.

- Esophageal reflux: The esophagus is the muscular tube that allows passage of food into the stomach. Opioids inhibit relaxation of the esophageal sphincter that normally occurs when we swallow. Also, opioids increase the amount of time food remains in the stomach by as much as 12 hours, which is another risk for reflux. One significant risk with esophageal reflux is that regurgitated food, especially during sleep, can be aspirated into the lungs and lead to pneumonia.

- Diarrhea, most typically associated with withdrawal.

- Nausea and vomiting are common side effects, especially in unhabituated opioid users. It's likely due to a combination of gastric slowing and direct stimulation of an area in the brain that controls the urge to vomit (*area postrema* of the medulla).

Urinary

- Urinary retention and hesitancy: This is a common side effect and can prove bothersome in clinics and practices where frequent urine tests are required. Because of this, it's helpful to remind clients to drink plenty of fluid and to not void prior to coming to the clinic. In severe instances of urinary retention, catheterization (the insertion of a tube into the bladder) may be necessary.

Central Nervous System

- Analgesia.

- Euphoria and mood enhancement.

- Sedation, which is dose- and tolerance-dependent. Most individuals on maintenance therapy (methadone and buprenorphine) may experience some initially, but this usually goes away in time, unless there is co-administration of another central nervous system depressant, such as alcohol, benzodiazepines, and prescription sleeping medications.

- Cough suppression: Morphine and other opioids decrease the cough reflex.

- Miosis (pupil constriction).

- Nausea and vomiting.

Skin

- Facial and truncal flushing.

- Itching.

- Sweating.

- Injection site reactions, from rashes to infections.

- Track marks: Where and how a client injects their drugs should be explored with them. Have they needed to move from one site to another due to sclerosed blood vessels? Is there meaning connected to where they inject? Such as choosing sites that can go undetected.

Hormonal (Endocrine)

- Decreased testosterone levels in both men and women. Testosterone is necessary for the mineralization of bones. This can have long-term implications with higher rates of osteoporosis and osteopenia, with increased risk for breaks and fractures. It may also be a factual underpinning for the statement, "Dope rotted my bones."

- Along with decreased levels of testosterone comes decreased libido, and over time there can be changes in secondary sexual characteristics, such as breast enlargement in men, and shrinking of the testicles. This is likely fueled by opioid-induced increases in prolactin levels (the hormone associated with breastfeeding).

- Women on chronic opioids may experience irregular and even absent menstrual cycles. This can lead to a false sense that they are not able to get pregnant. The mechanisms for this have to do with decreased levels of both luteinizing hormone and follicle stimulating hormone—both integral to the normal menstrual cycle.

Cardiovascular

- Decreased blood pressure when changing from a lying to standing position (orthostatic hypotension). This is experienced as light-headedness and, if extreme, can result in fainting.

- Decreased heart rate.

Dental

- Opioids can cause dry mouth. Because saliva is important to wash away the bacteria that cause plaque, the lack of this leads to cavities. Clients need to be advised to use a fluoride toothpaste and mouthwash, especially if they're not on fluoridated water. Regular dental care is recommended.

Psychiatric

- As we've touched on throughout this book, one potent reason that people turn to opioids is for their euphoric and mood-enhancing properties. Beyond this, many individuals with anxiety, depression, and PTSD report relief, at least initially, from some, or all, of these painful emotional states. Clinically this is both useful and interesting when getting a client started on replacement therapy, and is one reason why a full psychiatric evaluation is best done after the induction, especially if there are withdrawal symptoms. It may be that someone you think will require treatment—including pharmacotherapy—for their depression or anxiety no longer appears clinically depressed or anxious once stable on methadone or buprenorphine.

Intravenous Drug Use

Intravenous drug use carries three broad categories of potential and serious harms: blood-borne diseases through unsafe injection practice, which introduces bacteria and other pathogens into the body through the injection site, and poisoning and overdose—through substances mixed with the drugs, as well as unknown drugs, potencies, and combinations. A cautionary truism from the harm-reduction community is: "Once you put it in your body, you can't take it out."

Blood-Borne Diseases

The human immunodeficiency virus (HIV) weakens the body's immune system and can lead to development of opportunistic infections and the full-blown acquired immunodeficiency syndrome (AIDS). There is no cure for HIV, but there are effective treatments. Risks for transmission include: unsafe intravenous drug use, sexual transmission, or from an infected pregnant woman to her newborn during pregnancy, at childbirth, or through breastfeeding.

- Early detection of HIV is associated with improved outcomes, both for the individual and to decrease further transmission of the virus.

Hepatitis B is transmitted via blood and mucous membranes. Frequent means of transmission are from mother to child at birth, close physical contact, and blood-borne transmission—such as can occur with unsafe injection practices and the sharing of needles and cookers. There are effective vaccines for hepatitis B and the recommendation from the CDC is that at-risk individuals, including those with multiple sexual partners, healthcare workers, and IV drug users, get vaccinated.

- Testing for hepatitis B and C is recommended for any person with a history of intravenous drug use or other risk factors.

Hepatitis C is mostly transmitted through blood—such as occurs with the sharing of needles, unsterile tattoo equipment, and accidental exposures—but can also be sexually transmitted. The current recommendation from the CDC is that all baby boomers (people born between 1945–1965) get screened. This is due to high rates of infection—3%, in this age group. Most people with hepatitis C infection are asymptomatic and likely unaware of their status. However, over time, hepatitis C infection can cause liver damage that ranges from mild to cirrhosis (scarring of the liver and liver failure) and liver cancer (hepatocellular carcinoma).

- Since 2011, highly effective treatments with greater than 90% cure rates have come onto the market (protease inhibitors). These typically involve 8–12 weeks of oral therapy.

- The CDC website for viral hepatitis contains all the information you and your client will want. It is found online at: https://www.cdc.gov/hepatitis/hcv/index.htm

Adverse Reactions Due to Injection Use

Our skin is colonized with a variety of organisms, including bacteria and fungi. Any time someone pierces a needle through the layers of the skin, especially if it's not been sterilized with alcohol or another antimicrobial agent, there is a risk that microbes will be introduced into the skin, the blood stream, the muscle, and even the bones.

- Cellulitis: This is an infection in the layers of the skin. It typically starts at an injection site and spreads out. Symptoms include redness, warmth, pain, and swelling. If caught early, oral and topical (creams/ointments) antibiotics may work. If not, this can turn into a medical emergency and require hospitalization and intravenous antibiotics.

- Endocarditis: Here, bacteria or fungi from an injection site find their way to the leaflets of the heart and establish colonies. This can damage and destroy the heart valves and other structures. If unchecked, this can be fatal. Treatment is most often provided in a hospital and requires up to four weeks of intravenous antibiotics. In some cases, surgery will be required to replace or repair damaged valves, or to directly treat a fungal infection. Signs and symptoms of endocarditis can include:

  - Fever

  - Chills

- Headache

- Joint pain

- Shortness of breath

- Dizziness and fainting

- Chest pain

- Osteomyelitis: These are infections of the bone and bone marrow, which are painful and serious. If untreated these can result in loss of limb and life.

- Abscesses: These are pus-filled localized infections. They may require surgical drainage; they can be both acute and chronic.

- Sepsis and septicemia: This occurs when bacteria, or other organisms, enter the bloodstream, which should be sterile (free from any infectious organism). Symptoms vary, but may include fevers, chills, confusion, and changes in blood pressure and pulse. Sepsis is life-threatening and represents a medical emergency.

- Sclerosed blood vessels: Likely due to a combination of contaminants in the drugs, the drugs themselves, and frequent injections, many intravenous drug users develop inflammation within their veins that render them unusable. Sclerosed veins that can be felt through the skin have a tough, hard feel.

  Sclerosed veins make it increasingly difficult for an intravenous drug user to find access and may eventually lead to higher-risk forms of injection. For healthcare providers, this may be an issue if a client needs an intravenous line started and there are no usable peripheral veins.

- Resistant bacteria: Methicillin-resistant *Staphylococcus aureus* (MRSA) has become prevalent in individuals who inject their drugs. These bacteria evolved due to the over-prescription of antibiotics and require aggressive treatment, which includes both oral and intravenous medications. Dubbed the "flesh-eating" bacteria, MRSA infections need to be taken seriously. If left untreated, they can result in amputation and/or loss of life.

Injection of Unknown Substances and Unknown Quantities

In the wake of the current fentanyl overdose phenomenon, people who inject drugs often do not know what's in the bag, or the pill—at times with catastrophic results. Prior to this, high-purity heroin, unlike what had been found on the street in the 60s, 70s, and 80s, contributed to the upward trend in overdose deaths. Again, the harm-reduction truism resonates: "Once you put it in, you can't take it out."

The following images from the DEA website speak volumes to the current dangers found with street drugs, from the miniscule quantities of fentanyl required for a fatal overdose, to the sophistication of drug dealers who counterfeit OxyContin and other pills, to where not even an experienced drug enforcement agent, pharmacist, or experienced drug user, can tell the real from the fake.

Amount of fentanyl (2mg) required for a fatal overdose. *Source: DEA*

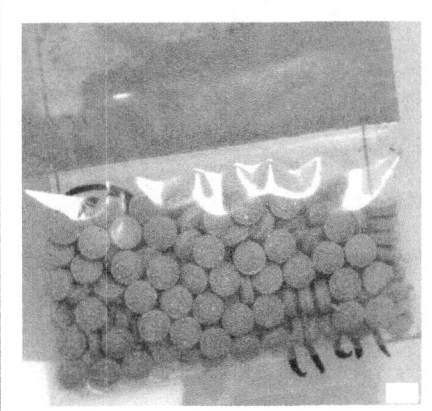

Counterfeit pills containing fentanyl and heroin. *Source: DEA*

How to Decrease Harms Associated with Intravenous Drug Use

The harm reduction movement began in the Netherlands when people who injected drugs asked the government to look at things from a public health perspective, to help stem the rising tide of HIV and hepatitis transmission. This led to the first needle-exchange programs, enhanced access to methadone, education provided to people in the community about safer practices, condom distribution, naloxone education and distribution, and more recent developments, which include quick-read strips to see if a substance has been tainted with fentanyl (not 100% accurate), and even Safe Injection Facilities (SIFs) where people can take their drugs in the presence of a healthcare team who can intervene if they get into trouble.

Harm-reduction strategies take the approach that people have always and will always engage in risky behavior. But if they understand what the risks are and have the means to decrease the potential for harm, they will do so.

People who inject drugs should:

- Thoroughly clean the injection site with alcohol or another antimicrobial—such as is done by a nurse or phlebotomist—to decrease the risk of introducing bacteria, fungi, and other potentially infectious agents found on our skin into the tissues or bloodstream.

- Never share needles.

- Use new, sterile needles.

- Don't share cookers. Hepatitis C can survive outside of the body for up to three weeks and can be transmitted via anything that's been contaminated by blood.

- Don't inject your drugs alone and take turns. That way if someone overdoses, someone is awake and can revive them.

- Have naloxone (Narcan) with you.

CHAPTER 9

The Therapeutic Relationship, Readiness for Change, and Establishment of Goals

- Overview
- Engagement
- Setting Your Goals and Priorities
- Level of Motivation and Stage of Change Theory
- Matching Stage of Change to Intervention
- Case Study and Discussion

OVERVIEW

Before we dive into specific therapies, wellness strategies, and the like, this chapter explores what matters in treatment. How do you and this person in your office or clinic get along? Do they look forward to seeing you and vice versa? Do they use what they've learned outside your office or clinic? Just as important, and connected, are you on the same page? Have goals been articulated and are they the client's, the clinician's, or some other entity's such as a criminal justice or a child protective service agency? Some people may struggle to identify and voice specific goals. We'll explore techniques that can help. Because without goals, where is this therapy or treatment headed? Finally, we'll discuss how all of this gets tied to the client's motivation for change, and why this is a moving target, especially with opioid use disorders.

ENGAGEMENT

Engagement, what happens at the start of any relationship—therapeutic or otherwise—sets the stage for the work to come. Can this person trust you? Do they feel heard? Do they believe that you have their best interest at heart? Engagement starts at "hello" and continues forward. There is no set time frame, but if the engagement process is not valued, or is glossed over, the foundation of a working relationship is not strong. While the above might seem basic, the lack of a solid relationship and mutually agreed-upon goals can lead to ineffective and failed treatments.

SETTING YOUR GOALS AND PRIORITIES

Next come goals. While I've separated these from engagement, they often develop together. People can struggle with this crucial process: what is it you want to work on? Why are we here today? In dialectic behavior therapy, one approach has been to use a generic goal—"A life worth living"—when a client is unable to articulate goals, especially at the start of a therapy.

For people with opioid use disorders—which is likely why they came to treatment—their substance use is a great place to start. What is their goal around the opioids? Are they looking to stop? To cut down? To get on MAT? What about other substances?

"I want to get on bup, but I don't want to stop smoking pot."

"I need to stop the street drugs. I don't want to die with a spike in my arm."

"I don't get high anymore. I'm just trying not to be dope sick. I'd love to be off everything, but it's not realistic right now. Maybe I should do methadone for now."

As we move away from substance-specific goals, things open up and can lead to other big-ticket items—the things the client really wants that have been compromised, lost, or delayed due to their substance use: family, work, a love relationship, inner peace. … This also provides a wonderful opportunity to get to know this person you're sitting with and to help them look at what a life in recovery might include.

The following worksheet can be used to help a client hone in on those goals they consider important. This can be completed in session, given as a homework assignment for group or individual therapy, or used as a structured, or semi-structured, interview (which might be useful for a client who can't read).

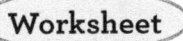
Setting Your Goals & Priorities

Below, and on the following pages, are lists of things many people find important. Next to each item is a place for you to check those that matter to you. Check as many as you like. If you come up with something not on these pages, write it down. Remember these are yours and not what you think others might want for you.

Relationships:
- I want to be in a committed/romantic relationship _____
- I want to improve my relationship with my partner _____
- I want to improve my relationship with my children _____
- I want to improve my relationship with my parents _____
- I want good relationships with other family members _____
  Be specific and write in who: _____
- I want to have lots of friends _____
- I want one or two good friends _____
- I like to be around people _____
- I like a lot of time alone _____
- Other: _____

Health:
- My health is important _____
- I need to work on my health _____
  Be specific: _____
- Exercise is important to me _____
- I want to exercise more, and/or more regularly _____
  Write in how much and what type: _____
- Sleep is important to me _____
- I want to watch what I eat _____
- I want to lose weight _____
- I want to gain weight _____
- I want to take medication as prescribed _____
- Other: _____

Copyright © 2018 Charles Atkins. *Opioid Use Disorders*. All rights reserved.

Drug and Alcohol Use:
- I want to stop using (write in the drug/drugs here): _____
- I want to cut down (write in the drug/drugs here): _____
- My recovery from drugs and/or alcohol is important to me _____
- I want to stop smoking cigarettes _____
- My continued abstinence from cigarettes is important _____
- Other: _____

Emotions:
- I want to be more emotionally stable _____
- I want to be less depressed _____
- I want to be less anxious _____
- I want inner peace _____
- Other: _____

Money:
- I want to have a lot of money _____
- Money is not so important to me _____
- I want enough money to be comfortable _____
- Other: _____

Spirituality:
- Being a part of a church/temple/synagogue is important to me _____
- I don't like to be a part of organized religion _____
- My spirituality is important _____
- My faith in God is important _____
- Giving back to others is important to me _____
- Meditation is important to me _____
- Prayer is important to me _____
- Other: _____

Creativity:
- Being creative is important to me _____
- I like to make stuff (be specific): _____
- Playing music is important to me _____
- I want to learn some kind of creative skill _____
- Other: _____

Copyright © 2018 Charles Atkins. *Opioid Use Disorders*. All rights reserved.

Work:
- I want to work a full-time job _____
- I want to work a part time job _____
- My current job is important _____
- Any job is important _____
- I don't want to go to work _____
- I want to do volunteer work _____
- Other: _____

School:
- School is important to me _____
- I want to go back to school _____
- These are my school goals (be specific): _____

Home:
- My home is important _____
- Where I live is important _____
- I like to spend most of my time at home _____
- I like to spend most of my time out of my house/apartment _____
- I want to find a stable place to live _____
- Other: _____

Hobbies & Fun Activities:
- Spending time on my hobbies is important _____
- I want to have more fun _____
- Scheduling time for activities and/or hobbies is important _____
- I want to spend time on fun things. (List at least three.)

   _____

   _____

   _____

- Other: _____

Pets:
- My pets are important _____
- I would like to have an animal(s) _____
- Other: _____

Copyright © 2018 Charles Atkins. *Opioid Use Disorders*. All rights reserved.

Step Two

Go back through the items you identified as important and circle two or three that are extremely important and that you want to work on <u>now</u>. Write them here.

1. _____

2. _____

3. _____

Step Three

Of the two or three things you identified as most important, rank them in order: first, second, and third. Put a star next to the one that you want to/need to address right away (this may or may not be number one). Look at what you've written down and see if these are indeed your most important goals/priorities. If not, make necessary adjustments. Remember these are for you and no one else.

1. _____

2. _____

3. _____

Copyright © 2018 Charles Atkins. *Opioid Use Disorders*. All rights reserved.

LEVEL OF MOTIVATION AND STAGE OF CHANGE THEORY

Nestled in the discussion of goals comes the matter of readiness. How eager, willing, and ready is your client to make the changes that will bring them closer to their goals? Stage of change theory (Prochaska and DiClemente) is a model that can be applied to any behavior. It's a way to think about where someone is at with their goals, priorities, and substance-use behavior.

The stages are broken down as follows:

Precontemplation: The person does not believe there is a problem.

- Jack: "I just snort on the weekends. I don't get withdrawals or anything. It's not a problem. If I had to stop I could. I just don't want to. I love the way heroin and the pills make me feel—like everything is good in the world. It's magic."

Contemplation: The individual acknowledges there may be a problem but is not yet ready/ willing to take action.

- "I think the cold symptoms I get every Monday after a weekend of snorting pills is withdrawal. But it's not that bad. I've got this handled … but maybe I don't."

- "I just spent two hundred bucks on oxys. I needed that money for the rent. What am I doing?"

Preparation/Readiness: The person plans and prepares to change the behavior.

- Jack researches different types of treatment on the internet. He finds programs in his area that provide buprenorphine. He finds out which ones take his insurance.

Action:

- He calls the clinic, makes an appointment, and goes. He starts on the buprenorphine or methadone and begins to attend groups. He learns about addiction. He has frequent cravings and urges to use. He gets a Narcotics Anonymous (NA) sponsor who doesn't hassle him about being on MAT.

Maintenance: The behavior is managed in an ongoing way and does not reoccur.

- Jack continues in treatment for three years. He steadily and slowly decreases his dose of buprenorphine or methadone. He attends 12-step groups in the community and a monthly relapse prevention group. He can go months between when he even thinks about using pills. On the rare occasion he gets a craving, he distracts himself or calls his sponsor.

Termination: The problem behavior has been completely extinguished. Many in recovery, even long-term recovery, view this as more theoretical than real.

- He completes his taper off the medication but continues to work on his recovery. Even the thought of using an opioid seems odd to him. He has no cravings or urges to use. He continues to attend 12-step and leads a meeting. He now sponsors three other people in recovery.

Relapse: The problem behavior reoccurs.

- Jack goes to an emergency room with abdominal pain. He is diagnosed with diverticulitis and given two shots of hydromorphone (Dilaudid). The pain subsides. He's sent home with two antibiotics and 30 oxycodone to take as needed. He crushes and snorts the pills. They're gone in two days. He thinks about calling his sponsor, but instead tracks down the number for his old dealer and purchases pills. He makes plans to see a GI doctor, who he hopes will order him a script if he complains about pain.

Readiness for change is not linear and it's a moving target. Following an overdose someone may desperately want to break the cycle of their addiction (preparation/readiness). However, as withdrawal symptoms worsen and cravings return, it's easy to slip back into contemplation and precontemplation. Now the motivation is to treat the withdrawal with drugs, often from the same dealer who sold them what they'd overdosed on.

Matching Stage of Change to Intervention

Readiness for change is crucial as to whether someone is willing and able to enter and continue with treatment. A person's stage of change can guide clinicians to match where they are with recommendations and interventions they are more likely to follow. Someone with a high level of motivation who is ready to act is the ideal candidate for many treatment options, including MAT and self-help groups.

Someone in precontemplation or contemplation is best served with motivational and engagement approaches, including approaches such as community reinforcement and family training therapy (CRAFT-T; discussed in Chapter 10), which mobilizes family and/or a concerned significant other (CSO) to help.

To tell someone who does not think they have a problem with opioids that they should attend an NA meeting once a day for the next 90 days, or enter a drug treatment program, is unlikely to be effective. "Are you crazy? I'm fine."

Treatment failures often occur when a client's motivation and readiness for change is not where the treatment team, or family, wants it to be. This kind of disconnect, at best, creates a treatment impasse and, at worst, destroys the relationship. The Stage of Change Readiness and Treatment Eagerness Scale (SOCRATES), while initially studied with people in treatment for alcohol-use disorders, is a useful tool to clarify a client's current readiness to work on their opioid misuse and other problematic substance behavior.

Copyright © 2018 Charles Atkins. *Opioid Use Disorders*. All rights reserved.

Questionnaire

Personal Drug Use
(SOCRATES 8D)

Instructions: Please read the following statements carefully. Each one describes a way that you might (or might not) feel about your drug use. For each statement, circle one number from 1 to 5, to indicate how much you agree or disagree with it *right now*. Please circle only one number for every statement.

	NO! Strongly Disagree	No Disagree	? Undecided or Unsure	Yes Agree	YES! Strongly Agree
1. I really want to make changes in my use of drugs.	1	2	3	4	5
2. Sometimes I wonder if I'm an addict.	1	2	3	4	5
3. If I don't change my drug use soon, my problems are going to get worse.	1	2	3	4	5
4. I have already started making some changes in my use of drugs.	1	2	3	4	5
5. I was using drugs too much at one time, but I've managed to change that.	1	2	3	4	5
6. Sometimes I wonder if my drug use is hurting other people.	1	2	3	4	5
7. I have a drug problem.	1	2	3	4	5
8. I'm not just thinking about changing my drug use, I'm already doing something about it.	1	2	3	4	5

9. I have already changed my drug use, and I am looking for ways to keep from slipping back to my old pattern.	1	2	3	4	5
10. I have serious problems with drugs.	1	2	3	4	5
11. Sometimes I wonder if I am in control of my drug use.	1	2	3	4	5
12. My drug use is causing a lot of harm.	1	2	3	4	5
13. I am actively doing things now to cut down or stop my use of drugs.	1	2	3	4	5
14. I want help to keep me from going back to the drug problem that I had before.	1	2	3	4	5
15. I know that I have a drug problem.	1	2	3	4	5
16. There are times when I wonder if I use drugs too much.	1	2	3	4	5
17. I am a drug addict.	1	2	3	4	5
18. I am working hard to change my drug use.	1	2	3	4	5
19. I have made some changes in my drug use, and I want some help to keep from going back to the way I used before.	1	2	3	4	5

Copyright © 2018 Charles Atkins. *Opioid Use Disorders*. All rights reserved.

SOCRATES Scoring:

Transfer the client's answers from the questionnaire (see note below):

	Recognition	Ambivalence	Taking Steps
	1 _____	2 _____	
	3 _____		4 _____
			5 _____
		6 _____	
	7 _____		8 _____
			9 _____
	10 _____	11 _____	
	12 _____		13 _____
			14 _____
	15 _____	16 _____	
	17 _____		18 _____
			19 _____
TOTALS	Re _____	Am _____	TS _____
Ranges	7–35	4–20	8–40

INSTRUCTIONS: From the SOCRATES Scoring Form transfer the total scores in the empty boxes at the bottom of the profile grid below. Then, for each scale, CIRCLE the same value above it to determine the decile range.

DECILE SCORES	Recognition	Ambivalence	Taking Steps
90 Very High		19–20	39–40
80		18	37–38
70 High	35	17	36
60	34	16	34–35
50 Medium	32–33	15	33
40	31	14	31–32
30 Low	29–30	12–13	30
20	27–28	9–11	26–29
10 Very Low	7–26	4–8	8–25
RAW SCORES (from Scoring Sheet)	Recognition=	Ambivalence=	Taking Steps=

Source: Miller, W.R., & Tonigan, J.S. Assessing drinkers' motivation for change: The Stages of Change Readiness and Treatment Eagerness Scale (SOCRATES). *Psychology of Addictive Behaviors.* 1996;10:81–89.

These interpretive ranges are based on a sample of 1,726 adult men and women presenting for treatment of alcohol problems through project MATCH (Matching Alcohol Treatment to Client Heterogeneity). Note that individual scores are therefore being ranked as low, medium, or high relative to people already presenting for alcohol treatment.

High scores in both recognition and taking steps correspond with a higher level of motivation to change the behavior. Ambivalence is tied to the recognition score. That is, a high score may represent willingness to address the behavior. But a low score, in someone who knows/recognizes that there is a problem, may also indicate openness to change.

An alternative screen that looks at readiness to change for any behavior, is the University of Rhode Island Change Assessment Scale (URICA), developed by Carlos DiClemente. This 32-item metric looks at the stages of change, and a client's current level of motivation using 5-point Likert scales. A downloadable version with instructions is available at: http://www.fadaa.org/archive/Annual_Conference/2010/Handouts/Wednesday/Glebe_handout4-UnivRI_Change_AssessScale.pdf

Case Study

20-Year History of Opioid Use

Ray is a 36-year-old married mental health social worker with a 20-year history of opioid use—currently 5–10 bags of intravenous heroin, or the equivalent in pills. He comes in for an outpatient treatment intake, stating, "I feel like a hypocrite, telling people they have to stay clean, and then I'm shooting up in the bathroom." He has concerns that his current job at a local mental health clinic is in jeopardy due to his frequent absences, and he received a written warning last month when he fell asleep at his desk. "I nodded off. It wasn't the first time. Just the first time I got caught. I know that if I don't get a handle on this I'm going to be another dead junkie." He last injected prior to coming to this appointment.

Ray's wife, Annie, is in recovery. "We met in rehab. Her drug of choice is cocaine. That and booze, but she's doing great—eight years without anything. It's just a matter of time before she kicks me out … It won't be the first time. Last time it did get me into detox and then onto bupe. I stayed mostly clean for two years. But about six months ago I got the 'eff its,' stopped the bupe, and scored some oxys. I'm such an idiot. I hear my patients talk about 'just one more time.' I know it's bull, but when I have those thoughts … moron." They have no children, and both work in the mental health and addiction fields.

Ray first used opioids following a high school soccer injury, where he suffered a torn meniscus and fractured patella. "I liked them the first time I tried them, and everyone talked about which pills to get. You know, ask for them by name, and wouldn't you know it, the doctor gave them to me. After a couple weeks of swallowing pills, one of my teammates told me about snorting. Wow. This is great, I thought. That first rush was unlike anything I'd ever experienced."

He first injected drugs in college, "But I use clean needles and never share." He has been to more than eight detox programs and three, monthlong residential programs. He has never been on psychiatric medications, denies symptoms of anxiety, depression, or dangerousness to self or others. He has no active legal issues. "The couple times I've been pulled over and holding, I've always managed to talk my way out of it." He completed a SOCRATES questionnaire in the waiting room, which shows high levels of a willingness to take steps and recognition of his substance-use problems. His ambivalence is low, as he knows that there is a problem.

In addition to sports injuries, his only other active medical problem is chronic hepatitis C, which he has had for over 10 years. "I know there's super-expensive pills you can take to cure that. I should probably do it—especially while I've still got a job and insurance. I don't want to get liver cancer."

A review of the PDMP is positive for multiple emergency room visits with small prescriptions for opioids. His report of being on buprenorphine is corroborated with monthly prescriptions for 16mg/day that ended five months ago. His urine toxicology is positive for morphine and codeine (expected metabolites of heroin).

DISCUSSION

Diagnostically, Ray meets criteria for an opioid use disorder, severe. His kept appointment, along with a high expressed level of motivation for change, are positive signs.

He presents with a stated goal to get off illicit opioids. While he has both an extensive history of opioid use and is in the mental health profession, it's important to both respect his expertise, but not assume he has all the necessary information he'll need to make informed decisions.

First, we want to help him better flesh out realistic and desirable short- and long-term goals. Either by using a worksheet, such as was presented earlier in this chapter, or through careful interviewing and listening, we'll want to explore:

- What level of care might work best?

  - Based on his history he would be a candidate for a higher level of care, such as a detox with MAT induction followed by a rehab stay.

  - Alternatively, with adequate support and supervision, he might do well with either an IOP or other structured program combined with MAT. If this is not successful, a higher level could then be sought.

- Options for MAT

  - Review the pros and cons of all three forms of MAT, again focusing on his goals. If he opts for either buprenorphine or methadone, this should be initiated as soon as possible. For methadone, that could be today. For buprenorphine, you'd want him to be in mild to moderate withdrawal, so a next day induction is optimal. If he opts to go on naltrexone XR, he would need to be completely detoxed from opioids, and that might be the deciding factor to get things started on an inpatient detox unit.

- Family involvement

  - Encourage him to include/invite his wife into the treatment/recovery process.

  - Consider CRAFT-T, which educates those concerned to help motivate the identified patient to get them in, and keep them in, treatment.

- Relapse prevention and other interventions, possibly CBT or rational emotive behavior therapy (REBT), to address his most recent relapse. A careful chain and subsequent solution analysis, presented in the next chapter, might help him identify problem triggers, cognitions—"One more time"—the "eff its," and behaviors and strategies to decrease the likelihood for relapse.

- Work: Help him problem solve around maintaining his job while getting the help he needs, possibly under the Family and Medical Leave Act (FMLA).

- Insurance and affordability: While no stranger to the options discussed, Ray will need to look at what his insurance covers, along with deductibles and co-pays.

- Look at self-help groups geared toward other mental health professionals with opioid-use disorders. He, and/or his wife, might already know about these.

- Medical follow-up for hepatitis C.

- Throughout the process, explore and support his interests and help him construct meaningful habits and wellness strategies, to include exercise, healthy diet, and the inclusion of activities he enjoys and finds meaningful.

CHAPTER 10

Treatment: A Thousand Paths to Recovery, from Professionals to Peers

- **Overview**
- **Interview with Rebecca Allen, MPH**
- **Contingency Management**
- **Motivational Interviewing/Enhancement/Technique**
- **Cognitive Behavioral Therapy (CBT)**
- **Dialectic Behavior Therapy (DBT)**
- **Community Reinforcement and Family Training for Treatment Retention (CRAFT-T)**
- **Don't Forget the Family**
- **Pros and Cons/Decisional Matrix**
- **12-Step Programs and Groups**
- **Self-Management and Recovery Training (SMART Recovery)**
- **Refuge Recovery**
- **All Recovery Meetings**
- **Online Groups and Recovery Communities**
- **Harm Reduction**
- **Case Study (With Diary Card and How to Construct a Behavioral Chain Analysis)**

OVERVIEW

There is no single, or right, road to recovery. Over the course of my career, and in writing this book, I have encountered thousands of people in recovery from substance-use problems. While stories have similarities, each is unique. The 12-step program that saved one person's life, just didn't appeal to someone else, who found help when she was ready in a long-term rehab. So too, professionals need to remember that the populations and people we work with can skew our big-picture perspective. Millions of people get into recovery without ever seeing an addiction specialist. They do it on their own, they do it with peer-support groups, they do it with their family, their faith, their …

The Power of Peers

Rebecca Allen, MPH
Connecticut Community for Addiction Recovery (CCAR)

I'm a woman in long-term recovery from heroin, although I did dabble in other things. I got into recovery about 20 years ago after a 10-year struggle with treatment and incarcerations.

Nicotine was my gateway drug at 12, maybe 13. Then it was pot, acid, a little bit of speed, some cocaine, but not much. At college I met some friends who'd progressed to heroin. I tried it, and very quickly I was addicted. I started snorting, was skin popping within two weeks, and IV mainlining after a month. I spent every dime I had on heroin. My first arrest—for shoplifting—came about six months into my addiction.

I've been imprisoned eight times, but most (five) of them were only for six months or less. My longest was 9–12 months. I gave birth to my youngest daughter while incarcerated in 1991. Back then, as long as you were not a high security risk, you were given a "medical furlough." When I went into labor, the guards brought me to L&M Hospital in New London. After I was admitted, they left. Once I gave birth and the hospital released me, they picked me up and brought me back to Niantic. I wasn't on MAT (although probably should have been—although that's a longer story) so my daughter didn't have to stay hospitalized. Her father ended up taking her from the hospital and I was released six weeks later.

Being locked up saved my life numerous times. It's true. I like to share my history of incarceration, because I'm not the only one who struggled and found recovery in prison.

My last time in Niantic was 1996. When I got out, I decided I had to do something different. I went to a long-term halfway house in Willimantic. It was a structured environment, though we could work. I spent almost a year there. I got a job. I worked in a factory. Not the type of thing I was used to, having always done office jobs. But the

my story

physical activity helped, and I found that mind-body connection and was able to manage my stress.

And yes, I got urges to leave. But I learned to sit with those feelings. Something connected for me while I was in there. I thought, why do I keep making stupid decisions? I couldn't figure out how to not use heroin. There was this running conversation in my mind, like my addiction was talking to me. I knew I was a smart person. Why did I keep making bad choices? Especially when I knew they'd bring me back to heroin. I started to pay attention and didn't act on those impulses. I began to recognize the addiction talking. It would tell me that all my counselors were full of shit. That I didn't need help. That I didn't have to be here. Or that I could do this on my own. When I recognized those thoughts and what they led to, I could sit with them and not act on them.

My path to working with others is sort of funny. I got a part-time job at the halfway house as a client supervisor—not a peer, more like a babysitter. But I was also open with the fact that I was a program alumnus. I used my story strategically to let others know that I knew at least some of what they were dealing with.

Eventually, I found my way to CCAR. I was aware of them, but not certain what they were. When a position opened, I applied. What attracted me were their foundational principles. You're in recovery when you say you are, and they're there to support people regardless of their path.

I'd never been a group person. My first encounter with a 12-step group was when I was early in addiction. That was the path you were supposed to take. Go to NA meetings, get a sponsor, do 90 meetings in 90 days. But no one looked like me. It was a bunch of old white men. I knew it wasn't for me. It was never my pathway to recovery. And the concept I found at CCAR—different things work for different people— was validating. It was my entry into peer-based services.

People need to be able to talk to someone with a shared experience. You have to vent and not worry about the other person being afraid you're about to relapse. You need that person in your life, and it must be in a way that you can hear it free from shame and blame. Now, I train others to be recovery coaches. We meet people where they're at, including in emergency rooms after an overdose. We've trained coaches since 2008—our curriculum is used worldwide and has trained over 20,000.

my story

This chapter provides an overview of therapies, wellness strategies, and other techniques that can help an individual move forward in their recovery. Some are provided or taught by professionals, others harness the power of one person in recovery helping another. We'll include contingency management, cognitive-behavioral approaches (including dialectic behavior therapy), diagnosis-specific therapies for clients with co-occurring mental health issues, motivational interviewing, mindfulness, case management, and the importance and utility of a whole-person approach to recovery. We'll look at peer-based and self-help therapies, approaches, and communities, and discuss harm reduction and abstinence models. Key techniques, such as constructing a pros and cons list, and behavioral chain analysis will be reviewed. For clinicians, it's important to remember: We are involved in a tiny portion of our clients' lives. How they move through their days outside of our offices and facilities is where the real work happens. Our challenge is to help them develop the skills, motivation, and resiliency they will need to succeed.

Psychosocial interventions and counseling are recommended in the prescribing guidelines for all three forms of FDA-approved MAT. However, studies assessing the efficacy of different interventions and therapies show inconsistent, and at times discouraging, results. So too, there is little careful research on the complex human beings who walk into our clinics and offices with co-occurring substance, mental health, physical, and social problems. This can create disconnects between what makes it into a study or journal article, and what makes sense with this person in your clinic/office. With careful and ongoing assessment, attention to the therapeutic relationship, and a rigorous focus on your client's goals, treatment will stay on course. Yes, there may be setbacks and relapses, but a strong therapeutic relationship, along with clear goals, will provide your client the greatest chance for recovery at their pace and on their own path.

CONTINGENCY MANAGEMENT

Contingency management is one of the better-studied interventions, and uses behavioral approaches, rewards, and reinforcers, to help the client achieve specific goals. Behaviors to put on a contingency plan might include:

- Clinic attendance.

- Abstinence from substance misuse, often linked to results of drug tests.

- Abstinence from risk behaviors for sexually transmitted diseases, HIV, and hepatitis.

- Abstinence from other problem behaviors, such as cutting and eating disorder behaviors.

- Homework completion.

Reinforcers and rewards can take different forms and are not extravagant. They might include:

- Praise: This should be genuine and authentic. "Awesome job. That's five weeks in a row with perfect attendance."

- Punch-card-style gift cards or vouchers, where after five negative urine screens in a row, the client gets a free coupon for a local coffee shop or store. An alternative is the "fish-bowl" style incentive program, developed by Nancy Petry, PhD, where a client who has exhibited a desired behavior, such as a negative drug screen, draws a slip of paper from a bowl. Sometimes they will win a prize, sometimes they won't. This employs the powerful behavioral technique of intermittent reinforcement. Tickets with no prize will have a positive message, such as "Good job!" Others will have small prizes, with a few larger ones scattered in the bowl.

- Increased numbers of take-home doses for methadone, or a longer prescription for buprenorphine based on desired behavior.

- Entry into a lottery drawing, where every negative urine or group attendance produces a ticket to be entered.

- In dialectic behavior therapy skills groups, the simple reinforcer of giving a sticker for group attendance, and another sticker for completed homework, are effective. Group members often cover their workbooks with these.

- Increased time between clinic visits (for some people this will be a reward, while for others a reinforcer might be an extra individual session).

For some, there may be specific goals that are well suited for a contingency plan. This could include people who have external motivators for treatment, such as active legal issues, probation, a child protective services case, housing issue, or so forth, that can be tied to clinic attendance and negative drug screens. "Wonderful, that's two months with perfect attendance and negative urines. Your mom said if you did that she'd let you move into the apartment over the garage. Well done."

Aversives/punishments are less effective and should be avoided, but if necessary, only used in the interest of the person's goals. The reason behind this can be likened to trying to get a donkey out of a room. If you wave a carrot or apple, that will usually do the trick. If you hit the donkey with a stick, it might move ... or kick you, but the chances of getting it through that door are slim.

When unwanted behaviors occur, the contingency moves in the opposite direction. The reward is withheld, and the behavior is addressed. "Hey, a relapse is not the end of the world. But I do think we need to ramp up the frequency we see you, until we figure this out and get you back on track." "Your last urine came back positive for fentanyl, let's talk about that. Because if you're not worried about that, I am."

When using contingency management, the client and the clinician should work off the same playbook; reinforcers should make sense and be connected to the behavior in real time. For programs with reward systems, give the client a copy of the menu of how many ticket punches they need for a prize. The goal is to make rewards and reinforcements frequent and easy to obtain, especially early into recovery when the pull of addictive behavior is the strongest.

The Reward Shop Menu

With each negative drug screen and kept appointment you receive a punch on your reward ticket—well done! When you have an adequate number of holes punched, you can trade your card for the following (subject to availability):

Item	Number of Holes Punched
$5 Donut House Gift Card	15
$10 Donut House Gift Card	20
Personal Hygiene Gift Basket	15
Recovery T-Shirt	10
Week Pass to Local Gym	10
Pair of Movie Tickets	30
$10 Internet Gift Card	20
Mystery Box	25

Motivational Interviewing/Enhancement/Technique

Developed by psychologists Miller and Rollnick, motivational interviewing (MI) provides a judgment-free, empathic, and validating approach to work with people with problem behaviors. It's change-based and helps a person articulate what it is they'd like to improve, weigh the pros and cons (see worksheet later in this chapter), and support steps toward their goal(s). It employs techniques that include:

- Reflective listening: Here you want to make certain that you have completely understood what a client is telling you. And that they're aware you got it.

  - "On the one hand, you loved that awesome rush you used to get from snorting oxycodone, but it's been getting harder and harder to get that back. Is that about right?"

- Nonjudgmental stance: In MI, clinicians need to monitor their own internal feelings and attitudes about the client's behaviors and not voice them, especially if they are negative. Do not turn into their mother.

  Judgmental: "Can't you see your IV drug use is killing you?"
  Nonjudgmental: "Tell me about your IV drug use."

  Judgmental: "I think methadone is just replacing one addiction for another."
  Nonjudgmental: "There are many paths to recovery."

- Nonconfrontational/Noncoercive: MI steps back from confrontation and meets the person where they're at, not where the clinician wants them to be.

- Roll with resistance: Ambivalence about substance misuse is normal. People engage in high-risk drug use for a variety of rewarding reasons. To give up getting high, or to lose the relief from depressive and anxious symptoms that opioids provide, is no small thing—especially when coupled with the reality of withdrawal. The approach is empathic and supportive.

  - "I can see how giving up getting high is a lot. You've had some great times with your friends."

  - "I can see how scary not using dope is—not just the sick part but wondering about how you'll cope with your PTSD stuff. Does that about sum it up? Or am I missing a piece?"

- Heighten the internal dissonance around the problem behavior. Here the therapist becomes a repository of change talk the client brings into the room. As the person entertains the notion of change (preparation/readiness stages of motivation) the clinician nudges toward action. This includes helping them voice steps they'd like to take, along with a time frame.

  - "On the one hand, you love the ritual with the cooker and the needle; and on the other you just told me that two of your friends had fatal overdoses. That sounds awful. How do you balance these two things?"

  - "Wonderful, you've thought about getting into a MAT program. Well done. Is it more than thoughts? If so, what's the plan? I'm very proud of you."

- Validation: MI—as with many of the strategies discussed in this book—deliberately employs the positive reinforcement of validation. All positive change needs to be acknowledged and reinforced in a sincere and genuine manner.

  - "You walked through that door to get help. That's no simple thing. Good for you."

  - "One month without a pill or dope—awesome."

Cognitive Behavioral Therapy (CBT)

Initially developed as a research tool by Dr. Aaron T. Beck, CBT has been well studied and found effective across a broad swath of psychiatric and substance-use disorders. It employs a here-and-now teaching model that helps people understand the connections between their thoughts, emotions and feelings, behaviors, and even physical (physiologic) responses to a variety of situations. In CBT, every emotional change can be traced back to thought.

- "What were you thinking and doing before you decided to call your dealer?"

- "Let's look at what went through your head when you started to get angry with your mother."

CBT works with clients to challenge distorted thoughts and to practice new approaches out in the real world. Homework assignments are a typical part of CBT. Similar to DBT and REBT, CBT uses behavioral chain analyses to better understand the connections among thought, emotion, and behavior.

Key concepts in CBT include:

- Automatic thoughts: These are fleeting (milliseconds) scripts that pass through our heads, which can trigger profound emotional changes, including flight-fight-freeze responses. These thoughts are connected to deeper-held views about oneself, the situation at hand, and other personal beliefs, which may or may not be accurate reflections of reality.

  - An 18-wheeler cuts you off on the highway. An automatic thought might be, "Oh my God, I'm going to die!" Adrenalin pumps, you swerve to avoid catastrophe, your pulse quickens. Free from the immediate danger, you think of all the horrible things you'd like to do to that truck driver.

  - For a person with chronic pain, an automatic thought might be, "If I don't get something for this pain, I'm not going to make it."

  - Urges and cravings to use can be triggered by automatic thoughts: "I'm hungry." "I need." "I'm sick, I can't take this."

  - Or, for someone with an opioid use disorder, the thoughts might support the substance use: "I can do this one more time." "These therapists don't know what they're talking about. I've got this covered." "I can stop whenever I want, I just don't want to."

- The cognitive model shows the ways we respond to situations. How we perceive an event leads to emotional responses, physical changes, and behaviors. An example could be an unopened letter from a law office: for one person it could signal a lawsuit, while another might joyously expect news of an inheritance from a relative they never knew.

- Cognitive distortions and cognitive restructuring: CBT looks at patterns of habitual thought to see if they're accurate and valid. Distortions, which take many forms, are identified and challenged. Some common distortions are:

  Mind-Reading: Does your boss really hate you, or is her silence as you walk by a sign that she's thinking about something else?

  Generalization/Filtering: This is when a piece of a situation is magnified into the whole. Is this an "awful day," or have you just had a difficult few minutes with a coworker?

  Catastrophizing: Does the phone message from your doctor's office saying, "Your test results are in, please call," indicate that you have an inoperable brain tumor, or that they just want to give you the normal results?

  Fallacy of Fairness: Is everyone else better off than you?

Control Fallacies: Here others become responsible for our actions (external)—

"Look what you made me do." Or that we're responsible for the way others feel or behave (internal)—"I didn't mean to make you feel bad."

Black or White Thinking: This is when things, or people, are all one way or another. There is no gray. "You're either with me or against me. You pick."

Labeling: This is where we reduce people, their behaviors, or situations to a global label—often a negative or pejorative one.

- "She's a junkie, what do you expect?"

- "He's so manipulative."

Shoulds: These are expectations we set for ourselves and possibly others.

- "I should be able to work a full-time job, take care of the kids, clean the house, and bake the 12 types of Christmas cookies my mother did."

Emotional Reasoning: This is when we take how we feel, about ourselves or others, to reflect a greater reality.

- "I'm pathetic, I can't do anything right."

- "I gained another pound … I'm such a fat loser."

DIALECTIC BEHAVIOR THERAPY (DBT)

Developed by Marsha Linehan, PhD, dialectic behavior therapy—initially targeted for individuals with suicidal and self-injurious behavior, accompanied by profound emotional vulnerability—has shown efficacy as a powerful multi-diagnosis therapy. This is not surprising when one looks under the hood at the components that constitute DBT. These include: mindfulness, CBT, and a dialectic approach that emphasizes a balance of radical acceptance (validation of the individual and their experiences, emotions, and perceptions) with the need to change. "I can see you're working very hard, but it's not getting you where you want to be. We need to figure out ways to make you work better and more effectively."

DBT views problematic behaviors, including substance misuse, self-injury (cutting, burning), and suicidal thought and action, as maladaptive solutions the client has found to address problems of living and, for some, unbearable emotional pain. DBT examines—using weekly diary cards and behavioral chain analyses—every aspect of a targeted behavior to fully understand the who, what, where, when, and why of the most recent relapse, cutting episode, overdose, fight with the child protective service worker, etc. Once the chain analysis is complete, the clinician and client can see where the use of skills might have made things go in a different direction. DBT emphasizes the teaching, practice, and reinforcement of skills. These are divided into four modules, which can be taught both in individual sessions, or in a structured, and typically weekly, skills training group.

The modules—which contain dozens of skills and hundreds of worksheets, which a clinician can download an unlimited number of times once they've purchased Dr. Linehan's manual—include:

- Mindfulness: Founded on Zen mindfulness, DBT breaks down the components into:

  - The three "how" skills: Observe, Describe, and Participate.

  - The three "what" skills: Nonjudgmentally, One-mindfully, Effectively (doing what works).

  Also covered in this module is a model for states of mind: Emotion Mind, Wise Mind, and Reasonable Mind.

- Interpersonal Effectiveness: This module helps clients learn effective ways to ask for what they want, and how to tell someone no.

- Emotion Regulation: Here the cognitive model, and all of CBT, are taught. Issues of emotional vulnerability are discussed and approaches to wellness are woven in. Other skills and worksheets encourage the deliberate and strategic increase in pleasurable—non-substance—behaviors, while others help the client better delineate and define their goals and priorities.

- Distress Tolerance: Here the focus is on crisis management. How to make it through a bad or difficult situation—such as getting pulled over by a cop, or having an active CPS case—without making it worse. Also taught in this module are strategies to manage problem substance-use behaviors and how to cope with urges to use (urge surfing).

There are many wonderful online DBT resources, samples of diary cards, mindfulness meditations, and even apps. Here are a few:

- https://behavioraltech.org/

- www.DBTselfhelp.com

- www.tara4bpd.org/

COMMUNITY REINFORCEMENT AND FAMILY TRAINING FOR TREATMENT RETENTION (CRAFT-T)

Not to be confused with the CRAFFT screening tool for adolescents presented in the following chapter, this intervention involves the identified client/patient and a CSO, such as a family member, partner/spouse, or friend. Developed by Robert Meyers, this dyadic intervention involves working with the CSO of a person with a substance-use disorder to help motivate them into treatment. It has also been studied with people already in treatment, where the CSO works to help them stay in treatment.

Studies that have looked at the effectiveness of CRAFT-T have demonstrated strong positive results for getting a person into treatment, treatment retention, and decreased substance use.

Don't Forget the Family

People in recovery from opioid use disorders often discuss the things that they lost as their addiction progressed: jobs, relationships, material goods, self-respect, and most importantly, their families. This psychosocial spiral frequently brings the adult child back into the family home—if they ever left. This creates tense and emotion-fraught scenarios where parents live in fear of finding their child dead on the other side of a bedroom or bathroom door. There can be intense feelings of shame and guilt—"Is this something I did?"—and isolation. As a culture, we tend to keep our problems to ourselves—"What am I supposed to say? My daughter is an addict?"

As seen in the CRAFT-T model, family and loved ones can be a tremendous asset to help motivate a person to get help and to instigate change and promote recovery. For clinicians, bringing in the family is more than window dressing. It's a chance to help your client maintain, or rebuild, important relationships. Where substance disorders often run in families this may also provide an opportunity for a pre-contemplative parent, partner, or sibling to also seek help. It's common for a child with an addictive disorder to get help at the same time their parent(s) pursue recovery—"Tell you what, Dad. If you go to rehab, so will I."

Family work also mobilizes powerful in-the-moment supports. It's often the mom or dad who will help make the calls, field the insurance issues, and drive their son or daughter to the intake appointment.

As clinicians, it's important to take the time and encourage our clients to include their families in the process. Most of the time, it's in everyone's interest.

For family members, involving them in the recovery process provides vital education and support. Family work can occur at many levels, although if done in a clinic, program, or practice setting, releases must be obtained and maintained. It's best to get these at the start and keep them up to date.

Approaches include:

- Peer-based such as Nar-anon family groups: http://www.nar-anon.org/

- Local support groups specific to the opioid crisis have arisen. These vary and clinicians and agencies might consider assembling a list with local contact information to provide to their clients and their families.

- Family work within all levels of treatment from outpatient to inpatient and residential. This can be provided in both multifamily groups and individual formats.

Pros and Cons/Decisional Matrix

Most of us use pros and cons every day. Do I get up or do I lounge in bed and play Candy Crush on my iPad? Well, it's Monday and if I don't get up and go to work, eventually I'll lose my job. I like my job and it pays the bills. I'd better put the iPad down and get up.

For someone in the grip of an addiction, a pros and cons list, developed during calm moments, serves multiple purposes. From a motivational perspective, this is a wonderful technique to elicit change talk. When a person puts something down in writing, it becomes real and retrievable on the printed page. Beyond that, a written pros and cons, which the client carries with them, can be read when the urge to use, or engage in, the problem behavior strikes. It's an interesting truth that when cravings hit, all the good reasons not to use are out of mind, or are cast in shadow by the urge. A pros and cons list reviewed in a high-risk moment may help a client regain perspective and make a different decision, such as not to use, to get something to eat to lessen the hunger/craving, to call a friend, to go to a meeting, to call their therapist, to pray, to …

The following worksheet and completed sample provide a simple two-by-two grid that includes both the reasons to engage in a behavior and not to. This can be given as a homework assignment or completed in group or individual session. The important step is to get someone to agree to keep it with him/her, and when the urge hits, to take it out and read it before doing the identified behavior.

Sample Worksheet

Pros & Cons

Name: Vic Filipetti

Date: 9/8/2018

Behavior to work on: Using heroin while on methadone

Instructions: Fill out your pros and cons for the above behavior in each of the squares below.

Pros of doing the behavior:	Cons of doing the behavior:
• Get super high. • I like the whole process of cooking and shooting dope. I miss it. • I miss the people I used to get high with.	• Risk getting kicked out of the methadone clinic because of positive urines. • I could overdose, because there's really powerful drugs on the street. • It's expensive and I don't have the money ... unless I sell some of my take-homes to pay for it. • People will be upset with me if they find out. • Some of the people I did drugs with were creeps.
Pros of not doing the behavior:	**Cons of not doing the behavior:**
• I'll be in good standing at the clinic and won't have to go so often. • Get more take-homes. • People might start trusting me. • I'll save money. • I won't die from an overdose. • I won't be around people who make me do things I don't want to do.	• I won't get high. I like to get high. I miss it.

Copyright © 2018 Charles Atkins. *Opioid Use Disorders*. All rights reserved.

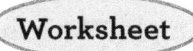

Pros & Cons

Name: _____ Date: _____

Behavior to work on: _____

Instructions: Fill out your pros and cons for the above behavior in each of the squares below.

Pros of doing the behavior:	Cons of doing the behavior:
Pros of not doing the behavior:	**Cons of not doing the behavior:**

Copyright © 2018 Charles Atkins. *Opioid Use Disorders.* All rights reserved.

12-STEP PROGRAMS AND GROUPS

Alcoholics Anonymous (AA), founded in 1935, is the oldest existing peer-based, self-help community. NA, begun in 1953, uses a similar format based around the 12 steps, which get woven into a person's program ("working the steps"). This is an abstinence-based model where people come together in meetings (no professional facilitator), tell their stories, discuss key topics (such as one of the steps or traditions), and share in a community that has come together with a single purpose: to get and stay clean and sober. The only membership requirement is "a desire to stop using." There are both open-to-the-public meetings, and closed meetings restricted to people with substance-use disorders.

Similar to AA, groups begin and end with a prayer, such as the serenity prayer:

"God give me the strength to accept the things I cannot change.
Courage to change the things I can,
And the wisdom to know the difference." (Reinhold Niebuhr)

The concept of giving over to a higher power is presented in step one, though there is no endorsement of a specific religious orientation. People are free to choose whatever a "higher power" means to them.

A mindful, "one day at a time" philosophy is embraced.

Sponsorship is urged, where one member with long-term abstinence becomes a coach to a newer person. AA and NA have groups around the world.

In regard to people on MAT, NA has brochures that discuss their position, which is to take no opinion on any outside matters including medical treatments and medication. They are clear, however, that the NA model is abstinence. This can potentially create barriers for people on MAT who could benefit from the fellowship, support, and education found within the NA rooms. Here, the recommendation is for a person to try attending different meetings within their geographic sphere, and find ones where they feel comfortable, supported, and accepted. For professionals, I urge attendance at one or more open meetings to obtain a firsthand sense of just how powerful these can be. Also, consider gender-specific groups, groups for teens, and groups geared toward members of the LGBTQ communities.

More information, including a meeting finder, is available at their website: https:// www.na.org/. There is also an NA app.

SELF-MANAGEMENT AND RECOVERY TRAINING (SMART RECOVERY)

Not a 12-step group, SMART recovery is an inclusive and secular program that emphasizes autonomy and self-management in the face of addictive behaviors.

The program incorporates Albert Ellis's REBT, a form of CBT that emphasizes a four-point program focusing on motivation; managing cravings and urges; understanding the connections between thoughts, emotions, and behaviors; and developing a full and balanced life.

The SMART recovery website, which includes information and a meeting finder, is: https://www.smartrecovery.org/

REFUGE RECOVERY

This is a mindfulness-based approach to recovery that draws upon Buddhist principles. It emphasizes knowledge of addiction and empathy and compassion toward oneself, especially in the face of suffering that has come from the addiction(s). They have both online and in-person meetings. Their website is: https://refugerecovery.org/

ALL RECOVERY MEETINGS

All Recovery Support Meetings are just that. They are inclusive and open meetings that welcome everybody, regardless of their path. Like 12-step there is no professional facilitator, and the following format, courtesy of the CCAR, can be followed. There is no insistence on a higher power; and rather than open and end with prayer, they start with a moment of silence and close with an affirmation. People on medication-assisted treatment are welcome.

All Recovery Meeting Format

Opening:

I would like to welcome everyone to the _____ (*Your Organization*) All Recovery Meeting. We welcome all who struggle with addiction, are affected by addiction, and/or support the recovery lifestyle.

Coming from a place of mutual respect and understanding, let's observe some basic meeting agreements:

1. Please respect the opinions and remarks of others.
2. Please, only one person speaks at a time.
3. Please turn your cell phones off or place them on vibrate.
4. Please refrain from the overuse of profanity in order not to offend others.

Are there any announcements?

Let's begin by introducing ourselves to one another. How you introduce yourself is completely up to you. My name is _____ and I am _____. *{You might consider saying, "I am a person in long-term recovery and for me that means …}*

Let's have a moment of silence to remember why we are here … Thank you.

This is a topic discussion meeting and the topic I have chosen is _____. Please feel free to share on the topic or anything that you feel will enhance your recovery. Please be mindful of the number of people in the room and the amount of time you talk.

{Start the sharing with some thoughts on the meeting topic. When finished, say something like: "That's it for me. Who'd like to share?" As best you can, refrain from commenting on other people's sharing. The less you say as facilitator, the better.}

Closing:

In closing, I would like to thank everyone for coming today. Let's close this meeting with a positive affirmation about ourselves or about our recovery. *{Start this by giving a positive affirmation like: "I'm proud of my recovery today," or "Life is good today." After everyone has shared say, "Thank you."}*

Reprinted with permission, CCAR

Copyright © 2018 Charles Atkins. *Opioid Use Disorders*. All rights reserved.

ONLINE GROUPS AND RECOVERY COMMUNITIES

The largest global network of online self-help/mutual support groups can be found through www.InTheRooms.com. This robust and free website asks for minimal information that is kept confidential and helps a person in recovery find in-person, online, and video meetings 24/7. There are resources and meetings for friends and family, and it is not restricted to 12-step AA/NA-style groups. In addition to self-help/mutual support resources, the website has searchable links to a broad array of treatment facilities.

HARM REDUCTION

Originally developed in response to the rise of HIV, hepatitis, and other blood-borne and sexually transmitted pathogens among intravenous drug users in the Netherlands, harm reduction offers life-saving strategies to people engaged in high-risk behaviors. The central philosophy of harm reduction revolves around the principle that people have always, and will always, do harmful things. The goal is to decrease the risk from the behavior so it's more likely that the person survives and is healthy. Harm reductionists "meet the person where they're at." This is a non-abstinence stance, though abstinence may be the ultimate goal. A motivational approach (reviewed in the previous chapter) is a natural fit with harm reduction, with its emphasis on nonjudgment and validation of all positive change. Harm reduction strategies for people who use opioids include:

- Clean needle and cooker exchanges, along with alcohol swabs or other antimicrobials.

- Condom distribution.

- Education on how to use your drugs more safely.

    - Don't use alone.

    - Take turns.

    - Never share works.

    - Test your drugs for fentanyl.

- Naloxone (Narcan) distribution and education.

- Safe Injection Facilities (SIFs). These are places where people can use their drugs without fear of being arrested and where there are medical personnel onsite should someone overdose and need to be revived. These are not available in most cities at the time of publication, but this is a growing trend with good results to support its efficacy—especially in the midst of the current fentanyl overdose spike.

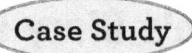

Sam's Relapse

Sam is a 46-year-old successful accountant in a cognitive behavioral therapy program for substance use (alcohol and opioids) and recurrent anxiety and depression.

He first used alcohol when he was 14 and an exchange student in Italy. "All the kids drank wine at dinner. It was part of the culture and who was I to argue? Of course, me and a couple friends started to sneak a little extra when everyone was asleep."

When he returned to the United States he began to steal liquor from his parents. "Booze makes me feel more comfortable in my skin. Sometimes my anxiety gets so bad that I just have to get away from everyone because I know a panic attack is coming."

He first tried an opioid following a double wisdom tooth extraction. "My dentist gave me 30, but told me I wouldn't need them all and to throw away the rest. I went through all of them in two days. I felt amazing, like I'd found something magic." By 16 he began to purchase prescription pain medications from kids at school. "It was everywhere, and suddenly I felt like one of the cool kids." He first snorted oxycodone as a high school senior. Despite his drug and alcohol use he continued to do well at school, he completed college, got his master's in accounting, and is a certified public accountant with his own business.

His is married and has two children aged 13 and 17, but has been separated from Melissa, his wife of 20 years, for the last year. "I can't blame her. She told me it was either the drugs or her and the kids. I tried to stop, went to rehab … a few times." His goals from the start of this therapy eight months ago were to stop drinking and drugging and become reunited with his family. He is prescribed 16mg/day buprenorphine for his opioid use disorder and has been abstinent from any alcohol or illicit opioids for six months.

At today's session he is distressed and readily admits to a relapse with both heroin and alcohol. As part of his therapy he completes a weekly diary card, which he presents at the start of the session.

Sam's Diary Card

Rate urges to use: 0–10 (0 low, 10 high)

Rate depression and anxiety: 0–10 (0 low, 10 high)

Monday	A decent day. 0 urges to use. Therapy in the morning. Work went okay; headed into tax season. Got out reminder emails to clients, but know damn well they'll all want appointments in March and April. It is what it is. Went to the gym. Called Melissa. Spoke to the kids; plan to go hiking with them, maybe Kent Falls this weekend. Depression/anxiety both a 0.
Tuesday	Not a good day. First time in a couple months with significant urges 5/10. Bad call with my mother. I'm 46 years old and she still makes me crazy. Wants me to fly to Chicago for cousin Michael's wedding. In the middle of tax season. And worse, wants all of us to cram together into a couple hotel rooms. Tried to tell her no and she started with the guilt thing. It took all I had to not slam down the phone and tell her to eff off. Anxiety is high 8/10, but more like pissed off and angry. Not depressed, but worried. Driving home, had strong impulse to get off I-691 and drive to Meriden where I used to score dope. Did go to the gym. It helped. Too angry to call Melissa. There was a message from her on my machine, but I didn't return it. Tried to do an online meeting; logged off after 10 minutes.
Wednesday	Shit day. Did not sleep more than two hours last night. Obsessed over this wedding BS. I don't want to go. Why does she always do this? Urges are through the roof 8/10, if just to get my mind to shut up. Was able to focus at work. Thought about calling my therapist, but didn't. Called Melissa. She'd had a bad day and I didn't want to make things worse by telling her I was struggling. Didn't go to the gym and should have. Ate a granola bar as I drove home; it helped to cut the craving. I know I'm on the bup so if I use dope, I'll have to use a lot, and with all that bad shit out there it would probably kill me. But thinking a lot about booze. Anxiety 5/10, little depressed 3/10. Worried. No meeting.
Thursday	I don't want to write this. I fucked up. Bad sleep again. Thought about calling Mom to tell her it was a flat-out no, but didn't. Obsessed about dope at work. Didn't take my bup this morning. Made it through the day. Did not eat lunch. Driving home called dealer—did not thoroughly delete his information. He told me he had real oxy 40s. It's like a switch went off in my head. "Just this once. I can do this." I'm an idiot. Bought 10. Crushed and snorted one in the car. Felt amazing. Bought liter and a half bottle of bourbon. Did not take nighttime bup.

Friday	Hung over beyond belief. Woke up on the floor of my home office. Third of the bottle gone. Snorted four of the oxys. Thought about flushing bourbon and the other six pills. Didn't. This is bad.
Saturday	Cancelled hike with kids. Told them I was sick. Melissa asked me if I'd used. I told her no. Feel like shit. Went to gym. Focused on remaining pills and vodka. Craving getting worse; started low, mid-afternoon 8/10. I'm going to use, just being honest.
Sunday	One pill left, took it. Booze mostly gone, dumped it down the sink. I'm screwed. Depression/anxiety 6/10. Don't want to go back to rehab. Dope sick. Took two bups. I'm going to have a positive urine. Maybe I'll skip therapy. Just kidding, I'll be there. Please don't make me go back to rehab. No matter what I am going to work tomorrow. I can't do this to myself again.

How to Construct a Behavioral Chain Analysis

Behavioral chain analyses help both the clinician and client better understand what leads up to a problem behavior and its aftermath, and provides important clues as to where and how interventions can be used to make the scenario go in a different direction. It's useful to think of doing a chain analysis in stages. The first is to clarify what happened (the problem behavior) and all the things that led up to it. This includes:

- Emotional vulnerabilities and emotions: Hungry, angry, lonely, tired (HALT), feeling sick, pain, being high, depression, anxiety, boredom, and so forth.

- Prompting event(s)/triggers: What led up to the problem behavior? When did the person notice that their mood or thinking changed?

- Automatic thoughts: What ran through their head prior to the behavior and at the various points that led up to it?

- Physical changes: Heart rate, breathing, physical sensations.

- What did the person do to try and stop the behavior?

- Other.

In session the therapist will encourage Sam to go through all the above so they can reconstruct the events that led up to the relapse and the aftermath, which is where he is now. While samples of chain analysis are neat and tidy, in my experience they get messy as details are recalled and scribbled in. A blank copy is included at the end of the chapter, but a plain piece of paper works well.

Behavioral Chain Analysis
Sam's Relapse

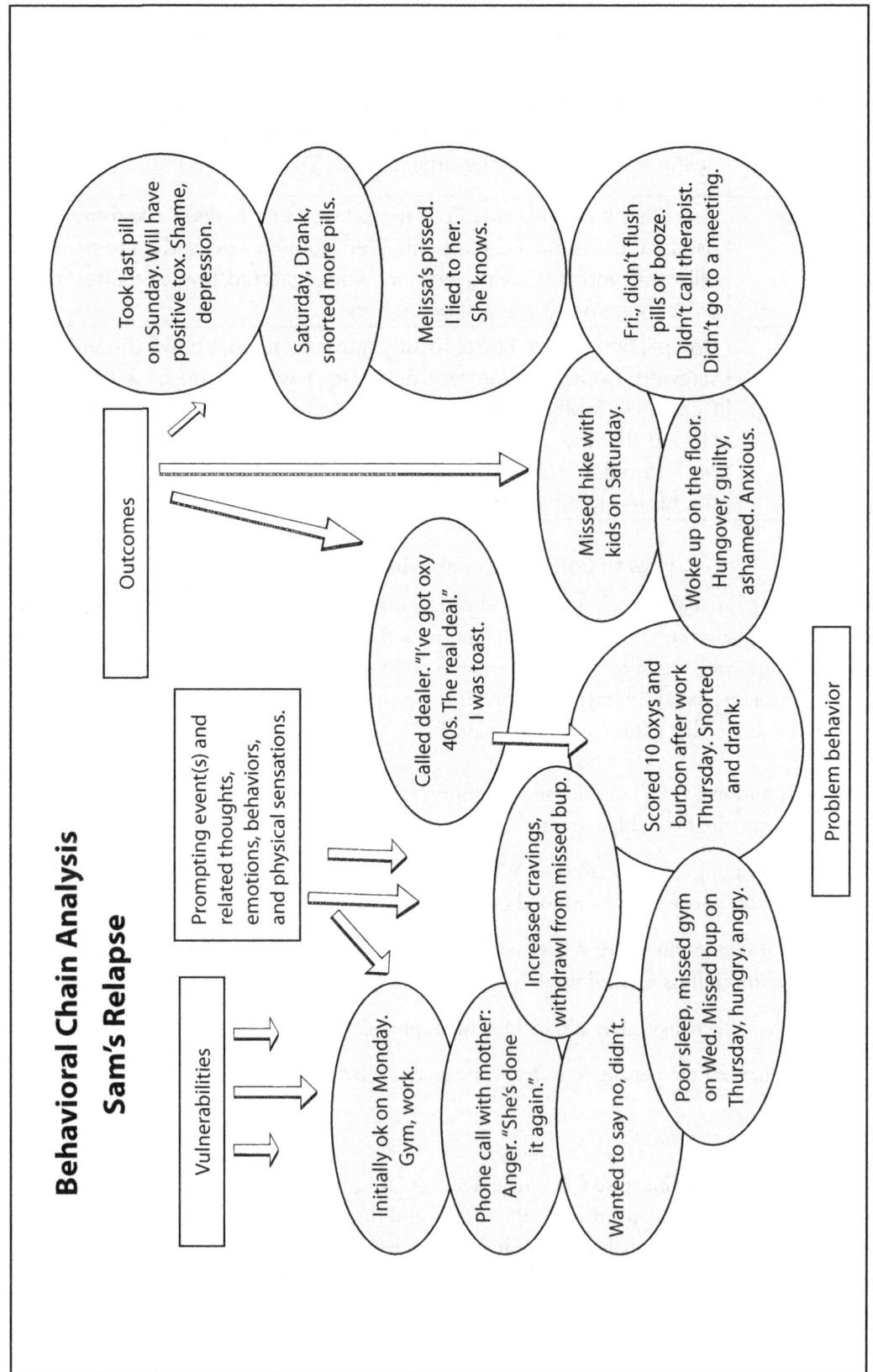

Vulnerabilities

Prompting event(s) and related thoughts, emotions, behaviors, and physical sensations.

Outcomes

Problem behavior

Initially ok on Monday. Gym, work.

Phone call with mother: Anger. "She's done it again."

Wanted to say no, didn't.

Increased cravings, withdrawl from missed bup.

Poor sleep, missed gym on Wed. Missed bup on Thursday, hungry, angry.

Scored 10 oxys and burbon after work Thursday. Snorted and drank.

Called dealer. "I've got oxy 40s. The real deal." I was toast.

Woke up on the floor. Hungover, guilty, ashamed. Anxious.

Missed hike with kids on Saturday.

Fri., didn't flush pills or booze. Didn't call therapist. Didn't go to a meeting.

Melissa's pissed. I lied to her. She knows.

Saturday, Drank, snorted more pills.

Took last pill on Sunday. Will have positive tox. Shame, depression.

Finding Solutions to Problem Behavior/Solution Analysis

Once the chain is fleshed out and both the client and therapist understand the sequence, prompting events, vulnerability factors, thought processes, cognitive distortions, and the like, it's time to review the chain with an eye toward finding solutions that might derail this behavior in the future.

In Sam's relapse, it appears the conversation with his mother kicked the ball into play (prompting event). He attempts to tell her he does not want to attend the wedding and backs down when she voices her disappointment. A skill that might prove useful, and could be worked on in therapy, is how to effectively say no to his mother and mean it. This could be accomplished through role-plays with his therapist. There is a wonderful DBT skill set with the acronyms DEARMAN, GIVE, and FAST, that breaks down the steps for effectively and mindfully asking for what you want and telling someone no. He could then be encouraged to call his mother, tell her he's not going to the wedding, and not back down. (A good explanation of DEARMAN skills can be found online at: https://www.dbtselfhelp. com/html/interpersonal_effectiveness.html.)

As he obsessed about the conversation and the upcoming wedding, and being crammed into a cheap hotel room with too many family members, he loses sleep and begins to let go of things that keep his emotions, and sobriety, on keel: the gym, adequate nutrition, nightly calls with his estranged wife and children, online meetings. These healthy habits support his recovery and goals (reunification with his family and sobriety) and need to be reinforced and strengthened.

- Urges to use are closely linked to hunger. Having something to pop into his mouth when cravings hit can be a useful strategy to get through the moment.

- Sleep is crucial to alertness and functioning. Sleep deprivation correlates with increased depression and anxiety. There are numerous effective non-pharmacologic techniques to help initiate and maintain sleep. These include progressive-muscle relaxation, white-noise machines, sleep hygiene, and regular exercise earlier in the day.

- As he moved through the week, he cut off ties with his emotional supports: his wife, his recovery network, and his therapist. Here it would be helpful to understand what ran through his head (cognitions) and get him to observe those thoughts and impulses, but not act on them. Are additional supports needed, such as a sponsor or recovery coach?

Another critical behavior that tipped him into the relapse was the missed dose of buprenorphine on Thursday morning. That might warrant its own chain analysis. What went through his head? When did he realize he'd missed it? Was he already thinking he'd use and didn't want the blocking effects of buprenorphine in his system? As buprenorphine is a replacement therapy, even though it's long-acting, a missed dose carries the risk of precipitating withdrawal symptoms, which will increase cravings and the likelihood of a relapse.

Other issues to explore and address include: eliminating the dealer's number from his telephone, asking point-blank about any remaining drugs or alcohol, assessing his current level of depression and any thoughts of self-harm, and of course, determining his level of motivation to get back on track (it appears high on Sunday) and what level of care makes sense. Can this relapse be managed in an outpatient setting, an IOP, or does he need a rehab to get some distance between him and the drugs?

CHAPTER 11

Adolescents and Opioids

- Overview
- Interview with Ally Kernan
- Facts and Figures
- The Developing Adolescent Brain
- Signs There Could Be a Problem
- Screening
- Screen for Co-Occurring Mental Health Problems
- Treatment
- Multi-Dimensional Family Therapy (MDFT)
- Multisystemic Therapy (MST)
- Other Treatment Approaches
- The Use of Drug Screens with Adolescents
- MAT with Adolescents
- Confidentiality
- Case Study and Discussion

OVERVIEW

"Adolescence" is most often defined as the period between puberty and legal majority. In the United States that would be between ages 12–18. WHO broadens this to ages 10–19. While others take a longer view and consider adolescence as the time from puberty into full adulthood, or up until age 25. For this book I'll break things into two groups: adolescents (12–18) and young adults (19–25).

Adolescence is a time of exploration, creativity, a desire for increased independence, and intense emotion. After puberty an individual has adult levels of sex hormones (testosterone, estrogen, progesterone) without an adult's ability to weigh the pros and cons that come with maturation and wiring of the prefrontal cortex. For boys, increased testosterone can be associated with aggression, and for girls the monthly fluctuations through the menstrual cycle can have profound effects on mood.

155

Ally Kernan

"I went to heroin and my life fell apart."

My substance abuse started in grade school. I tried cigarettes at eight and marijuana in fourth grade, so I was maybe 10. I took it from my bio dad's stash. I thought it was okay.

In middle school I didn't really get into drugs. That's when I found out my brother had a problem with crack cocaine. *This is bad.* I thought it was my fault because we'd smoked pot together. I didn't want to be like him, so I didn't use.

I started again in sophomore year of high school. I was dating a guy—it's always a guy. He smoked weed, but I didn't. I had standards. He'd smoke pot and I'd smoke cigarettes. But then it got to where we sat around passing a blunt, and I thought, *I'm not my brother. I can do this.*

I got back in with the party crowd. I felt like I belonged. I hid it from my parents. Plus, I figured, *it's just weed.* I wasn't into alcohol. My experience with it wasn't great. I hated beer and that's what I thought all booze was. But once I tried mixed drinks, I thought, *this isn't bad. It's great.*

Sophomore year into junior year I started doing shots. I had my license and a car. I'd drink and drive and smoke weed and skip class. I got attention and could hide my anxiety and depression. They diagnosed me with ADHD, but that's not why I couldn't focus. I had horrible anxiety, depression, and PTSD from stuff I went through when I was younger. I didn't like myself and didn't want to burden my family with how bad I felt. Plus, my boyfriend was abusive. It was a whirlwind of domestic violence and I felt isolated.

Then came the pills. I caught my boyfriend crushing up a Percocet, the 10mg yellow ones, bananas. I saw all these lines. "What are you doing?"

"I'm sniffing a Perc." He said. "You can't have any."

"Doesn't it hurt? Don't you feel something going up your nose?"

"You don't feel a thing."

"What's it like?" I asked.

"It's great. Like weed, but stronger and more convenient. You want a line?"

"Well, I don't know …" I said.

Right before I did it, he said, "Just so you know, it can be very addicting." He wanted me to do it. Wanted me to do drugs.

I was hooked that first time. I wasn't anxious. I had self-esteem that I never had before. He didn't hit me and he didn't call me names. It did wonders. *This is a cure.* Until it started to get bad. The Percs weren't enough. Then came the oxys, the blues. Just a little line could get you high. I even did it in school, right on the desk or in the bathroom. I got attention. "Wow you're sniffing something. You're cool." People talked. "Ally's doing hardcore drugs."

I was high at graduation. I thought that was so cool. Having pills in my pocket as I walked across the stage. It was my secret cure.

Then came college. I moved onto campus and I thought I was going to be the only one doing drugs. But wouldn't you know it, there was this place where everyone was going around asking, "Anyone have drugs? Anyone have blues?"

Well, yeah, I thought, this is how I can make friends. People came to me to get drugs. So I had a free habit. No one suspected me because I was female and I was slick. My habit grew. That's when I first experienced withdrawal. I woke up and thought I had the flu. I smoked some and took a Nyquil. It got worse. I did a little bit of a pill and 5 or 10 minutes later I didn't have the flu anymore. That's when I knew.

It was pills from 16 to 19. Then I went to heroin and my life fell apart. I was 22 when I went to prison on conspiracy charges. I served 9 out of 18 months and had three years' probation. I had one horrible relapse three months after I got out, and I came close to dying. I was desperate and suicidal. I prayed, "God, if you have a plan for me that's not with a needle in my arm every day, tell me." I tied the tourniquet, and the needle was inches from my vein with what I knew was a fatal dose of heroin, when the phone rang. It was a treatment facility, "We have a bed, if you can get here right now."

I'll be 26 in 30 days. I have been clean for over two years. I'm in college with a 3.8 average. I get to go around and tell my story to kids in high school, and trust me, there are hard drugs in every single one. I work for Turning Point CT, an organization that helps kids and young adults with all kinds of problems. I'm a member of the Connecticut Commissioner's Alcohol and Drug Policy Council (ADPC), and things I thought would be barriers—like having a felony—help me.

My relationship with my mom is better than ever, and God gives me strength. I still have my breakdowns, but I've learned how to ground myself. And when I'm rocking back and forth on the verge of a panic attack, I stare at my mug shot—I weighed 86 pounds when I went to prison—pray, write, and hug my cat, Pete.

To find out more about Turning Point CT, an excellent resource for adolescents and young adults both in Connecticut and nationally, its website is: https://turningpointct.org/

my story

Adolescents create families outside of their biologic ones. The peer group, and fitting in, become the priority. Risk-taking behavior, without a clear sense of negative consequences, is the norm.

"Hey, let's jump the fence and go into that pool."

"Sounds good to me."

They experiment and push boundaries. This can manifest in intense romantic relationships, sexuality, alcohol, drugs, and exploring new things. There is a high sensitivity to the reinforcing/rewarding aspects of pleasurable experiences, including the euphoria and "high" of drugs and alcohol. Once these behaviors are established, and found pleasurable, they become deeply rooted, more so than for an older individual first trying a drug, alcohol, or other pleasurable behavior.

The earlier the exposure to any substance, including nicotine (e-cigarettes/vaping included), the greater the likelihood a person is to develop a subsequent use disorder. This has everything to do with brain development and hijacking of the dopamine reward system. While children and adolescents don't typically initiate substance use with opioids, there has been an upward trend in recent years. This is likely linked to a significant increase in prescription pain medications written for adolescents. Those who do develop opioid misuse and use disorders often trace their substance use histories back to high school, middle school, and earlier, with nicotine, alcohol, and cannabis.

FACTS AND FIGURES

- Alcohol has been tried by 26% of 8th graders, 43% of 10th graders, 61% of 12th graders, 81% of college students, and 86% of young adults.

- Opioid pain medications were tried by 2.1 million adolescents in 2016.

- 2.1% of high school students have used heroin (Youth Risk Behavior Survey [YRBS], 2015).

- 21.7% of high school students had been offered, sold, or been given drugs on school property in the last year (YRBS, 2015).

- 20% of adolescents prescribed opioids report using them to get high or to enhance the euphoria from alcohol or other drugs.

- Use of prescribed opioids in high school carries a 33% increased risk of developing a later disorder, even among individuals who initially reported a strong disapproval of illicit drug use.

- Misuse of opioids in high school is a strong predictor of later heroin use.

- One study that looked at medical and pharmacy claims between 2007–2008, found that of over 8,000 adolescents that presented with a complaint of headache, 48% received a prescription opioid and 29% received ≥3 prescriptions.

- Adolescent males who participate in organized high school sports have higher rates of being prescribed opioids and higher rates of misuse than those who do not.

Reasons cited by adolescents as to why they use opioids versus other substances include:

- Easy to obtain from the medicine cabinet.

- Not illegal.

- If caught, can claim they're prescribed.

THE DEVELOPING ADOLESCENT BRAIN

During adolescence and into the mid-20s the brain continues to mature. Unused synapses are pruned back, and white matter—which enhances smooth and rapid neuronal transmission—is enhanced. The prefrontal cortex, the last part to be fully wired, sees increased connections with deep brain structures, including those involved with pleasure-seeking behavior and memory.

Functions of the prefrontal cortex include:

- Decision making

- Complex social behavior

- Striking a balance between emotion and behavior, and reflective delay.

  - "I'd really like to go out with my friends and party, but if I do, I'll be wrecked for the big test in the morning."

SIGNS THERE COULD BE A PROBLEM

While emotional upheavals and "drama" are associated with normal teen development, it's important to educate families about warning signs. These include:

- An abrupt change in attitude, often with increased oppositional behavior.

- A decline in school and/or home functioning.

- Missing classes, skipping classes, and truancy.

- Moodiness.

- Secretiveness.

- A change in peer group.

- Giving up activities, such as music or sports, that they once valued and enjoyed.

- A deterioration in hygiene and appearance.

- Changes in sleep and eating behaviors and patterns.

- Appearing high or stoned.

SCREENING

It's rare for an adolescent to acknowledge, or disclose, that they have a problem with drugs or alcohol. Yet the evidence supports early identification and interventions. Screening can be done in a pediatrician's office, school-based clinic, or other setting can be of use.

Adolescent Screening, Brief Intervention and Referral to Treatment (ASBIRT): ASBIRT is the adolescent version of SBIRT. It's an early-intervention approach to identify youth with problem substance use, as well as those at an increased risk for developing a problem. It can be used in a broad range of settings from a pediatrician's office, to a school nurse, school-based healthcare setting, or as part of a pre-program enrollment for an extracurricular activity, such as a sport. One such screening tool—The CRAFFT Interview (Version 2.1)—is presented in full next.

CRAFFT Screening Tool: Developed by John R. Knight, MD, at the Center for Adolescent Substance Abuse Research (CeASAR), the CRAFFT is an acronym for six questions, where each positive response is scored as one point. A score of two indicates a need for further assessment and increased risk for a substance-use problem. It can be completed as a self-report, or as part of an interview. It is reprinted here with permission and is also available for free in pdf form in a number of languages: http://www.ceasar-boston.org/CRAFFT/index.php

Brief Screener for Alcohol, Tobacco, and Other Drugs (BSTAD): An electronic form is available at https://www.drugabuse.gov/ast/bstad#/

The CRAFFT Interview

To be orally administered by the clinician

Begin: *"I'm going to ask you a few questions that I ask all my patients. Please be honest. I will keep your answers confidential."*

Part A
During the PAST 12 MONTHS, on how many days did you:

1. Drink more than a few sips of beer, wine, or any drink containing **alcohol**? Say "0" if none.

   > *# of days*

2. Use any **marijuana** (weed, oil, or hash, by smoking, vaping, or in food) or "**synthetic marijuana**" (like "K2," "Spice") or "vaping" **THC oil**? Say "0" if none.

   > *# of days*

3. Use **anything else to get high** (like other illegal drugs, prescription or over-the-counter medications, and things that you sniff, huff, or vape)? Say "0" if none.

   > *# of days*

Did the patient answer "0" for all questions in Part A?

Yes ☐	No ☐
↓	↓
Ask CAR question only, then stop.	Ask all six CRAFFT* questions below.

Part B

		No	Yes
C	Have you ever ridden in a **CAR** driven by someone (including yourself) who was "high" or had been using alcohol or drugs?	☐	☐
R	Do you ever use alcohol or drugs to **RELAX**, feel better about yourself, or fit in?	☐	☐
A	Do you ever use alcohol or drugs while you are by yourself, or **ALONE**?	☐	☐

Copyright © 2018 Charles Atkins. *Opioid Use Disorders.* All rights reserved.

F   Do you ever **FORGET** things you did while using   ☐   ☐
         alcohol or drugs?

F   Do your **FAMILY** or **FRIENDS** ever tell you that you   ☐   ☐
         should cut down on your drinking or drug use?

T   Have you ever gotten into **TROUBLE** while you were   ☐   ☐
         using alcohol or drugs?

*Two or more YES answers suggest a serious problem and need for further assessment.

NOTICE TO CLINIC STAFF AND MEDICAL RECORDS:

The information on this page is protected by special federal confidentiality rules (42 CFR Part 2), which prohibit disclosure of this information unless authorized by specific written consent. A general authorization for release of medical information is NOT sufficient.

1. **Show your patient his/her score on this graph and discuss their level of risk for a substance-use disorder.**

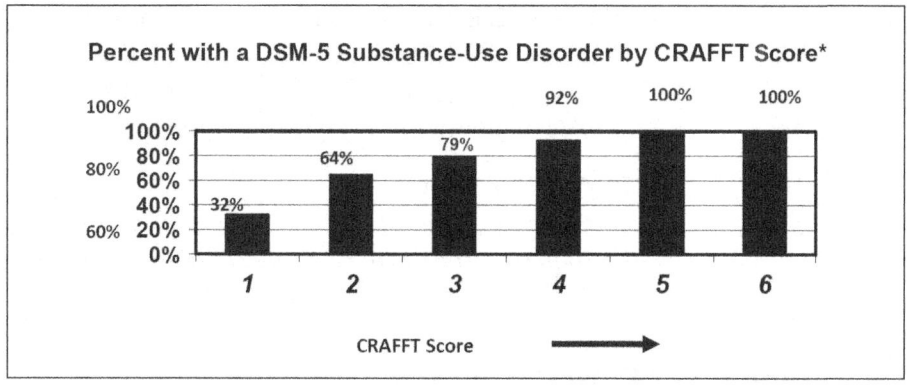

*Data source: Mitchell, S. G., Kelly, S. M., Gryczynski, J., Myers, C. P., O'Grady, K. E., Kirk, A. S., & Schwartz, R. P. (2014). The CRAFFT cut-points and DSM-5 criteria for alcohol and other drugs: a reevaluation and reexamination. *Substance Abuse*, 35(4), 376–80.

Copyright © 2018 Charles Atkins. *Opioid Use Disorders.* All rights reserved.

2. Use these talking points for brief counseling.

1. **REVIEW** screening results.
   For each "yes" response: *"Can you tell me more about that?"*

2. **RECOMMEND** not to use.
   "As your doctor (nurse/healthcare provider), my recommendation is not to use any alcohol, marijuana or other drug because they can: 1) Harm your developing brain, 2) Interfere with learning and memory, and 3) Put you in embarrassing or dangerous situations."

3. **RIDING/DRIVING** risk counseling.
   "Motor vehicle crashes are the leading cause of death for young people. I give all my patients the Contract for Life. Please take it home and discuss it with your parents/guardians to create a plan for safe rides home."

4. **RESPONSE:** Elicit self-motivational statements.
   Non-users: *"If someone asked you why you don't drink or use drugs, what would you say?"* Users: *"What would be some of the benefits of not using?"*

5. **REINFORCE** self-efficacy.
   "I believe you have what it takes to keep alcohol and drugs from getting in the way of achieving your goals."

3. Give patient Contract for Life. Available at www.crafft.org/contract

© John R. Knight, MD, Boston Children's Hospital, 2016.
Reproduced with permission from the Center for Adolescent Substance Abuse Research (CeASAR), Boston Children's Hospital.
(617) 355-5433 www.ceasar.org
For more information and versions in other languages, see www.ceasar.org.

Copyright © 2018 Charles Atkins. *Opioid Use Disorders.* All rights reserved.

SCREEN FOR CO-OCCURRING MENTAL HEALTH PROBLEMS

In addition to screening for substance use, it's important to obtain historical data from the parent or guardian, as well as from the youth, about mental health issues and prior treatment. Screening tools and metrics can help flag co-occurring mental health concerns. An assortment of both cross-cutting and diagnosis-specific tools can be found online and free-to-use with your clients at the American Psychiatric Association's DSM-5 website. This includes screening instruments completed by the parent/guardian and by the minor: https://www.psychiatry.org/psychiatrists/practice/dsm/educational-resources/assessment-measures

Diagnoses and areas you'll want to screen for include:

- Trauma

- Depression and bipolar disorder

- Anxiety disorders

- Attentional problems and ADHD

- Presence of psychotic symptoms (hallucinations and delusions)

- Delinquent behaviors (truancy, running away, criminal acts)

- Autism spectrum

- Cognitive limitations and impairment

TREATMENT

When minors present to treatment, it's usually at the recommendation or insistence of someone else. This could be a parent/guardian, the school, CPS, or the courts. This creates challenges for the clinician, as the identified client may have little to no motivation to enter treatment. They are there because they must be. This means establishment of trust is crucial if forward gains are to be made. Clinic and program rules and expectations should be spelled out at the start, including drug screens. Issues related to confidentiality—"Your parents don't need to know what we talk about in here"—must be addressed.

MULTI-DIMENSIONAL FAMILY THERAPY (MDFT)

MDFT is a family-focused integrative treatment that addresses issues of adolescent substance use, truancy, criminal and other problem behaviors. The target ages are 9 to 26, although there can be program variability. It is highly rated as an evidence-based practice and has numerous studies to support its efficacy. The fundamental treatment objectives of MDFT include:

- Treatment engagement and maintenance

- Family functioning

- Substance abuse

- School performance

- Criminal and delinquent behavior

- Family stability

- Mental health symptoms

MDFT has been studied and found effective in a broad range of settings. These include substance use and mental health programs, juvenile justice and drug courts, and in both rural and urban locations. It can be used for early intervention and when more significant problems have developed. In MDFT the therapist creates relationships with the adolescent, individual family members, and others who are part of the teen's world. A motivational approach is taken, and the therapist fosters conditions that make change possible and sustainable. While typically provided in the community and home, it can be adapted to office and clinic-based work.

Multisystemic Therapy (MST)

Developed by Scott Henggeler, PhD, MST is an intensive, team-based approach for at-risk youth (juvenile offenders, survivors of abuse and neglect). It employs a model (ecological) that considers all dimension of the youth's interconnected world: family, peers, school, community, neighborhood. A typical client is one with juvenile justice involvement, who may be at risk for out-of-home placement due to delinquent behaviors, including substance use, sexual offenses, or other illegal or delinquent activities.

In MST the family is viewed as the solution and collaborates in the treatment to help effect positive and sustained change. The treatment is predominately delivered in the home and in the community.

MST has been extensively studied and, among the results when compared to control groups, are:

- Decreased arrest rates and decreased future criminal behaviors.

- Decreased long-term out-of-home placements.

- Improved family relations and satisfaction.

- Decreased adolescent substance misuse.

- Decreased psychiatric symptomatology.

MST trainings are through MST Services, which is licensed by the University of South Carolina. Its website is: www.mstservices.com

Other Treatment Approaches

There are numerous viable treatment options for adolescents with substance use, with or without co-occurring mental health problems. These include cognitive and dialectic behavior therapies and approaches that target specific symptoms or diagnoses, such as PTSD, anger, impulsivity, depression, and anxiety. A family component, which can be in both group and individual formats, is needed to provide families with education, support, and skills. So too, many clinicians and clinics effectively employ an eclectic approach to their work, which is often a mixture of psychodynamic and cognitive-behavioral strategies. While difficult to obtain studies on such multivariable therapies, outcomes at the level of the individual can be determined based on factors such as: treatment retention, negative drug screens, use of metrics to track symptoms, client satisfaction, and progress toward goals.

The level of care and intensity of services required will be based on the individual's need, preferences, and available resources. At times, outside forces such as juvenile justice or a child protective agency may encourage or mandate the level of care.

THE USE OF DRUG SCREENS WITH ADOLESCENTS

When and how to obtain drug screens (most often urine, but could be saliva, sweat, hair, or blood) is somewhat different for adolescents than adults. There needs to be a balance between invasiveness and privacy, with the clinical utility drug tests offer, especially after an adolescent has been diagnosed with an opioid or other substance-use disorder. Programs and practices should have written guidelines/policies around drug testing. In addition, rules around confidentiality and consent need to be clear. Some states allow minors of various ages to enroll in substance-use treatment without their parent's consent, others do not.

Drug tests should be viewed as a clinical tool. Results should be shared with the client, and whether they choose to tell those results to a parent may be encouraged, but is their decision. The following FAQ sheet can be provided to an adolescent and their parent or guardian at the start of treatment to clarify the rules around drug tests. Also, there may be instances in your state where confidentiality could be breached, in which case you'd want to include that in your written guidelines.

FAQs for Drug Testing of Youths in a Substance Treatment Setting

As part of our treatment program we do both scheduled and random drug and alcohol tests. While this will generally involve the collection of a urine sample or blowing into a tube, it might also include blood, saliva, sweat, or a portion of hair. The results of a drug test will be shared with you and evaluated alongside other clinical information, self-report, and historical data.

How we use the results of your drug test.

Your treatment/recovery plan will incorporate drug tests as a sign of progress.

Negative drug tests (ones that are free of drugs or alcohol) may be connected with some form of reward (voucher, coupon, small gift). A series of negative tests over time may indicate you're ready for a less-intensive treatment.

Positive drug tests (ones that indicate the presence of drugs or alcohol) may be a sign that the current treatment/recovery plan is not working or not working well enough for you. Multiple positive tests may signal the need for more intensive therapy, or a higher level of care.

Expected positive results will include positive screens for medications you have been prescribed, such as those for the treatment of opioid use disorders or ADHD. In the case of desired positive results, these could also be worked into a reward/contingency part of your treatment/recovery plan.

Who sees the results?

Your treatment team (prescriber and clinical staff) will review the results. These will be shared with you, and you alone. You may be encouraged to include your parent(s) or guardian in that discussion, but that's your choice.

Drug tests are confidential. If there are to be exceptions to this, you must give written permission. This includes your parent(s)/guardian(s) or workers from other agencies, such as juvenile justice and CPS.

Copyright © 2018 Charles Atkins. *Opioid Use Disorders*. All rights reserved.

What if I refuse or can't give a sample?

Refusals, or not being able to produce a sample, are clinical matters to be reviewed between you and your counselor, or other member of your treatment team.

What if I disagree with the results?

Drug tests can make mistakes. There can be both false positives (showing the presence of a drug when it's not there) and false negatives (showing no drug when it's present). Because of this, if you disagree with the test results we can send the sample to a laboratory for a more definitive reading.

What if I just tell you what I've used? Do I still have to do the test?

Honesty clearly is the best policy and may make a test unnecessary. However, where it's often unclear what is present in drugs gotten from friends/family or purchased on the street, a drug test might still be recommended.

How often do I have to give a test?

Frequency of drug tests is tied to your treatment/recovery plan. In general, as people move forward with their recovery and abstain from substance use, the frequency of drug tests decreases, but does not stop altogether.

Does someone have to be in the bathroom with me?

Supervised urines provide the most accurate results and discourage tampering with the sample. At times nonsupervised sample production may be considered, but this is a treatment decision made between you and your team. However, we promise to respect your modesty and dignity during sample collection.

Copyright © 2018 Charles Atkins. *Opioid Use Disorders*. All rights reserved.

MEDICATION-ASSISTED TREATMENT WITH ADOLESCENTS

None of the three available forms of MAT—buprenorphine, methadone, naltrexone—have been thoroughly evaluated in adolescents. One large retrospective cohort study that looked at 20,822 youths with commercial insurance between the ages of 13–25 with opioid use disorders found that 1 in 4 received either buprenorphine or naltrexone. And that younger, female, Hispanic, and black patients were less likely to be given medication.

Methadone

In the *Federal Guidelines for Opiate Treatment Programs* are the following related to the use of methadone:

- "For the purpose of this document, adolescents are defined as youth ranging in age from 13 to 18. Programs develop and implement policies to ensure that adolescents are provided with developmentally appropriate treatment and evidence-based psychosocial support, such as family involvement, for that treatment. Screenings and assessments tailored to adolescents ensure that MAT is the most appropriate treatment for these patients."

- Title 42 of the *Code of Federal Regulations*, offers the following regarding methadone maintenance treatment in adolescents:

  "A person under 18 years of age is required to have had two documented unsuccessful attempts at short-term detoxification or drug-free treatment within a 12-month period to be eligible for maintenance treatment. No person under 18 years of age may be admitted to maintenance treatment unless a parent, legal guardian, or responsible adult designated by the relevant state authority consents in writing to such treatment."

On the federal level, there are no absolute prohibitions to the use of methadone in adolescents. However, it is uncommon, and most methadone programs are not equipped to meet the federal regulations for age-appropriate screenings, assessment, family work, and other psychosocial supports.

Buprenorphine

Studies of sublingual (dissolved under the tongue) buprenorphine in adolescents are promising, and have shown increased treatment retention, lower relapse rates, and lower rates of hepatitis C exposure. The length of treatment with buprenorphine/naloxone in this age group has not been well defined, although the emerging trend, as with adults, is that this should be tailored to the individual, their goals, preferences, length and severity of opioid use, relapse history, and other factors. Buprenorphine is FDA-approved for the treatment of opioid use disorders in those aged 16 and older.

- One study with patients aged 15–21 compared a buprenorphine/naloxone two-week detox versus ongoing treatment and slower taper with buprenorphine/naloxone (12 weeks). The 12-week group showed greater treatment retention and fewer opioid-positive urines, at six-, nine-, and 12-month follow up. Both groups had high rates of relapse (41–56% in the 12-week group and 65–76% in the detox group).

- A study of 36 opioid-dependent youths aged 13–18 compared buprenorphine/ naloxone to clonidine. Both groups received three times a week counseling and incentives around their opioid use. Those on buprenorphine/naloxone had higher rates of treatment retention and lower rates of opioid-positive drug screens.

On a case-by-case basis buprenorphine/naloxone might be considered for a minor who has not succeeded with other forms of treatment for opioid use disorder. The parent or guardian will need to monitor the medication to prevent its misuse or diversion. The medication should be a part of a comprehensive treatment plan, which includes a family component.

Naltrexone and Naltrexone XR

The opioid blocker naltrexone (Revia and Vivitrol) has some studies to support its usefulness with adolescents to both help keep them in treatment and decrease relapse, especially the longer-acting monthly injection. In order for someone to be prescribed naltrexone they must be completely opioid free, as it can precipitate withdrawal. This might be an ideal option for a youth prior to leaving a residential program, or one who has completed a detox. An initial test dose injection of naloxone, or several days of the oral form of naltrexone—both to insure tolerability and that there is not a precipitated withdrawal—is recommended.

CONFIDENTIALITY

Federal guidelines (the Public Health Services Act) provide confidentiality to anyone seeking, or in, drug treatment with a licensed substance abuse counselor, which includes minors. This includes results of drug tests. The only conditions under which confidentiality may be breached are when there is a serious threat to the minor's life or physical well-being and it is determined that this threat can be diminished by disclosure to the parent(s)/guardian(s).

At the state level, there is variability, although most are in line with the federal guidelines which favor the rights of the minor, especially for outpatient drug treatment. There is greater variation when inpatient services are sought. One resource for state laws regarding a minor's right to consent for medical treatment is available online through the National District Attorney's Association; this includes a number to contact for updates: http://www.ndaa.org/pdf/Minor%20Consent%20to%20Medical%20Treatment%20(2).pdf

Confidentiality for young people raises concerns across a range of issues that go beyond substances and include reproductive health, gender, and gender identity. It's unlikely that a teenager will establish a trusting relationship with a therapist if they believe that what they say in session will be retold to their parents or guardian. It's incumbent on clinicians, crisis workers, and others who work with people under 18 to be clear on what the rules are at both the state and federal levels and to communicate these in a clear fashion to their clients. This will include times a clinician may have to breach confidentiality, such as can occur with imminent risk of suicide or harm to others, or through other mandated reporting statutes around suspected child abuse or neglect. Also, if a parent's or guardian's medical insurance is billed this can create an inadvertent disclosure and should be discussed prior to initiating services.

Behavioral Changes, Depression, Anxiety

Part One

Jason is a 15-year-old sophomore at Southford High School. He is brought to today's evaluation at a child guidance clinic by his mother, Evelyn. They are self-referred for behavioral changes, depression, and anxiety.

This is their third scheduled intake. The first two were cancelled at the last minute by his mother. "He refused to get in the car. The only reason he came this time is I had to bribe him with a video game."

Jason sits in the waiting room, playing a shooter game on his iPhone, while simultaneously listening to music. He is dressed in jeans, a Nirvana T-shirt, and sneakers. He has gauges in his ears, and two nasal piercings. He refuses to fill out any forms, which his mother does for him.

When they go in to meet with the clinician, Jason is nonverbal and needs to be asked multiple times by his mother to put away his phone. He complies, stares at the floor, and states, "This is a waste. I don't need to be here."

Evelyn takes a conciliatory tone with her son and explains how up until two years ago Jason had been a "wonderful" child. He excelled in academics and athletics, soccer especially. When he transitioned from middle school to high school, "things changed." He dropped out of all athletics and went from being an A student in honors classes, to scraping by with Cs in lower level classes. He's had multiple detentions this year for talking back to teachers, and she's received numerous emails about incomplete or missing homework assignments. He's in jeopardy of failing multiple classes, which could result in needing to repeat the year.

His response: "Who cares? They're all in it for the money."

Evelyn says that what prompted her to call is that two months ago Jason was brought home by Southford police at 2 a.m. He was intoxicated and had been trespassing and swimming with friends in a hotel pool. No charges were brought. She reports it's not the first time he's been drunk, and she's found pot in his room, which she flushed. "It's ever since he started hanging around with that Zane kid."

Social/Developmental/Family

Jason was delivered at term and achieved all expected developmental milestones. He is the oldest of three; younger sisters are Gillian (14) and Kaitlyn (12). His mother describes his early childhood as a happy one.

His parents separated when he was nine and divorced three years later. His mother states that there were heated fights with her and her ex. "No one got hit, but it came close." There is a split custody arrangement where he spends every other weekend with his father and stepmother, Sheila, in Bedford Falls. The rest of the time is spent with his mother and sisters in a townhouse purchased following the divorce (the family home had to be sold).

His father, Alex, is a truck driver and Evelyn works as a physical therapist for a large orthopedic practice where she's been for 15 years.

DISCUSSION

Adolescents don't typically bring themselves in for mental health or substance-use treatment. They usually come at the insistence of a parent, their school, or due to involvement with juvenile justice or a CPS agency. This can create immediate barriers to treatment and the establishment of a trusting therapeutic relationship. Why should this young man trust you? How will you let him know that what is said in session will be between the two of you and not shared with his parents or anyone else without his express permission?

To begin, while his mother has done the bulk of talking in the prior scenario, she needs to leave the room. In an intake scenario with both children and adolescents it's a good idea to leave a balance of time. Yes, you need the parent's input; but if the minor isn't given adequate time without his mother in the room, there's little chance to begin the crucial first step of establishing rapport.

Once his mother has left the room validate Jason's reality that, "You don't want to be here. Correct?" Let him talk, listen, and avoid common pitfalls of trying to take on youthful slang or an overly familiar attitude. A nonjudgmental motivational stance allows you to hear where he's coming from and all the reasons why coming to your office is a global waste of his time. Be honest and genuine, and if there are confidentiality disclosures that need to be made, let him know about that. If you have a plain-speak printout regarding confidentiality of minors in your state, give him a copy.

Once he's had a chance to talk, or chooses to sulk and remain quiet, ask open-ended questions about why he's here. "Why do you think it's so important to your mom for you to come here?" Or, "You said they're all in it for the money, tell me about that."

Whether or not he returns for a second visit—other than his mother cajoling or throwing another video game into the mix—will be based on how he gets along with you and if he's able to see any value in a second visit.

At this point the most-concerning issues relate to drugs, alcohol, decline in school and home functioning, and potential criminal behavior. He reports no imminent risk of self-harm or harm to others. His level of motivation is pre-contemplative.

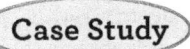

Jason's Story–Four Months Later

Part Two

Four months later, Jason and his mother return to the child and family clinic. They kept none of their scheduled appointments and were discharged. This is a new intake at the request of the New Bedford Juvenile Court.

Six weeks ago, Jason was arrested with two other minors trespassing in a neighbor's barn. Between them they had an ounce and a half of marijuana, and an assortment of 32 pills that appeared to be OxyContin, lorazepam, and Vyvanse® (a stimulant used to treat ADHD). There was also some minor damage to the structure from a bonfire they'd started. The police report indicates that this was likely not the first time this barn had been used.

Jason has a promise to appear in court in four weeks. The judge stipulated that he must comply with treatment recommendations, which will include negative drug screens and regular attendance at some form of substance-use treatment, or face eight months in juvenile detention.

The therapist first meets with his mother, who is distraught and discouraged. "I don't know what to do. He won't do anything I say, and now. … He's disrespectful, he stays out till all hours, and he's missed more days of school than attended. I don't know how many detentions he's had. I don't like the effect he's having on his sisters, and his father is less than useless. I'm at the point where if he goes to detention, maybe it wouldn't be the worst thing. I feel like a horrible mother, but I don't know what to do anymore. And those kids they caught him with, one has already done time. And Jason says they're best friends. How do I get my son back? You've got to help me."

Jason is more cooperative at this visit. "I'm here because if I don't do this, I'm going to juvie."

The therapist asks him how he feels about that. "I'd rather not. But I don't think it's that bad. I mean Zane went for three months and he said it was like a farm or something. He milked cows. It sounds kind of lame, but whatever."

The clinician administers the CRAFFT screening tool. Jason candidly admits to alcohol consumption multiple times/week, often to the point of drunkenness. He says he first tried alcohol when he was 12, and would steal from the liquor cabinet, watering down what remained so it wouldn't look like anything was missing. "I like the buzz."

Similarly, he admits to daily cannabis and occasional pills. "Whatever is around, but I'm trying to cut down on those, there's some scary stuff out there." Prior to giving his drug screen, he tells the counselor, "It's going to be positive for weed, but that should be it. I haven't used any pills since the arrest."

Over the course of the session he reveals that he's given up on the school year. "No way I can make it up. So, either I repeat next year, or drop out and maybe get my GED. It's not like the end of the world or anything."

When asked about things at home: "Mom is driving me crazy. I'm going to ask my dad and Sheila if I can stay with them. Maybe a start in a new town isn't the worst thing. Though knowing me, I'd probably screw up there, as well."

On a screen for depression he is mildly positive, but adamantly denies any thoughts or history of self-harm or harm to others.

DISCUSSION

At this second, court-mandated visit, Jason's level of motivation, fueled by the threat of juvenile detention, is contemplative. A more thorough assessment of his substance-use behaviors is obtained, and he will meet criteria for multiple substance-use disorders—most notably cannabis, which he continues to consume despite knowing he will give positive drug tests. That at age 15 he's taking opioids, at times with benzodiazepines, is dangerous and concerning. Important activities, which once mattered to him, such as school and relationships with his sisters and mother, have been neglected and damaged by his current behaviors.

His mother reports considerable oppositional behavior—detentions, staying out, and being disrespectful to her and other authority figures. While a normal part of adolescence involves separating from parents and affiliating with peers, he's clearly chosen a group that is engaged in drug-related and other illicit activities—such as breaking into a barn and lighting a bonfire.

The presence of depressive symptoms needs to be monitored and addressed. While he denies any suicidal thoughts, he's in a high-risk group—adolescent males with oppositional and conduct disordered behavior. The highest-risk period for this group is in the setting of active legal issues, such as he has.

Level of care decision making must balance what Jason wants with what is likely to be effective. As he's never been in treatment—other than the single intake he attended four months ago—it's reasonable to consider an outpatient level of care, possibly even an intensive adolescent substance use/co-occurring program. From a pragmatic perspective, even if a residential program were sought, it's unlikely his insurance would cover it at this point. However, in certain states, juvenile justice may have special programs, or priority status with programs, that could get him a residential slot. If available, either MST or MDFT would be good options.

$$\boxed{\text{Case Study}}$$

Jason's Story–Crisis

Part Three

Another four months have passed. Jason has shown up for weekly substance-use counseling and a weekly relapse-prevention group. His mother has been active in a monthly parents' support group, which his father and stepmother have been invited to, but never attended.

His urines have been negative for illicit substances and he tells you that he's cut way back on his alcohol consumption. He currently admits to drinking on the weekends and does not believe it represents a problem. He has been told that all his charges will be "nollied" if he remains in treatment and has negative urines. He did move in with his father and stepmother and four-year-old half-brother, Caleb, and is retaking his junior year in Bedford Falls.

At today's session he is visibly upset, reeks of alcohol, and has a black eye. When asked, "What's going on?" he's noncommunicative. Finally, he states, "My life is over, what's the point?"

The therapist presses, "What happened?"

The normally stoic teen struggles to find words. What emerges is that four days ago his stepmother walked in on him with his best-friend Zane, making out.

Jason has told no one that he thinks he is bisexual, and possibly gay. This is compounded by his promise to his mother to have nothing to do with Zane after they were arrested together. Jason begged his stepmother, Sheila, not to tell his father. She did. A fight ensued between Jason and his father, and he was told to leave the house and not return. "He said he didn't want me around my brother Caleb. Like I was going to infect him or something."

You ask if the fight turned physical. Jason denies this and states he tripped and landed on his face, which is how he got the shiner. He moved back with his mother and sisters, has no way to get from Southford to Bedford Falls for school, and has not divulged to his mother why he was kicked out of Alex and Sheila's house. To make matters worse, Zane refuses to take his calls and has outed him on Facebook and other social media sites. "Why would he do that? I thought he loved me."

The counselor asks, "Jason, how are you going to get through this?"

He replies, "Anyway you look at it I'm screwed. What's the point?"

"Are you having thoughts of hurting yourself? Or of even killing yourself?"

"It hurts so bad," he answers tearfully. "How can it hurt so bad? How could he have done that to me?"

"How much have you had to drink?"

He says, "All of it."

His quick-read urine is positive for cannabis and hydrocodone. His breathalyzer is 1.5.

His mother, Evelyn, is in the waiting room, and told the therapist, "I have to talk to you. I don't know what's going on. No one's telling me anything. And if my ex did that to him, I'm calling the cops."

DISCUSSION

In this final scenario Jason presents intoxicated, with multiple substances—alcohol, cannabis, and hydrocodone—and in crisis. It's possible there are other substances involved that may not have been detected with the quick-read cup or strip. His fatalistic statements need to be explored: "My life is over." "I'm screwed." "What's the point?" Along with his being outed by his stepmother to his father, and perhaps more painfully, to his friends and classmates via the internet, by someone whom he trusted and was in love with.

His overall level for risk of self-harm in this moment is high. Factors that fuel this and increase the likelihood of suicidal behavior include:

- Intoxication

- Male gender

- Recent loss or disruption of multiple significant relationships (father, stepmother, younger brother, Zane)

- Feelings of abandonment, humiliation, and possibly fear. The outing on Facebook is significant and may carry real concerns about both cyber and in-person bullying.

- Hopelessness

- Active legal involvement

- LGBT youth carry a much higher rate of suicide versus non-LGBT, especially in this type of nonsupportive coming-out situation. According to the CDC's YRBS, there is a nearly threefold increase in attempts and a fourfold increase in attempts requiring medical treatment.

There is no one right approach in this vignette, but Jason's safety will guide decisions that need to be made in the coming minutes and hours. How this is handled requires finesse, and what Jason chooses to divulge and to whom, must be respected. That he's shared as much as he has with his therapist is encouraging. But his current emotional and substance-fueled state further complicate things and will require an emergency room evaluation, and likely an inpatient admission. All of which can add trauma on top of what he's going through.

To soften this, evaluate whether his mother—who has demonstrated her commitment to her son through regular attendance and obvious concern—can be taken into Jason's confidence, even if specifics are avoided at first. Where he meets criteria for an inpatient hospitalization, even if just for brief crisis stabilization, her involvement and support can make the difference.

"Jason, would it be okay if I brought your mom into the room and we told her some of what's going on?"

"You're not going to tell her I'm gay or nothing."

"No, that's for you to decide when you're ready. But she needs to know how much pain you're in and that we're going to have to keep you safe so you can get through this."

"Just don't tell her about me and Zane."

"Got it."

Once through the crisis, the previous recommendation for an IOP/PHP or either MST or MDFT, would still be good options, as well as connections with peer-and-youth-based LGBTQ 12-step or other recovery-based groups.

CHAPTER 12

Women, Babies, Pregnancy, and the Post-Partum Period

- **The Eat, Sleep, and Console Model for Neonatal Abstinence Syndrome**
- **Overview**
- **Facts and Figures**
- **Gender Differences in Substance-Use Disorders**
- **Opioid Use in Pregnancy**
- **Unintended Pregnancy**
- **One Key Question**
- **Treatment for the Opioid-Dependent Pregnant Woman**
- **Medication-Assisted Treatment (MAT) During Pregnancy**
- **Psychosocial Supports and Therapies**
- **The Partner, Family, and Other Supports**
- **High-Risk Behavioral Health Concerns During Pregnancy and the Post-Partum Period**
- **Therapeutic Approaches and Other Interventions to Consider**
- **Breastfeeding and MAT**
- **Barriers to Care**
- **Incarcerated and Recently Incarcerated Women**
- **CAPTA and CARA as They Relate to Pregnant Women**
- **Effects of Opioids on the Fetus and Newborn**
- **Neonatal Abstinence Syndrome (NAS)/Neonatal Opioid Withdrawal Syndrome (NOWS)**
- **Case Study with Discussion and Treatment/Recovery Plan**

Matthew Grossman, MD
Yale New Haven Hospital

The Eat, Sleep, and Console Model

my story

I'm a pediatric hospitalist. I take care of sick kids in the hospital. That didn't usually include babies in withdrawal, what we call neonatal abstinence syndrome (NAS) or neonatal opioid withdrawal syndrome (NOWS).

This is what used to happen. Babies would be born to a mother on methadone, or other opioids, and taken from delivery to the neonatal intensive care unit (NICU). They would be put in an isolette— a hi-tech crib—and monitored using the Finnegan scale. It's used by about 95% of hospitals worldwide. It has a list of 29 withdrawal symptoms and gives a point value. Above 8 three times and you medicate with morphine.

It was standard. There are lots of studies on what's the right medication, but they all say the first-line treatment is non-pharmacologic care: swaddling, feeding, holding. But that wasn't considered "real" treatment. In our original protocol you had to have two days in a row with Finnegan scores below 8 and then we'd decrease the morphine by 10% every other day. The average length of stay was 28 days when I started.

It was the protocol. I followed it. But then we noticed that kids did better when their parents were around. And rather than wait two days to decrease the dose, we started to go down every day. Those two things cut the length of stay by six days. Another hospital—Middlesex —found out about that and wanted me to give a talk. Problem was, I only had 90 seconds of material. I had to review the literature.

There were all these studies looking at different medications. But there was this crazy range in the length of stay. For one it was between 10–79 days, and 8–30 for another. I didn't have an explanation, but it didn't seem right. What did it mean? And what could we do about it?

So, I went back to the guidelines and looked at the non-pharmacologic treatment as real treatment. We started with two things. Let's pay attention to the non-pharmacologic, and we looked at the Finnegan scale, which came out in 1975. We asked, why are we doing the things we're doing? The answer was: because that's what we did yesterday and the day before. That was it—tradition. That's dangerous in medicine. To do a thing just because that's how we've always done it.

It seemed wrong to separate these irritable babies from their parents and put them in a noisy NICU in a sterile plastic crib with tubes and wires. We focused on the parents. We got them more engaged and had them room-in with their newborn. There was an immediate drop in stay by over a week.

Now, if we had a pill that cut length of stay by a week, we'd make sure everyone got it. If you have a colicky baby, which I did at the time, you pick them up and hold them. The parents were the treatment. Or as one nurse manager overheard a mother say, "I have everything my baby needs."

We decided to treat the baby like it's a baby. This had a dramatic impact on the length of stay. But we were still sending them to the NICU, which is loud and beeping, and highly stimulating. It was hard to deliver the non-pharmacologic care. We sent babies to a unit where they couldn't be with their parents, like withholding steroids from someone having an asthma crisis.

We stopped sending them to the NICU. We treated those babies aggressively from day one; we didn't use medications as much. Next, we looked at the Finnegan tool. It didn't make a lot of sense. It lists the signs of withdrawal. All these babies have withdrawal signs. There's stuff on there like yawning, and sneezing, and nasal stuffiness. And three scores of 8 got you started on morphine. Mothers would tell me how terrified they were of certain nurses who'd score higher, because it could mean an additional two weeks in the hospital. Three sneezes wouldn't get you a point, but that fourth sneeze could push you over 8. The other problem with the Finnegan tool is to administer it you disturb the baby and un-swaddle it. It was doing harm.

my story

Another big issue was when you start medication with these protocols you give a dose of morphine followed by at least another 100 doses to complete the taper. That's why the national average is about three weeks.

We weaned faster when they roomed-in with the parents. And then we went to dosing only when they needed it. The last three kids got a total of nine doses combined versus 300.

We took things down to basics. What is a baby's job description? They have to eat, they have to sleep, and they have to be consoled. We looked at that instead of these scores. How's the baby? How did it go last night? That's the approach: eat, sleep, and console.

Our length of stay for the last two and a half years is below six days. That wasn't our goal. It was to make things go better for the parents and the babies.

It's also brought about a huge culture shift. At the start there was a lot of animosity. The families and staff didn't get along. The moms described troubling experiences in the hospital. No one knew what they were going through. They knew that their opioid use had caused their babies to go through this. They had tremendous guilt and shame. They felt judged by nursing staff, who were angry at them. It was a non-supportive, and unpleasant environment.

These were always difficult babies. But now they do really well. And staff are there to help the parents. If a mom is on a higher dose of methadone—as happens toward the end of pregnancy—and she's sleepy, staff know what's going on. They can tell her, "I'll do the afternoon feed so you can sleep." Instead of judgment, we support them. In the old way of doing things parents couldn't bond. Now they do. They used to want a couple extra days before taking their baby home because they weren't prepared. Now they do all the care in the hospital, and at five days they're ready to go. It's better for the staff, the parents, and the babies. Not to mention higher rates of successful breastfeeding.

It's early on and we're looking for longer-term data. That hospital in Middlesex came back and visited us a year ago. We took them around, met some families, and on their 45-minute drive back they adopted our model and went from over three weeks to under 10 days. We published our study last summer and have seen hospitals in 25 states and Canada move to this new approach.

my story

OVERVIEW

This chapter explores gender differences as they relate to opioids and opioid use disorders, pregnancy, breastfeeding, and neonatal abstinence syndrome (NAS)/neonatal opioid withdrawal syndrome (NOWS)—the terms used to describe opioid-exposed newborns who display withdrawal. We'll look at best-care practices, legislation that impacts pregnant opioid-dependent women, and barriers to care.

FACTS AND FIGURES

Current statistics around women and opioids reveal a disturbing trend of women rapidly catching up to men in rates of usage and overdose deaths.

- From 1999 to 2015 overdose deaths in women increased by 471% versus an increase of 281% among men.

- 48,000 women died from prescription pain medication overdose between 1999–2010.

- Heroin use increased 100% in women between 2002–2013 versus 50% in men.

- One large study found that one in five Medicaid-enrolled pregnant women filled at least one prescription for an opioid.

- Rates of NAS/NOWS increased by 300% between 2000–2009.

GENDER DIFFERENCES IN SUBSTANCE-USE DISORDERS

Statistical patterns of substance use and reasons for substance use differ between men and women. It's important to remember that these numbers reflect trends, which may not hold true for the individual in your office or house.

What follows is a non-exhaustive list of gender differences as they relate to substance misuse in general and opioids in particular.

- On average more women use drugs to medicate away negative mood states, such as anxiety and depression.

- On average more men use drugs to get high.

- Women report much greater rates of sexual trauma, including childhood trauma. There is a positive correlation between sexual trauma and subsequent use disorders. A literature review by Lisa Najavits showed rates of reported trauma in women between 55–99% versus 36–51% in men.

- Women experience higher rates of chronic pain and are prescribed opioids more frequently than men.

- Women progress to opioid tolerance and dependence at lower doses than men and more rapidly than men. This is referred to as the "telescoping rate" of substance abuse.

- Women report higher rates and intensity of cravings.

- On average women initiate opioid use later than men.

- Women often initiate use in the setting of a domestic partner who uses.

- Men are more likely to initiate use with peers.

- Women are more likely to be prescribed higher doses of opioids and use them longer than men.

OPIOID USE IN PREGNANCY

About one-third of people with opioid use disorders are women of reproductive age (4.4% of pregnant women admit to illicit drug use in the last 30 days, and 1% report illicit use of opioids during pregnancy). Two large, recent U.S. studies showed 14–22% of pregnant women are prescribed opioids at least once, and 2.2% are prescribed three or more times.

For women who misuse opioids during pregnancy, especially those who inject drugs, there are increased risks, which include viral illnesses (hepatitis, HIV) and the potential transmission to their baby, sexually transmitted diseases, and other infectious sequelae of injection drug use (abscesses, cellulitis, endocarditis). Other impacts of illicit drugs include prematurity and spontaneous miscarriage. Women of lower socioeconomic status may also be at greater risk for prostitution, homelessness, arrest, incarceration, and violence.

UNINTENDED PREGNANCY

Rates of unintended pregnancy are high and usage of contraception fall below the average for women with substance-use disorders. Reasons for this include lack of access to reproductive education and care, and family planning services. Opioids are associated with irregular, and even absent, menses, which can lead to misconceptions about the risk of getting pregnant.

It's common to admit a woman into a treatment program, obtain a pregnancy test prior to the initiation of MAT, and discover she's pregnant. The response to this needs to be handled in a caring, nonjudgmental way, where the individual is given adequate time to process the information. She needs to be reassured that the pregnancy will not impact her ability to get started on MAT, although the options will change somewhat and are reviewed in the following sections.

Education about her options needs to be provided, as well as access to obstetrical care if she does not currently have a provider. There should be no attempt to talk her out of taking the pregnancy to term, or to discourage her from a termination. It's important to convey the message that MAT will not present a barrier to having a healthy child. Indeed, either buprenorphine or methadone are considered the standard of care.

ONE KEY QUESTION

As part of an assessment with any woman of reproductive age is the inquiry into her reproductive goals. This conversation can begin with what has been called the One Key Question: "Would you like to become pregnant in the next year?"

This approach helps us understand a woman's reproductive goals. Her response provides a basis for referral and follow-up care. National organizations in women's health—such as the American College of Obstetricians and Gynecologists, the National Association of Nurse Practitioners, and the American Public Health Association—have endorsed this proactive intervention because it addresses causes of unintended pregnancy, poor birth outcomes, and racial and social disparities in the health of mothers and their newborns.

TREATMENT FOR THE OPIOID-DEPENDENT PREGNANT WOMAN

There is good evidence to support the use of MAT, combined with psychosocial supports, other therapies, and wellness strategies. Detoxification during pregnancy—especially rapid detox—is not recommended and is associated with poorer outcomes, including high relapse rates, prematurity, miscarriages, and overdose deaths.

Level-of-care decisions must include the women's preferences and address potential barriers, which can be significant. In some states, based on the implementation of federal regulations, legal considerations and reporting statutes can add levels of complexity and stress, including fears around reports to CPS, and loss of autonomy as it relates to decision making and basic civil rights.

Ideally, care is coordinated, and frequent contacts are maintained with the client, her support system, and involved providers. Good prenatal care, coordination of services, and close follow-up with her OB/GYN, are recommended. Level of care, from inpatient, residential, to partial hospital, intensive outpatient, and outpatient should be based on need and preference.

In 2005 SAMHSA published guidance about recommended services for pregnant women on MAT in their Treatment Improvement Protocol (TIP) 43. These included:

- Special groups to address problems of pregnant women who are opioid addicted

- Available treatments for women addicted to opioids, including pharmacotherapies

- Education and discussion groups on parenting and childcare

- Special groups and services for children and other family members

- Couples counseling

- Case management and assistance in locating safe, affordable housing.

MAT During Pregnancy

MAT is the standard of care for an opioid-dependent pregnant woman, yet the rates of women who receive it continue to be under 50%. This may reflect issues with access, concerns a woman may have about treatment, or feelings of shame or of being judged.

Two forms of MAT, methadone and buprenorphine (without the naloxone component), are the standard options for opioid-dependent pregnant women. Studies, including the Maternal Opioid Treatment Human Experimental Research Study (MOTHER), show better maternal and fetal outcomes for women and their babies when compared to women using street drugs. Some of the findings from this study and differences between the two medications are outlined in the following chart.

Buprenorphine and Methadone in Pregnancy

Buprenorphine	Methadone
Decreases relapse to illicit drugs.	Decreases relapse to illicit drugs.
Improved obstetrical care.	Improved obstetrical care.
Neonatal abstinence syndrome, but less severe than either methadone or illicit opioids (47%). Required less medication and shorter duration of treatment (MOTHER and other studies).	Significant neonatal abstinence syndrome, but less than with illicit opioids (50–81%).
Lower incidence of respiratory distress symptoms.	Higher incidence of respiratory distress symptoms.
Preterm labor 1.8% (MOTHER study).	Preterm labor 14.9% (MOTHER study).
Not liver toxic.	Not liver toxic.
Higher drop-out rate than methadone (33% versus 18%).	Lower drop-out rate than buprenorphine.
May require increased doses in the third trimester.	May require increased doses in the third trimester.
Available without the naloxone component (recommended for pregnant women).	Decreased risk of heroin-induced fetal withdrawal and intoxication.
Increased fetal growth.	Increased fetal growth.
Decreased fetal mortality.	Decreased fetal mortality.
FDA category C.	FDA category C.
No specific regulations around pregnancy unless provided in a SAMHSA-approved OTP.	Written federal regulations related to methadone and pregnancy, which include preferential and rapid, typically within 24 hours, admission of pregnant women.
Decreased new cases of hepatitis or HIV.	Decreased new cases of hepatitis or HIV.

Other factors to consider when deciding whether buprenorphine or methadone is the better choice include:

- Client preference.

- Is the client already on one or the other? If she is, and is stable on it, continue with it. The only variation would be if she's on a buprenorphine/naloxone combination, the naloxone component would be stopped. Also, for both methadone and buprenorphine the dosage may need to be increased, this is often done in the second trimester. This does not represent addictive behavior but is a product of the maternal-fetal circulation. Ways to assess this would be to ask about any symptoms of withdrawal and/or increased drug cravings. Typically, the dose can be adjusted back down within days after delivery.

    - A side effect of this dose increase is that after delivery, the mother may exhibit increased sleepiness and drowsiness, especially with methadone.

- Methadone, especially for new clients, requires daily attendance. This could be helpful for a woman struggling with early recovery. Or the frequent attendance might present an insurmountable obstacle due to childcare or transportation barriers.

- Buprenorphine allows for longer duration of prescriptions. For clients who are stable, this is up to a month.

- Insurance constraints, including Medicaid: Here the issue comes to the discussion of the "card in your wallet." In some states, buprenorphine is covered by Medicaid, in other states there will be restrictions, pre-authorizations, and/or limits to dosage and how long someone can be on the medication.

- Access: Methadone programs have explicit rules on admitting pregnant women in a timely fashion, usually within 24 hours. Rapid access to buprenorphine is more varied and will depend on willing providers and area clinics.

Regardless of the medication chosen, comprehensive treatment and social support are important for successful outcomes through pregnancy and the post-partum period. As there are risks for relapse and overdose, it's recommended that the client, and her supports if possible, are provided with naloxone (Narcan) and education in how to use it.

PSYCHOSOCIAL SUPPORTS AND THERAPIES

In working with a pregnant opioid-dependent woman, who may well have co-occurring mental health issues and other medical concerns, the ideal approach is a whole-person one that starts and ends with her and her goals. It includes an assessment of her existing resources, including her partner, family, finances, housing, and strengths, coupled with a look at her needs. All of which culminates in a working treatment/recovery plan that is fluid and comprehensive.

THE PARTNER, FAMILY, AND OTHER SUPPORTS

Who does the client identify as her support system? Who does she want to be a part of her treatment team? Ask, get the necessary consents signed, and invite them in. When she delivers, who would she like in the room with her? Does she have/want a delivery coach or a doula (a person who can support her emotionally and physically during the end of her pregnancy, through delivery, and even after)?

If possible, and desirable, include her partner. This can be especially useful if they also use opioids or other substances. Active drug use in the home can be a potent trigger for relapse. Education with the partner, which might include an agreement to not do drugs in the presence of the client, should be established. Perhaps this is the time where he/she might be interested in entering treatment.

HIGH-RISK BEHAVIORAL HEALTH CONCERNS DURING PREGNANCY AND THE POST-PARTUM PERIOD

For clinicians and teams working with women with co-occurring mood disorders, especially bipolar, it's important to remember that the risk of a serious mood episode is high throughout pregnancy, but especially in the last trimester and post-partum period. This risk increases if psychiatric medications have been precipitously stopped (rates as high as 90% for bipolar 1). Where many of the commonly used medications (both on and off label) for bipolar disorder are not recommended during pregnancy (such as valproic acid [Depakote], carbamazepine [Tegretol], the benzodiazepines, gabapentin [Neurontin], and others), it's often the case that there have been recent medication changes. Lithium, which does carry a slight risk for a cardiac defect (Ebstein's anomaly), may be continued during pregnancy with a careful discussion/informed consent of potential risks and benefits.

Women with a history of peripartum depression, bipolar disorder, peripartum psychosis, or mania, present challenges and concerns—both to their own well-being and that of their children. Rapid changes in mood and the presence of hallucinations or delusions, including paranoia and odd beliefs, represent a psychiatric emergency and require immediate attention, including the use of local crisis centers, 911, emergency rooms, and inpatient psychiatric units and hospitals.

Onset of a mood episode in a pregnant woman with bipolar disorder can happen fast—within a day or even hours. There is often not the prodrome to a depression, hypomania, or mania that is more typical.

Clinicians need to be alert to the onset of atypical behavioral or mood symptoms in their patients previously diagnosed with major depression. It's common for a first manic episode—often with psychotic features—to manifest during pregnancy, especially if the woman is on an unopposed antidepressant. The partner and/or other supports should be educated to respond immediately should symptoms develop.

While a risk assessment is part of any clinical visit, in pregnant women with mood and psychotic disorders, this takes on added importance. Questions need to be clear not just around suicidal thinking, but around thoughts toward the unborn child and other living children.

"If you were to kill yourself, who'd look after your children?" While clearly disturbing, if the response were: "My mother. They'd be better off with her." It becomes even more alarming to hear, "The world is an awful place. I have to take them with me." Studies looking at woman who have committed infanticide find high rates of bipolar and other mood and psychotic disorders.

A major mood episode in a pregnant or post-partum woman, especially with psychosis, is an emergency and needs to be handled as such.

The partner and other supports should be educated about ways to support the client both during her pregnancy and after. For women with mood disorders this will include planning how she will get adequate downtime and sleep to maintain her well-being. For women with bipolar disorder—who are already at tremendous risk of a mood episode during the peripartum—this should include eight hours of uninterrupted sleep, and frequent check-ins with their behavioral health providers.

THERAPEUTIC APPROACHES AND OTHER INTERVENTIONS TO CONSIDER

While not always available, research shows that women are more likely to attend and stick with programs that meet their specific needs and attend to common barriers such as childcare, transportation, and housing assistance. For residential programs, those that offer family options where a woman can be with her children, and actively involve her partner, can make her decision to enter that level of care more palatable. On the outpatient side, including intensive programs, common barriers, such as transportation and childcare need to be addressed. Again, coordination and collaboration between the client, her supports and her providers is key.

Education

This is tailored to the client and her needs/interests. Common topics include pregnancy, prenatal care, community resources, parenting, early childhood, treatment options, rights, medications, and such.

Motivational Interviewing/Harm Reduction

Women are more likely to modify risk behavior when pregnant, this includes decreasing illicit drug use, alcohol and cigarette consumption, and other behaviors that may impact their unborn child. A motivational approach to risk behaviors employs a nonjudgmental stance, active and reflective listening, genuineness, and recognition of all positive change. Validation and its expression by the clinician is key.

"You cut down to half a pack, well done. I'm so proud of you."

"That's four weeks without a bag of dope, wonderful."

When a woman makes positive changes during the pregnancy—often with the motivator of having a healthy baby—it's important for her to identify what will help her maintain these gains after delivery, as the post-partum is associated with high rates of relapse and overdose.

"You stopped smoking for six months, which is awesome. What are your thoughts about maintaining that after you deliver?"

"You got on and stayed on the buprenorphine and haven't touched a pill or needle, that's tremendous. Do you have concerns about a relapse after the baby comes?"

Cognitive Behavioral Therapy (CBT)

CBT can help identify triggers to relapse, as well as decrease symptoms of anxiety and depression. It can be provided in both group and individual formats.

Contingency Management

Contingency management is the strategic use of positive reinforcers (rewards, tokens, gift cards) and other behavioral strategies to promote desired behaviors and decrease unwanted ones.

Recovery Communities and Peer Mentoring

This can include 12-step and other self-help group formats, such as SMART recovery and All Recovery. Mentors with lived experience, possibly connected to a women-specific program or program for pregnant and/or parenting women, can provide one-to-one support.

Case Management/Care Coordinators

As we work with opioid-dependent pregnant women—often with co-occurring mental and physical health needs—care can become fragmented, and accessing resources can present additional barriers. Comprehensive case management can help address a broad range of needs, which might include:

- Care coordination between medical OB/GYN behavioral health and/or substance-use providers, such as a methadone or buprenorphine clinic.

- Linkages to social service agencies.

- Integration with other agencies already involved with the client, such as child welfare, parole, probation, Temporary Assistance for Needy Families (TANF), and others.

- Transportation.

- Legal services.

- Finance and budgeting.

- Education and vocational assistance.

- Daycare/childcare.

- Linkage to domestic violence programs and/or shelters.

- Housing.

BREASTFEEDING AND MEDICATION-ASSISTED TREATMENT

While both methadone and buprenorphine are found in breast milk in small quantities, there is consensus (ASAM, ACOG, American Academy of Pediatrics [AAP]) that the benefits of breastfeeding overwhelmingly exceed any risk. Additionally, there is evidence to support skin-to-skin contact to decrease symptoms of neonatal abstinence syndrome and promote infant-mother bonding, as demonstrated in Dr. Grossman's study at the start of this chapter.

The only contraindication to breastfeeding relates to active maternal viral infections, such as hepatitis and HIV.

BARRIERS TO CARE

It is common for pregnant women to underreport or not disclose opioid misuse or dependence for many powerful reasons:

- Shame.

- Fear of being judged.

- Fear of being reported to CPS.

- Fear of being mandated to treatment including forcible hospitalization, as can happen in some states.

- Fear of having custody of her existing children and/or the unborn child taken away.

Other barriers to treatment can include:

- Program hours are incompatible with her job.

- Lack of daycare.

- Transportation.

- Available services not geared toward women, especially pregnant women.

- Residential programs that do not allow the woman to bring her children.

INCARCERATED AND RECENTLY INCARCERATED WOMEN

There are over 100,000 women incarcerated in the United States, and 6–10% are pregnant. Some will learn this at the time of incarceration and their initial physical screening and examination. For incarcerated women with opioid use disorders, the recommendation—as it is with un-incarcerated women—is treatment with buprenorphine or methadone.

This is also a population at very high risk for fatal overdose following release.

CAPTA AND CARA AS THEY RELATE TO PREGNANT WOMEN

The Child Abuse Prevention and Treatment Act (CAPTA) provides grants to states for protective services for abused and neglected children. This was amended in 2003 so that for states to receive this money, they needed to implement policies and procedures that included reporting mandates to providers involved in the delivery process. Should a mother or infant test positive for drugs, or the newborn display signs of withdrawal, states needed to demonstrate how this would be referred to protective services or other agencies.

How states interpreted this mandate varied greatly, to where some equated substance use during pregnancy to child abuse. This led to civil, and in some states criminal, prosecution. There is extensive literature on how states have responded to the CAPTA requirements. This includes multiple states that view substance use during pregnancy as grounds for civil commitment. This can then lead to mandated treatment, both within a community, or involuntary admission to an inpatient or rehab setting.

In July 2016, Congress revisited this reporting issue and passed it into the larger Comprehensive Addiction and Recovery Act (CARA). Now, to receive CAPTA funds, states must demonstrate more rigorous identification and reporting of newborns affected by substances at birth to CPS. This includes an annual report on the number of infants, and how many of these had a plan of safe care.

This legislation has profound ramifications for women with opioid use disorders, including those receiving appropriate care with MAT. The expected and treatable neonatal abstinence syndromes seen with these medications is grounds for reporting. Again, we see state-to-state variation with this new twist in the mandates. Clinicians need to familiarize themselves with how these rules have been interpreted and implemented, especially as it relates to women with opioid use disorders and those on MAT. Key to this will be your state's notification guidelines in contrast to already existing child-maltreatment referrals and definition of a "substance-exposed infant" and "plan of safe care."

One helpful resource regarding state-to-state policies on substance use during pregnancy is through the Guttmacher Institute: https://www.guttmacher.org/state-policy/explore/substance-use-during-pregnancy. As of their January 2018 update, 24 states plus the District of Columbia consider substance use during pregnancy child abuse, and 3 states consider it grounds for civil commitment.

EFFECTS OF OPIOIDS ON THE FETUS AND NEWBORN

As opposed to alcohol, cocaine, and even the benzodiazepines, opioids have not been reported to have negative effects on the developing fetus. The notable exception is that codeine in the first trimester carries an increased risk for cardiac anomalies.

Opioid misuse is associated with low birth weight, prematurity, still birth, neonatal abstinence syndrome, and in the case of intravenous use, carries increased risk for maternal-fetal transmission of viral illnesses (hepatitis and HIV).

Methadone and buprenorphine both carry the risk for abstinence syndromes.

NEONATAL ABSTINENCE SYNDROME (NAS)/NEONATAL OPIOID WITHDRAWAL SYNDROME (NOWS)

These terms describe symptoms manifested by a newborn to an opioid-using mother. As might be expected, the number of babies born with NAS has multiplied in the setting of the current opioid epidemic, a nearly fivefold increase between 2000 and 2012, with rates higher in rural than urban settings. NAS symptoms can range from mild to severe, even life-threatening, and may be worsened by the presence of additional substances including SSRI antidepressants, benzodiazepines, gabapentin, and others.

For babies born to opioid-dependent mothers, NAS symptoms appear within 24–72 hours and may include:

- Gastrointestinal symptoms: vomiting (including projectile vomiting), loose stools and diarrhea, weight loss, poor feeding, abnormal sucking

- Central nervous system symptoms: irritability, crying, shakes, seizures, increased muscle tone, jerking of limbs, sleep disturbance

- Respiratory symptoms: abnormal or rapid breathing (greater than 60 respirations/minute), nasal stuffiness

- Autonomic nervous system symptoms: yawning, sneezing, tearing, sweating, rapid heart rate

Treatment of Neonatal Abstinence Syndrome (NAS)

Traditionally NAS has been treated with a combination of non-pharmacologic and pharmacologic means. Treatment that ties dosage of methadone, morphine, or other medications to the newborn's symptoms using the Finnegan scale had been the standard of care. Lengths of stay, often in NICUs, typically ran around three weeks.

Newer, and more pragmatic, approaches encourage rooming-in with the caregiver(s) and not using scales, but basing medication around whether or not the newborn displays expected behaviors, such as feeding, sleeping, being able to be soothed, and so forth. Studies, such as the one published by Dr. Grossman and his team in *Hospital Pediatrics* and described at the beginning of this chapter, have decreased lengths of stay from over four weeks to a few days. There are many benefits to this approach, which include:

- Enhanced maternal (or other caregiver)–fetal bond.

- Increased likelihood of breastfeeding.

- Decreased length of stay with overall decreased healthcare costs.

- Decreased early traumatization to the newborn.

    - The entire manual for this Eating, Sleeping, Consoling (ESC) model is available for free online at: https://docs.wixstatic.com/ugd/55ea1e_f6d23b76d 588408eb2f588e523155e79.pdf

Case Study

After An Overdose

Shayla is a 28-year-old unmarried mother of two. She was brought to the emergency room by ambulance following a drug overdose and reversal with two doses of naloxone administered by the medics. The ambulance paperwork states she was found unresponsive by an anonymous caller at an area hotel. On site, there was evidence of drug usage, a few pink glassine envelopes, syringes, and a cooker.

In the emergency room she is in opioid withdrawal with a COWS score of 32. Despite intense flu-like symptoms, dry heaves, tremors, and an elevated blood pressure and pulse, she clearly states, "If you can get me into a program or back on meth or bup, like right now, I'll do it. Otherwise, let me out of here."

She lives with her parents in Oakville, and they have custodial rights for her 11-year-old twins (voluntarily relinquished custody). There is no active involvement of protective services. "I never use in the house or anywhere near them."

Shayla has been opioid dependent for at least five years and has used sporadically since she was a teen. She mostly uses pain pills (oxycodone), but on occasion she resorts to heroin. Recently, she has used needles, "No more than five or six bags. I don't know what happened. There must have been some of that fentanyl in my dope." She has no active legal problems.

She admits to sporadic use of alcohol and cocaine, but does not feel that either of those represents an active problem. She smokes one pack per day.

Shayla also reports long-standing problems with depression and intense anxiety, for which she has been treated with a variety of antidepressants and sedatives—lorazepam (Ativan) and alprazolam (Xanax), which she is currently prescribed by her psychiatrist at a local mental health clinic. She has never divulged her opioid use to that provider. She is also on fluoxetine (Prozac®) and bupropion (Wellbutrin®).

She has never required inpatient psychiatric hospitalization, but has been to two detox programs in the past. The longest she has remained off illicit opioids was six months when she was on methadone three years ago. She was administratively tapered off for positive urines (cocaine).

Today she reports her depression is a 5/10, and her anxiety is a 9/10, which she relates to a combination of opioid withdrawal and benzodiazepine withdrawal—she overused her prescription and ran out a week early. She adamantly denies that this overdose was a suicide attempt. There is no evidence of psychosis.

Her urine toxicology is positive for opioids, including fentanyl, and benzodiazepines. Her pregnancy test is also positive. She believes her last period was two months ago, but reports her periods are irregular.

While distressed by the news of her pregnancy, Shayla reports that she intends to have the baby and expresses fear that protective services will again try to have her relinquish custody. Her mother has also made it clear, repeatedly, that she is unable and unwilling to care for additional children. She is unclear as to the identity of the biologic father as she occasionally makes money to pay for drugs by working for an online escort service. She does not consistently use barrier protection or other forms of birth control.

DISCUSSION

Shayla presents to an emergency room following an overdose and naloxone (Narcan®) reversal, a common circumstance. Her in-the-moment desire to get help speaks to the ephemeral nature of willingness-to-change with opioid use disorders. She sums up the core dilemma that both she, and her providers, face. She's in withdrawal, it's going to worsen. Either she gets help immediately, or she will leave the emergency room against medical advice and seek drugs that will alleviate her withdrawal.

Additional complexities, that need to be addressed include:

- A possible benzodiazepine withdrawal (tremors, and elevated blood pressure and pulse).

- The newly discovered pregnancy.

- As her near-death experience demonstrates, a habitual and dangerous mixing of opioids with benzodiazepines. She states that she ran out a week early, but she also tests positive for benzodiazepines. As both lorazepam and alprazolam (Ativan and Xanax) have short half-lives, it's likely that she has an additional source.

Regardless, her current pattern of substance use has brought her to a critical point and may kill her if she does not get the help she both needs and reports a willingness to obtain.

If we focus on her expressed goals, both of which should be supported—to get into treatment with MAT and to have her baby—the initial treatment/recovery plan has a clear direction. The challenge, based on the community where this unfolds, is what resources are immediately available?

Typically, when we discuss MAT, we look at outpatient options, which include OTPs that provide methadone, or clinics and practices where she could receive buprenorphine. OTPs have specific guidelines that relate to pregnant women, and she would be afforded a same-day or next-day admission. Availability of buprenorphine is more variable and does not have specific mandates around pregnancy. In a growing, though small, number of emergency rooms, buprenorphine can be started in the ED with a next-day follow-up appointment in a clinic or practice that offer this option. Also, some emergency rooms have people in recovery either on-site or on-call, who will meet with clients and help them access services and resources in the community, including peer- and wellness-based ones.

However, an inpatient option might be safer due to the benzodiazepines, her unclear pattern of use/overuse/misuse, current symptoms of benzodiazepine withdrawal, the overdose, and her desire to carry this pregnancy to term. A medically supervised detox from benzodiazepines—not opioids—would be a recommendation. However, if this cannot be coupled with initiation of MAT (either buprenorphine or methadone), it's unlikely that she would agree to this on a voluntary basis.

Finally, where she expresses concerns about CPS a proactive approach is warranted. While CPS was involved with her voluntarily relinquishing custody of her older children to her mother, they may also represent a rich source of in-home and community supports that will aid in her goal to parent her unborn child.

Treatment/Recovery Plan

Patient's Name: Shayla Botsford   **Date:** 9/2/2018
Date of Birth: 10/9/1989
Medical Record #: 000-00-0000

Level of Care: Inpatient Detox (Benzodiazepine)

Diagnosis	ICD-10 Code
Benzodiazepine withdrawal, with use disorder, severe	F13.239
Opioid withdrawal, with use disorder, severe	F11.23
Pregnancy	
Depressive disorder, other unspecified with anxious features	F32.9
Nicotine-use disorder, moderate	F17.200
Cocaine-use disorder, moderate	F14.20

The Individual's Stated Goal(s): "I want treatment. I want to have this baby. I don't want protective services anywhere near my kid."

1. **Problem/Need Statement:** Life-threatening pattern of substance use, as evidenced by recent near-fatal overdose with opioids in combination with benzodiazepines. Current poly-drug withdrawal state.

Long-Term Goal: To be abstinent from illicit opioids and benzodiazepines.

Short-Term Goals/Objectives/Target Date:
   1) To complete a safe and medically supervised taper off of benzodiazepines. 9/16/18
   2) To complete a buprenorphine induction to where the client is free from symptoms of opioid withdrawal and her cravings are less than 2 on a 10-point scale. 9/5/18

Copyright © 2018 Charles Atkins. *Opioid Use Disorders.* All rights reserved.

2. Problem/Need Statement: Newly discovered pregnancy. No current OB/GYN.

Long-Term Goal: To deliver and maintain custody of a healthy child.

Short-Term Goals/Objectives/ Target Date:
1) OB/GYN consultation. 9/3/18
2) Provide education regarding pregnancy, including MAT during pregnancy. 9/3/18 and ongoing
3) Obtain referral to and appointment for outpatient OB/GYN follow-up when ready for discharge.
4) Explore both outpatient and residential resources for follow-up, and review options with Shayla.
5) Education around reproductive health.

3. Problem/Need Statement: Moderate to severe anxiety and distress.

Long-Term Goal: To be free from symptoms of anxiety or distress greater than a 3/10.

Short-Term Goals/Objectives/Target Date:
1) Complete a full psychiatric diagnostic evaluation once the buprenorphine induction is complete. 9/6/18
   a. In conjunction with OB/GYN reevaluate efficacy and safety of current antidepressant regimen. 9/7/18
2) Obtain a release for current behavioral health provider and obtain records. 9/4/18
3) Engage in on-unit group and individual CBT and MI. 9/3/18

Interventions					
Treatment Modality	**Specific Type**	**Frequency**	**Duration**	**Problem Number(s)**	**Responsible Person(s)**
Benzodiazepine detox	Unit protocol	Based on protocol	7–10 days, based on protocol	1	Dr. Jayson
MAT induction	Buprenorphine without naloxone	Once	2 days	1,3	Dr. Jayson and team
Psychiatric evaluation	Individual	Once	One hour	1,2,3	Dr. Jayson
Medication management	Individual	Daily	15 minutes	1,2,3	Dr. Jayson
Nursing evaluation	Individual	Once, and as needed	One and a half hours	1,2,3	Jeanne Gray, RN

Copyright © 2018 Charles Atkins. *Opioid Use Disorders.* All rights reserved.

OB/GYN consultation and follow up	Individual	Per consultant's recommendations	Per consulting team	2	OB/GYN service. Dr. Incerti, Deb Draven, APRN
Individual therapy and substance-use counseling with MI	Individual	3 times/week	One hour	1,2,3	Laura Petricone, LCSW
12-step	Group	Daily	One hour	1	Morgan Harris/ Beverly Swift
Prenatal counseling	Individual	Per OB team	Per OB team	2	OB service. Deb Draven, APRN
Relapse Prevention	Group	Daily	One hour	1	Grace Dinali, LCSW
Peer navigator	Individual	5 times/week	15–60 minutes	1,2,3	Kathy Blake
Parenting and attachment counseling	Individual	Initial assessment with referral for f/u at next level of care.	One hour/ week	2,3	Jeanine Fishman (Doula)

Identification of Strengths: "I want to get it right this time. I know I can do it." Highly motivated for both treatment and to do what is necessary to be a competent parent.

Peer/Family/Community Supports to Assist: Parents.

Barriers to Treatment: Expressed fears regarding reporting requirements to CPS. Client would like to go into a women's residential program following discharge, but there are currently no beds available in an all-female program.

Staff/Client Identified Education/Teaching Needs: Prenatal and parenting. Rules regarding protective services. Concerns regarding community-based triggers.

Assessment of Discharge Needs/Discharge Planning: To have safely completed a detoxification from benzodiazepines, completed a buprenorphine induction, and have services in place at a less-restrictive level.

Copyright © 2018 Charles Atkins. *Opioid Use Disorders.* All rights reserved.

Completion of this treatment/recovery plan was a collaborative effort between the client and their treatment team:

SIGNATURES		Date/Time:
Client:	*Shayla Botsford*	9/3/18
Physician:	*Lionel Jayson, MD*	9/3/18
Treatment Plan Completed By:	*Laura Petricone, LCSW*	9/3/18
Primary Clinician:	*Laura Petricone, LCSW*	9/3/18
Doula:	*Jeanine Fishman*	9/3/18
Other Team Members:	*Jeanne Gray, RN*	9/3/18
	Grace Dinali, LCSW	9/3/18

CHAPTER 13

Opioids and Older Adults

- Overview
- Facts and Figures
- Neurocognitive Disorders (Dementias) and Implications with Opioid Use and Misuse
- Co-Occurring Behavioral Health Problems
- Co-Occurring Medical Problems
- Treatment Considerations for Older Adults on Opioids, Including Replacement Therapies
- Case Study and Discussion

OVERVIEW

Opioids in later life come with additional factors to consider. This starts with differentiating between biological age—how old someone is—and relative age, what shape a person is in. To use an analogy, it's not the year of a car you want to buy that matters, but its mileage. A 75-year-old who exercises regularly, doesn't smoke, has good genes, and has taken care of themselves, may appear decades younger than a 65-year-old with a sedentary lifestyle, obesity, diabetes, depression, and a drug habit.

As we age, our kidneys and liver are less-efficient at metabolizing medications. Older people are more likely to be on a greater number of medications, which increases the risk for drug-to-drug interactions, side effects, and adverse reactions. Opioids, especially when combined with other central nervous system depressants, carry additional risks for falls, fractures, cognitive dulling, memory impairment, and overdose.

Finally, there can be a bias or ageism with older individuals, where clinicians may not consider that this grandmother of 10 might also have a decades-long history of substance misuse.

FACTS AND FIGURES

- 40–50% of adults over age 65 report chronic pain.
- Use of opioids increases the risk of falls and fractures in older adults.

- Older adults are prescribed 1/3 of all prescription medications, often without adequate workup and indications for the medications they take.

- 19% of men and 23% of women take at least five prescription medications.

- As baby boomers age, there is an increase in older adults with substance-use disorders.

NEUROCOGNITIVE DISORDERS (DEMENTIAS) AND IMPLICATIONS WITH OPIOID USE AND MISUSE

By age 65, 5% of Americans will have at least a moderate degree of a neurocognitive disease (aka dementia). This risk doubles every 5 years. By age 85, 35–50% will have a dementia. The most common cause in the United States is Alzheimer's disease, followed by vascular dementias (multi-infarct), Lewy Body disease, Parkinson's, and others. Heavy drinkers carry a risk for alcohol-related dementia (Korsakoff's disease), and individuals with a history of HIV are at increased risk for viral dementias. While rare, there is a rapidly progressive and fatal dementia associated with smoking heroin—progressive spongiform encephalitis—which is likely caused by contaminants in the drug.

This background rate of neurocognitive disorders raises issues for clinicians and clinics that work with older adults on opioids, including replacement therapies for opioid use disorders. Even in an early/mild dementia, short-term memory loss is associated with inaccurate medication administration, at times with disastrous consequences. Early and moderate neurocognitive disorders are easily and frequently missed. This is most likely due to preserved social functioning—the person looks and sounds fine.

One solution is to complete an annual, or more frequent, mental status screening examination with every person over the age of 65, and with those whom you might suspect have difficulty with memory. There are several well-validated instruments, such as the Saint Louis University Mental Status Examination (SLUMS), which is used by the Veterans Administration. Another excellent tool is the Montreal Cognitive Assessment (MOCA), available online at: https://www.parkinsons.va.gov/resources/MOCA-Test-English.pdf

CO-OCCURRING BEHAVIORAL HEALTH PROBLEMS

Older individuals with opioid use disorders should be evaluated for a history of behavioral health treatments and problems over the course of their lives. It's important to note that the group with the single-highest rate of completed suicide in America is older white men. This often comes in the setting of a major loss, such as the death of a spouse, or diminished physical abilities and health. The Geriatric Depression Scale is a widely used metric that keys in to symptoms often found in older individuals with depression.

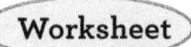
Geriatric Depression Scale: Short Form

Choose the best answer for how you have felt over the past week:

1. Are you basically satisfied with your life? YES / **NO**

2. Have you dropped many of your activities and interests? **YES** / NO

3. Do you feel that your life is empty? **YES** / NO

4. Do you often get bored? **YES** / NO

5. Are you in good spirits most of the time? YES / **NO**

6. Are you afraid that something bad is going to happen to you? **YES** / NO

7. Do you feel happy most of the time? YES / **NO**

8. Do you often feel helpless? **YES** / NO

9. Do you prefer to stay at home, rather than going out and doing new things? **YES** / NO

10. Do you feel you have more problems with memory than most? **YES** / NO

11. Do you think it is wonderful to be alive now? YES / **NO**

12. Do you feel pretty worthless the way you are now? **YES** / NO

13. Do you feel full of energy? YES / **NO**

14. Do you feel that your situation is hopeless? **YES** / NO

15. Do you think that most people are better off than you are? **YES** / NO

This scale is in the public domain. Apps and other language versions of this scale are available at: https://web.stanford.edu/~yesavage/GDS.html

Copyright © 2018 Charles Atkins. *Opioid Use Disorders*. All rights reserved.

Answers in bold indicate depression. Score 1 point for each bolded answer.

A score >5 points is suggestive of depression.
A score ≥10 points is almost always indicative of depression.
A score >5 points should warrant a follow-up comprehensive assessment.

CO-OCCURRING MEDICAL PROBLEMS

The most common reason an older adult develops an opioid use disorder is that they were started on opioids for a medical problem. As discussed in the chapter on pain, the clinician needs to tease apart when, and how, appropriate use led to misuse and a disorder. So too, guiding the identified patient through this process needs to be handled in a nonjudgmental fashion. Where there may be an underlying chronic pain condition, such as arthritis, sciatica, fibromyalgia, diabetic neuropathy, etc., there could also be the added difficulty of opioid-induced hyperalgesia. Referral to an experienced pain specialist is indicated, and if still prescribed opioids, coordination of all providers is essential. A couple truisms in geriatric medicine can help steer the overall amount of medication a person takes:

- Start low and go slow.

- It's often better to take away a medication than to add one.

TREATMENT CONSIDERATIONS FOR OLDER ADULTS ON OPIOIDS, INCLUDING REPLACEMENT THERAPIES

- Monitor mental status regularly. Complete a 30-item mental status screen, such as MOCA, SLUMS, or another standardized tool.

  - If the screen is positive and there is evidence of short-term memory loss, and possibly other cognitive decline, a referral to a geriatric assessment clinic or specialist might be indicated for a more thorough assessment and treatment planning.

- Avoid combinations of sedating medications, especially benzodiazepines, and prescription sleeping medications.

- Be alert to, and test for, other potential substance of misuse, including alcohol.

- Encourage clients to maintain written lists of all their medications and always keep them on their person. These should include dosages and the reasons why they take them.

- Check your state's PDMP. This will key you in both to prescriptions filled for controlled substances, as well as to how many prescribers and pharmacists your patient has been to.

- For individuals with memory loss and other cognitive deficits, employ strategies to ensure accurate medication administration. Depending on the degree of decline this could range from reminder calls from family members to in-home nursing/aide supports, to total care either in the home or a skilled-nursing facility.

- Encourage clients to involve family and significant others in their treatment. This is especially true if there is cognitive decline and memory loss.

- Get releases for all medical providers and coordinate treatment.

- Current Medicare restrictions, and large out-of-pocket expenses, may create barriers to treatment, especially MAT.

(Case Study)

Multidrug Misuse in an Older Adult

Dr. Gerry Lundquist is a 77-year-old semiretired dentist, with an honorable discharge from the Navy following 20 years as a career officer. He is brought to a local emergency room at 10 p.m. after he's observed driving erratically and is pulled over by state troopers. In so doing he hit a tree stump and the air bags in his vehicle deployed. He was breathalyzed in the field, it was positive, but well below the legal limit at 0.03.

The officers observed Dr. Lundquist had slurred speech and was unsteady on his feet. He complained of chest pain and appeared short of breath. Emergency services were called and he was transported to the ED.

In the hospital he becomes distraught, and at times is confused, giving the wrong date and year. A cardiac workup is obtained and he is examined for injuries. As the night wears on he becomes increasingly tremulous, complains of hot and cold flushes, his eyes tear, and he displays flu-like symptoms. The cardiac workup is negative and there is no evidence of physical injury.

His blood pressure is elevated, as is his pulse. He asks to leave the emergency room, and then moments later needs to be told where he is. His daughter, Joanne—a nurse—is contacted. Over the phone she informs the treating physician that her father has been drinking more heavily since the death of his wife three years ago. But she adds he has no history of being in treatment for his drinking and has no history of withdrawal symptoms that she is aware of. She does not have a current list of his medications but agrees to go to his condo in a local retirement community and will bring them to the emergency room.

To stabilize what appear to be symptoms of alcohol withdrawal, possibly with delirium, Gerry is started on a lorazepam (Ativan) drip. His vital signs stabilize, but he continues to shake, complains of cramping and muscle aches, his pupils are dilated, and he sweats profusely.

The treating physician queries the PDMP, which reveals monthly—some months more frequent—refills for oxycodone (OxyContin) 40mg three times a day, and alprazolam (Xanax) 1mg three times a day, and as needed. The database only goes back four years, but Gerry has been on these, or similar medications, for at least that long, all prescribed by the same physician. A urine drug test is positive for both oxycodone and alprazolam.

When his daughter arrives, she has empty bottles for the oxycodone and alprazolam, along with fuller bottles of an antihypertensive and a cholesterol-lowering medication. The physician observes that both the oxycodone and alprazolam were filled two weeks ago and should not be empty. His daughter was unaware of the high-doses of oxycodone her father was on and believes it's for a long-standing problem with chronic pain from knee injuries he suffered in the military for which he receives a partial VA service-connected benefit.

Gerry is admitted to a medical unit with presumptive multidrug withdrawal from alcohol, benzodiazepines, and opioids. The following day he continues to appear confused and in opioid withdrawal. He is given steady doses of benzodiazepines to control the symptoms of alcohol and benzodiazepine withdrawal. A psychiatric consult is ordered.

Gerry's speech is rambling, he reports seeing shadowy figures around his bed, but answers the psychiatrist's questions. To keep him comfortable, he has been restarted on a lower-dose of oxycodone, but still displays mild to moderate flu-like symptoms of opioid withdrawal. He admits to overtaking his medications but denies that it was a suicide attempt. He appears ashamed when he admits that at times he will crush his oxycodone and snort it, as he enjoys the high—especially when combined with alcohol and alprazolam.

He reports frequent loneliness and crying jags since the death of his wife. He brightens when talking about his grandchildren and his lengthy career as a military (and then civilian) dentist, including his current two day/week visits to a local nursing home where he provides dental care, along with his oldest son, who took over his practice. A mental status exam (SLUMS) reveals problems with short-term memory, focus, and concentration, but the psychiatrist reports this is likely due to the delirium and he cannot state at this time if there is an underlying dementia. He has Gerry complete the Geriatric Depression Scale, which shows him as having a moderately severe level of depression.

DISCUSSION

In the previous case, we're presented with an older man who has become dependent on multiple substances: alcohol, benzodiazepines, and opioids. The relative risk for dangerous, even fatal, withdrawal (delirium tremens—"the DTs") from alcohol and benzodiazepines increases with age, length of use, comorbid medical conditions, and a history of prior withdrawals. This complex combination is further complicated by loss (death of his wife), comorbid depression and grief, and opioid dependence and withdrawal.

The first goal of treatment will be to safely and successfully prevent his symptoms of alcohol/benzo withdrawal from worsening. The standard treatment for this involves benzodiazepines, often tied to a metric for alcohol and benzodiazepine withdrawal: the Clinical Institute Withdrawal Assessment (CIWA). Where Gerry is currently delirious with a waxing and waning level of consciousness, confusion, and visual hallucinations, establishing his goals as they relate to his polysubstance misuse will be addressed when his thinking clears. So too, a more thorough assessment of his cognitive functioning and level of depression can be performed once he is free of acute withdrawal symptoms. It's possible that the presence of opioid withdrawal has inflated the results of the depression scale. However, his depression must be taken seriously. His risk factors for suicide are high. These include: age, gender, race, loss of his wife, substance use, recent overdose—even though he says it wasn't a suicide attempt—access to lethal means, and being a dentist (profession with a high rate of completed suicide).

Gerry has clearly developed patterns of misuse with his oxycodone—snorting, overtaking his medications, and using them in dangerous and potentially life-threatening combinations. He will meet criteria for an opioid use disorder, based more on clinical judgment than actual DSM-5 criteria. This combined with his depression raise serious concerns about his risk for a future fatal overdose, whether intentional or accidental. Both should be addressed.

Because he has strong family attachments, one strategy will be to obtain releases for his daughter, son, and any others whom he identifies as supports, and begin to educate both the client, who may not retain much at this point, and his family about approaches both in the short-term and more long-range to address the three problematic substances and his depression. Family support and validation may also help lessen his feelings of loneliness and isolation, and possibly embarrassment, guilt, and shame over his substance misuse and current situation.

When the more serious and acute symptoms of alcohol and benzodiazepine withdrawal have passed, Gerry will meet criteria for a longer residential rehabilitation admission. To safely complete a taper off all benzodiazepines will take two to four weeks, and possibly longer. Because he is a service-connected veteran, there may be local programs and facilities especially suited to his needs. They may also provide a degree of comfort and familiarity as he has strong affiliations and memories of his years in the military.

In regard to his opioid use disorder, he will likely be a candidate for MAT, which could be initiated during his rehab stay. Releases should be obtained for his existing physician, so he can be apprised of the current scenario, with an eye toward better care coordination and more careful prescribing in the future.

Resources

For Families and Others Affected by Overdose

The Compassionate Friends (TCF)

- For general information and chapter locations for TCF: www.compassionatefriends.org
- For the direct link to TCF—Loss to Substance-Related Causes online closed support group on Facebook: www.facebook.com/groups/1515193738693712
- For the direct link to TCF—Sibling Loss to Substance-Related Causes online closed support group on Facebook: www.facebook.com/groups/1516508415263760

Grief Recovery After a Substance Passing (GRASP)

- For general information and chapter locations for GRASP: www.grasphelp.org
- For the direct link to GRASP's online forum: www.facebook.com/groups/grasphelp

Other Resources

Agency for Healthcare Research and Quality (AHRQ):

- *The Effectiveness and Risks of Long-Term Opioid Treatment of Chronic Pain:* https://www.ahrq.gov/research/findings/evidence-based-reports/opoidstp.html
- *Medication-Assisted Treatment Models of Care for Opioid-Use Disorders in Primary Care Settings:* https://effectivehealthcare.ahrq.gov/sites/default/files/pdf/opioid-use-disorder_technical-brief.pdf

American Psychiatric Association—DSM-5 Website:

- This site has dozens of downloadable PDF files of metrics. This includes cross-cutting, diagnosis-specific, and age-specific tools: https://www.psychiatry.org/psychiatrists/practice/dsm/educational-resources/assessment-measures

American Society of Addiction Medicine (ASAM):

- ASAM National Practice Guideline for the Use of Medications in the Treatment of Addiction Involving Opioid Use: www.asam.org
- *ASAM Opioid Addiction 2016 Facts and Figures:* https://www.asam.org/docs/default-source/advocacy/opioid-addiction-disease-facts-figures.pdf

Centers for Disease Control: www.cdc.gov

- *Guideline for Prescribing Opioids in Chronic Pain—United States 2016:* https://www.cdc.gov/mmwr/volumes/65/rr/rr6501e1.htm

Food and Drug Administration:

- List of Pregnancy Exposure Registries: https://www.fda.gov/ScienceResearch/SpecialTopics/WomensHealthResearch/ucm134848.htm

Massachusetts General Hospital Center for Women's Mental Health:

- This is a robust, content-rich website with a broad range of information, articles and resources that relate to women's mental health, including a medication registry for psychiatric medications: https://womensmentalhealth.org/

National Center for Biotechnology Information:

- Downloadable versions of many of the opioid scales mentioned throughout this book: https://www.ncbi.nlm.nih.gov/books/NBK143183/

National Institute on Alcohol Abuse and Alcoholism: http://www.niaaa.nih.gov

- *Alcohol Screening and Brief Intervention for Youth: A Practitioner's Guide.* (2015) NIH Publication No. 11-7805. http://www.niaaa.nih.gov/Publications/EducationTrainingMaterials/Pages/YouthGuide.aspx

National Institute on Drug Abuse (NIDA):

- NIDA for Teens: https://teens.drugabuse.gov/

Patient Care Support System (PCSS):

- This site, part of the American Society of Addiction Medicine (ASAM), is an invaluable resource for information—including trainings (both live and online)—relative to MAT and related subjects. It includes a wealth of downloadable forms, patient agreements, and metrics, such as the COWS and SOWS: https://www.asam.org/education/resources/pcss-mat

Substance Abuse and Mental Health Services Administration (SAMHSA):

- Buprenorphine Treatment Practitioner Locator. This link, searchable by state, provides names and contact information for practitioners approved to prescribe buprenorphine for opioid use disorders: https://www.samhsa.gov/medication-assisted-treatment/physician-program-data/treatment-physician-locator
- National Survey on Drug Use and Health (NSDUH 2016 Survey Results): https://www.samhsa.gov/data/

- Opioid Treatment Program Directory (SAMHSA). This is a searchable database of programs that can offer methadone: http://dpt2.samhsa.gov/treatment/directory.aspx
- SBIRT: This link provides resources about this screening process, which include the billable codes: https://www.samhsa.gov/sbirt

U.S. Surgeon General:

- This is a content-rich website geared toward prescribers. It includes useful fact sheets and checklists regarding the management of pain, opioid prescribing, and other treatment options: https://turnthetiderx.org

World Health Organization:

- WHO definition and criteria for dependence: http://www.who.int/substance_abuse/terminology/definition1/en/

References

Chapter 1: The Opioid Epidemic in America: How We Got Here and Why that Matters

Booth, M. (1996). *Opium: A hisotry*. New York: St. Martin's Griffin/Thomas Dunne Books.

DEA Intelligence Brief. (2016, Jul). *Counterfeit Prescription Pills Containing Fentanyls: A Global Threat*. DEA-DCT-DIB-021-16 (Unclassified). Retrieved online at: https://content.govdelivery.com/attachments/USDOJDEA/2016/07/22/file_attachments/590360/fentanyl%2Bpills%2Breport.pdf

FDA. *Part I: The 1906 Food and Drugs Act and Its Enforcement*. Retrieved online at: https://www.fda.gov/AboutFDA/History/FOrgsHistory/EvolvingPowers/ucm054819.htm

Miroff, N. (2017, Oct 17). From Teddy Roosevelt to Trump: How drug companies triggered an opioid crisis a century ago. *The Washington Post*.

Parker, R. R., Cobb, J. P., & Connell, P. H. (1974, Mar 9). Chlorodyne dependence. *British Medical Journal, 1*(5905), 427–429.

Porter, J., & Jick H. (1980, Jan 10). Addiction Rare in Patients Treated with Narcotics: Letter to the Editor. *The New England Journal of Medicine, 302*, 123.

Quinones, S. (2015). *Dreamland: The true tale of America's opiate epidemic*. Bloomsbury Press.

Vargas-Schaffer, G. (2010). Is the WHO analgesic ladder still valid? *Canadian Family Physician, 56*, 514–517.

Chapter 2: Opioids: Definitions, Neuroscience and the Hijacking of the Brain's Reward System

Al-Hasani, R., & Bruchas, M. R. (2011, Dec). Molecular mechanisms of opioid receptor-dependent signaling and behavior. *Anesthesiology, 115*(6):1363-1381. doi:10.1097/ALN.0b013e318238bba6.

Brunton, L.L., Hilal-Dandan, R., & Knollmann, B. C. (Eds.). (2018). *Goodman and Gilman's The Pharmacological Basis of Therapeutics, 13th Edition*. McGraw-Hill Education.

CDC. *Calculating Total Daily Dose of Opioids for Safer Dosage*. Retrieved online at: https://www.cdc.gov/drugoverdose/pdf/calculating_total_daily_dose-a.pdf

CMS. *Opioid Oral Morphine Milligrams Equivalent Conversion Factors*. Retrieved online at: https://www.cms.gov/Medicare/Prescription-Drug-Coverage/PrescriptionDrugCovContra/Downloads/Opioid-Morphine-EQ-Conversion-Factors-Aug-2017.pdf

Pharmacist's Letter/Prescriber's Letter. (2012, Apr). *Analgesic dosing of opioids for pain management*. Retrieved online at: http://www.nhms.org/sites/default/files/Pdfs/Opioid-Comparison-Chart-Prescriber-Letter-2012.pdf

Von Korff, M. et al. (2008, Jul-Aug). De facto long-term opioid therapy for non-cancer pain. *The Clinical Journal of Pain, 24*(6), 521–527.

Washington State Agency Medical Directors Group (AMDG). (2015). *Interagency Guideline on Prescribing Opioids for Pain*. Retrieved online at: http://www.agencymeddirectors.wa.gov/Files/2015AMDGOpioidGuideline.pdf

Chapter 3: The Face of the Epidemic and Those at Greatest Risk

Dube, S. R., Felitti, V. J., Dong, M., Chapman, D. P., Giles, W. H., & Anda, R. F. (2003). Childhood abuse, neglect and household dysfunction and the risk of illicit drug use: The Adverse Childhood Experiences Study. *Pediatrics, 111*(3), 564–572.

Felitti, V. J. et al. (1998, May). Relationship of childhood abuse and household dysfunction to many of the leading causes of death in adults. The Adverse Childhood Experiences (ACE) Study. *American Journal of Preventive Medicine, 14*(4), 245–258.

Gilbert, L. K. et al. (2015, Mar). Childhood adversity and adult chronic disease: An update from ten states and the District of Columbia, 2010. *American Journal of Preventive Medicine, 48*(3), 345–349.

Hedegaard, H., Warner, M., & Miniño, A. M. (2017). Drug overdose deaths in the United States, 1999–2016. *NCHS Data Brief*, No. 294. Hyattsville, MD: National Center for Health Statistics. CDC.

Jones, C. M. et al. (2015). Demographic and substance use trends among heroin users, U.S., 2002-2013. *Morbidity and Mortality Weekly Report (MMWR), 64*(26), 719–725.

SAMHSA. (2017). *Key substance use and mental health indicators in the United States: Results from the 2016 National Survey on Drug Use and Health* (HHS Publication No. SMA 17-5044, NSDUH Series H-52). Rockville, MD: Center for Behavioral Health Statistics and Quality, Substance Abuse and Mental Health Services Administration. Retrieved online at: https://www.samhsa.gov/data/

Wide-ranging online data for epidemiologic research (WONDER). (2016). Atlanta, GA: CDC, National Center for Health Statistics. Retrieved online at http://wonder.cdc.gov

Chapter 4: Making the Diagnosis: the DSM-5 and Beyond

American Psychiatric Association. (2013). *Diagnostic and statistical manual of mental disorders, Fifth Ed. (DSM-5)*. Arlington VA: American Psychiatric Publishing.

The World Health Organization. (2016 Ed.). *The international classification of diseases and related health problems, Tenth Edition (ICD-10)*.

Chapter 5: Opioids and Pain Management

American Pain Society. (2106). Guidelines on the management of postoperative pain. *The Journal of Pain, 17*(2), 131–157. Retrieved online at: www.jpain.org

Anderson, E., & Shivakumar, G. (2013). Effects of exercise and physical activity on anxiety. *Frontiers in Psychiatry, 4*, 27. Retrieved online at: https://www.ncbi.nlm.nih.gov/pmc/articles/PMC3632802/pdf/fpsyt-04-00027.pdf

CDC. *Current physical activity guidelines.* Retrieved online at: https://www.cdc.gov/cancer/dcpc/prevention/policies_practices/physical_activity/guidelines.htm

Chaparro, L. E. et al. (2104, Apr 1). Opioids compared with placebo or other treatments for chronic low back pain: An update of the Cochrane review. *Spine, 39*(7), 556–563. doi:10.1097/BRS.0000000000000249.

Craft, L. L., & Perna, F. M. (2004). The benefits of exercise for the clinically depressed. *Journal of Clinical Psychiatry/Primary Care Companion, 6*(3), 104-111. Retrieved online at: https://www.ncbi.nlm.nih.gov/pmc/articles/PMC474733/pdf/i1523-5998-6-3-104.pdf

Geneen, L. J. et al. (2017, Apr 24). Physical activity and exercise for chronic pain in adults: An overview of Cochrane Reviews. *Cochrane Database of Systematic Reviews, Issue 4*, Art. No.: CD011279. doi:10.1002/14651858.CD011279.pub3.

Kabat-Zinn, J. (1982). An outpatient program in behavioral medicine for chronic pain patients based on the practice of mindfulness meditation: Theoretical considerations and preliminary results. *General Hospital Psychiatry, 4*(1), 33–47.

Kabat-Zinn, J. (1990). *Full catastrophe living: Using the wisdom of your body and mind to face stress, pain and illness.* Delta.

Kim, B. J. et al. (2017). Impact of mindfulness-based stress reduction therapy on myocardial function and endothelial dysfunction in female patients with microvascular angina. *Journal of Cardiovascular Ultrasound, 25*(4), 118–123.

Kissin, I. (2013). Long-term opioid treatment of chronic nonmalignant pain: Unproven efficacy and neglected safety? *Journal of Pain Research, 6*, 513–529. doi:10.2147jpr.s47182.

Lee, M. et al. (2011). A comprehensive review of opioid-induced hyperalgesia. *Pain Physician Journal, 14*, 145-161. Retrieved online at: https://www.integration.samhsa.gov/pbhci-learning-community/Opioid-Induced_Hyperalgesia_Article.pdf

Lomas, T. et al. (2015). A systematic review of the neurophysiology on mindfulness on EEG oscillations. *Neuroscience Behavioral Review, 57*, 401–410.

Martell, B. et al. (2007). Systematic review: Opioid treatment for chronic back pain: Prevalence, efficacy, and association with addiction. *Annals of Internal Medicine, 146*(2), 116–127.

Murphy, J. L. et al. *Cognitive behavioral therapy for chronic pain among veterans: Therapist manual.* Washington, DC: U.S. Department of Veterans Affairs. Retrieved online at: https://www.va.gov/PAINMANAGEMENT/docs/CBT-CP_Therapist_Manual.pdf

Qaseem, A. et al. (2017, Apr 4). Noninvasive treatments for acute, subacute, and chronic low back pain: A clinical practice guideline from the American College of Physicians. *Annals of Internal Medicine, 166*(7), 514–530.

SAMHSA. (2012). Managing chronic pain in adults with or in recovery from substance use disorders. *Treatment Improvement Protocol (TIP) Series, No. 54*. Report No.: (SMA) 12-4671. Rockville MD: Substance Abuse and Mental Health Services Administration (US). Retrieved online at: https://store.samhsa.gov/shin/content//SMA13-4671/SMA13-4671.pdf

Santorelli, S. F. (Ed.). (2014, Feb). Mindfulness-based stress reduction standards of practice. The Center for Mindfulness in Medicine, Health Care, and Society. *University of Massachusetts Medical School*. Retrieved online at: https://www.umassmed.edu/co ntentassets/24cd221488584125835e2eddce7dbb89/mbsr_standards_of_practice_ 2014.pdf

Teater, D. *Evidence for the efficacy of pain medications.* National Safety Council. Retrieved online at https://www.nsc.org/Portals/0/Documents/RxDrugOverdoseDocuments/ Evidence-Efficacy-Pain-Medications.pdf

Turakitwanakan, W. et al. (2013). Effects of mindfulness meditation on serum cortisol of medical students. *Journal of the Medical Association of Thailand, 96*(suppl1), 90–95.

Vickers, A. J. et al. (2012). Acupuncture for chronic pain: Individual patient data meta-analysis. *Archives of Internal Medicine, 172*(19), 1444–1453. doi:10.1001/archinternmed. 2012.3654.

Wang, C. et al. (2010, Aug 19). A randomized trial of Tai Chi for fibromyalgia. *The New England Journal of Medicine, 363*(8), 743–754.

Weinstock, J. et al. (2008, Aug). Exercise-related activities are associated with positive outcome in contingency management treatment for substance use disorders. *Addictive Behaviors, 33*(8), 1072-1075. doi:10.1016/j.addbeh.2008.03.011.

Chapter 6: Co-Occurring Mental Health Problems and Opioids: Let's Get Integrated

Ardito, R. B., & Rabellino, D. (2011). Therapeutic Alliance and outcome of psychotherapy: historical excursus, measurements, and prospects for research. *Frontiers in Psychology, 2,* 270. doi: 10.3389/fpsyg.2011.00270.

Atkins, C. (2014). *Co-occurring disorders: Integrated assessment and treatment of substance use and mental disorders.* PESI Publishing & Media.

Hirshfeld, R. (2002). The Mood Disorder Questionnaire: A simple, patient-rated screening instrument for bipolar disorder. *Primary Care Companion. Journal of Clinical Psychiatry, 4*(1), 9–11.

Tarig, S. H. et al. (2006). Comparison of the Saint Louis University mental status examination and the mini-mental state examination for detecting dementia and mild neurocognitive disorder—A pilot study. *American Journal of Geriatric Psychiatry, 14*(11), 900–910.

Weathers, F. W., Litz, B. T., Keane, T. M., Palmieri, P. A., Marx, B. P., & Schnurr, P. P. (2013). *The PTSD Checklist for DSM-5 (PCL-5)*. Scale available from the National Center for PTSD at: www.ptsd.va.gov.

Chapter 7: Medication-Assisted Treatment (MAT) for Opioid Use Disorders and Overdose Reversals: What You Need to Know

ASAM Expert Panel. (2017, Apr 5). Consensus statement: Appropriate use of drug testing in clinical addiction medicine. *American Society of Addiction Medicine.*

ASAM. (2015). *National practice guidelines for the use of medications in the treatment of addiction involving opioid use.* Retrieved online at: https://www.asam.org/resources/guidelines-and-consensus-documents/npg

Center for Substance Abuse Treatment. (2004). *Clinical Guidelines for the Use of Buprenorphine in the Treatment of Opioid Addiction.* Treatment Improvement Protocol (TIP) Series 40. DHHS Report No. (SMA) 04-3939. Rockville, MD: Substance Abuse and Mental Health Services Administration. Retrieved online at: https://www.ncbi.nlm.nih.gov/books/NBK64245/pdf/Bookshelf_NBK64245.pdf

Dean, A. J. et al. (2006, Jan). Does naltrexone treatment lead to depression? Findings from a randomized controlled trial in subjects with opioid dependence. *Journal of Psychiatry and Neuroscience, 31*(1), 38–45.

Freyer, F. J. (2017, Oct 30). 10 percent revived by Narcan in Mass. died within year, study says. *The Boston Globe.*

Fullerton, C. A. et al. (2014, Feb 1). Medication-assisted treatment with methadone: Assessing the evidence. *Psychiatric Services, 65*(2), 146–157.

Ling, W. et al. (2012, Jul 2). Buprenorphine for opioid addiction. *Pain Management, 2*(4), 345–350. doi:10.2217/pmt.12.26.

Miotto, K. et al. (1997, Apr 14). Overdose, suicide attempts, and death among a cohort of naltrexone-treated opioid addicts. *Drug and Alcohol Dependence, 45*(1-2), 131–134. doi.org/10.1016/S0376-8716(97)01348-3.

Patrick, S. W. et al. (2016, Jul 1). Implementation of prescription drug monitoring programs associated with reductions in opioid-related death rates. *Health Affairs (Millwood), 35*(7), 1324–1332. doi:10.1377/hlthaff.2015.1496.

Schuckit, M. A. (2016, Jul 28). Treatment of opioid use disorders. *The New England Journal of Medicine, 375*(4), 357-368. doi: 10.1056/NEJMra1604339.

Thomas, C. P. et al. (2014, Feb 1). Medication-assisted treatment with buprenorphine: Assessing the evidence. *Psychiatric Services, 65*(2), 158–170.

Van Ryswyk, E., & Antic, N. A. (2016, Oct). Opioids and sleep-disordered breathing. *Chest, 150*(4), 934–944.

Wesson, D., & Ling, W. (2003, Apr-Jun). The Clinical Opiate Withdrawal Scale (COWS). *Journal of Psychoactive Drugs, 35*(2), 253–259.

Chapter 8: The Medical Fallout: It's Not Just Overdoses

CDC. *Viral Hepatitis Surveillance, United States (2015)*. Retrieved online at: https://www.cdc. gov/hepatitis/statistics/2015surveillance/pdfs/2015hepsurveillancerpt.pdf

Yaksh, T., & Wallace, M. (2018). Opioids, Analgesia, and Pain Management (Chapter 20). In Brunton, L. L., Hilal-Dandan, R., & Knollmann, B. C. (Eds.). *Goodman and Gilman's The Pharmacological Basis of Therapeutics, 13th Edition*. McGraw-Hill Education.

Chapter 9: The Therapeutic Relationship, Readiness for Change, and Establishment of Goals

DiClemente, C., Nidecker, M., & Bellack, A. S. (2008, Jan). Motivation and the stages of change among individuals with severe mental illness and substance abuse disorders. *Journal of Substance Abuse Treatment, 34*, 25–35.

Miller, W. R., & Tonigan, J. S. (1996). Assessing drinkers' motivation for change: The Stages of Change Readiness and Treatment Eagerness Scale (SOCRATES). *Psychology of Addictive Behaviors, 10*, 81–89.

Chapter 10: Treatment: A Thousand Paths to Recovery, from Professionals to Peers

Beck, J. (2011). *Cognitive behavioral therapy: Basics and beyond, Second Ed*. The Guilford Press.

Brigham, E. S. et al. (2014, May 1). A randomized clinical trial to evaluate the efficacy of Community Reinforcement and Family Training for Treatment Retention (CRAFT-T) for improving outcomes for patients completing opioid detoxification. *Drug and Alcohol Dependence, 1*(138), 240–3. doi:10.1016/j.drugalcdep.2014.02.013.

Dugosh, K. et al. (2016, Mar-Apr). A systematic review on the use of psychosocial interventions in conjunction with medications for the treatment of opioid addiction. *Journal of Addiction Medicine, 10*(2), 93–103. doi:10.1097/ADM. 0000000000000193.

Hanh, Tich Nhat. (1999). *The miracle of mindfulness: An introduction to the practice of meditation*. Beacon Press.

Kellogg, S. H. et al. (2007). *Contingency Management: Foundations and Principles. Unpublished Chapter*. Retrieved online at: http://attcnetwork.org/PAMI/PDF/Contingency_Mgt_F_P.pdf

Linehan, M. (2014). *DBT skills training, Second Edition*. The Guilford Press.

McKay, M. et al. (2007). *Dialectical behavior therapy skills workbook: Practical DBT exercises for learning mindfulness, interpersonal effectiveness, emotion regulation, & distress tolerance*. New Harbinger Publications.

Petry, N. M., & Bohn, M. J. (2003, Aug). Fishbowls and candy bars: Using low-cost incentives to increase treatment retention. *Science and Practice Perspectives, 2*(1). Retrieved online at: https://www.niatx.net/PDF/PIPublications/Petry_2003_NIDASPP.pdf

Chapter 11: Adolescents and Opioids

American Academy of Pediatrics. (2011, Oct). Substance use screening, brief intervention, and referral to treatment for pediatricians clinical report on SBIRT. Retrieved online at: http://pediatrics.aappublications.org/content/early/2011/10/26/peds.2011-1754.abstract?rss=1

Arain, M. et al. (2013). Maturation of the adolescent brain. *Neuropsychiatric Disease and Treatment*, 9, 449–461. Retrieved online at: https://www.ncbi.nlm.nih.gov/pmc/articles/PMC3621648/pdf/ndt-9-449.pdf

Borduin, C. M. et al. (1995, Aug). Multisystemic treatment of serious juvenile offenders: Long-term prevention of criminality and violence. *Journal of Consulting and Clinical Psychology*, 63(4), 569–578.

Center for Children's Advocacy. (2016). *Medical-legal partnership project: Adolescent health care: Legal rights of teens, 5th Edition.*

Dakof, G. A. et al. (2015, Apr). A randomized clinical trial of family therapy in juvenile drug court. *Journal of Family Psychology*, 29(2), 232–241.

DeVries, A. et al. (2014, Jul). Opioid use among adolescent patients treated for headache. *Journal of Adolescent Health*, 55(1). 128–133. http//dx.doi.org/10/1016/j.jadohealth.2013.12.014

Fishman, M. et al. Adoption of medication treatment for adolescent and young adult opioid dependence. *Johns Hopkins School of Medicine*. Retrieved online at: http://ctndisseminationlibrary.org/PDF/470.pdf

Fishman, M. J. et al. (2010, Sep). Treatment of opioid dependence in adolescents and young adults with extended-release naltrexone: Preliminary case series and feasibility. *Addiction*, 105(9), 1669–1676.

Hadland, S. E. et al. (2017, Aug 1). Trends in receipt of buprenorphine and naltrexone for opioid use disorder among adolescents and young adults, 2001-2014. *JAMA Pediatrics*, 171(8), 747–755. doi:10.1001/jamapediatrics.2017.0745.

Henggeler, S. (1999). Multisystemic therapy: An overview of clinical procedures, outcomes, and policy implications. *Child Psychology and Psychiatry Review*, 4(1), 2–10.

Kann, L. et al. (2016, Aug 12). Sexual identity, sex of sexual contacts, health-related behaviors among students in grades 9-12—United States and selected sites 2015. *Morbidity and Mortality Weekly Report (MMWR)*, 65(9), 1-202.

Kerwin, M. E. et al. (2015). What can parents do? A review of state laws regarding decision making for adolescent drug abuse and mental health treatment. *Journal of Child and Adolescent Substance Abuse*, 24(3), 166–176.

Knight, J. R. et al. (2002, Jun). Validity of the CRAFFT substance abuse screening test among adolescent clinic patients. *Archives of Pediatrics & Adolescents*, 156(6), 607–614.

Levy, S., & Siqueira, L. M. (2014). Clinical report: Testing for drugs of abuse in children and adolescents. *American Academy of Pediatrics*, 133, e1798-e1807. Retrieved online at: http://pediatrics.aappublications.org/content/early/2014/05/20/peds.2014-0865

Liddle, H. A., Dakof, G. A., Turner, R. M., Henderson, C. E., & Greenbaum, P. E. (2008, Oct). Treating adolescent drug abuse: A randomized trial comparing Multidimensional

Family Therapy and Cognitive Behavior Therapy. *Addiction,* *103*(10), 1660–1670. doi: 10.1111/j.1360-0443.2008.02274.x.

Liddle, H. A., Rowe, C. L., Dakof, G. A., Ungaro, R. A. , & Henderson, C. E., (2004, Mar). Early intervention for adolescent substance abuse: Pretreatment to posttreatment outcomes of a randomized controlled trial comparing multidimensional family therapy and peer group treatment. *Journal of Psychoactive Drugs, 36*(1), 49–63. doi: 10.1080/02791072.2004.10399723.

Liddle, H. A., Rowe, C. L., Dakof, G. A., Henderson, C., & Greenbaum, P. (2009). Multidimensional Family Therapy for young adolescent substance abusers: Twelve-month outcomes of a randomized controlled trial. *Journal of Consulting and Clinical Psychology, 77(1),* 12–25. doi: 10.1037/a0014160.

Massachusetts Department of Public Health. *Adolescent screening, brief intervention, referral and treatment (SBIRT) toolkit for providers.* Retrieved online at: http://www.mass.gov/eohhs/gov/ departments/dph/programs/substance-abuse/prevention/screening-brief-intervention-and-referral-to.html#pubs

McCabe, S. E, West, B. T., & Boyd, C. J. (2013, Apr). Leftover prescription opioids and nonmedical use among high school seniors: A multi-cohort national study. *Journal of Adolescent Heath, 52*(4), 480–485. http://dx.doi.org/10.1016/j.jadohealth.2012.08.007

Miech, R. J. et al. (2015). Prescription opioids in adolescence and future opioid misuse. *Pediatrics, 136*(5), e1169–e1177. http://dx.doi.org/10.1542/peds.2015-1364

National Archives and Records Administration. *Code of Federal Regulations*: 42 CFR 8.12e.

Olfson, M., Wall, M. M., Liu, S. M., & Blanco, C. (2018, Jan). Cannabis use and risk of prescription opioid use disorder in the United States. *American Journal of Psychiatry, 175*(1), 47–53.

Subramaniam, G. et al. (2013). Treatment of opioid-dependent adolescents and young adults using sublingual buprenorphine. *PCSS MAT Training.* Revised December 20, 2013. Retrieved online at: https://pcssnow.org/wp-content/uploads/2014/03/PCSS-MATGuidanceTreatmen tofOpioidDependantAdolescent-buprenorphine.SubramaniamLevy1.pdf

Tolman, R. T. et al. (2008, Dec). Outcomes from multisystemic therapy in a statewide system of care. *Journal of Child and Family Studies, 17*(6) 894–908.

Veliz, P. E. et al. (2014, Mar). Painfully obvious: A longitudinal examination of medical use and misuse of opioid medication among adolescent sports participants. *Journal of Adolescent Health, 54*(3), 333–340. http://dx.doi.org/10.1016/j.jadohealth.2013.09.002

Woody, G. E. et al. (2008, Nov 5). Extended vs. short-term buprenorphine-naloxone for treatment of opioid-addicted youth. *The Journal of the American Medical Association, 300*(17), 2003–2011. doi:10.1001/jama.2008.574.

Chapter 12: Women, Babies, Pregnancy, and the Post-Partum Period

ACOG Committee on Health Care for Underserved Women, & American Society of Addiction Medicine. (2012, May). ACOG Committee Opinion 524: Opioid Abuse,

Dependence, and Addiction in Pregnancy. *Obstet Gynecol, 119*(5), 1070-1076. doi: 10.1097/AOG.0b013e318256496e.

Behnke, M. et al. (2013, Mar). Prenatal substance abuse: Short-and long-term effects on the exposed fetus. *Pediatrics, 131*(3), e1009–1024.

Bishop, D. et al. (2017, Feb). Bridging the Divide White Paper: Pregnant women and substance use: Overview of research & policy in the United States. *Jacobs Institute of Women's Health*. George Washington University, Paper 5.

Brogly, S. B. et al. (2014, Oct 1). Prenatal buprenorphine versus methadone exposure and neonatal outcomes: Systematic review and meta-analysis. *American Journal of Epidemiology, 180*(7), 673–686. https://doi.org/10.1093/aje/kwu190

CAPTA Reauthorization Act of 2010. (2010). Pub. Law No. 111-320. https://www.gpo.gov/fdsys/pkg/PLAW-111publ320/content-detail.html

Comprehensive Addiction and Recovery Act of 2016 (CARA) (2016). Pub. Law No. 114-198. *114th Congress*. https://www.congress.gov/bill/114th-congress/senate-bill/524/text

Compton, W. M., Jones, C. M., & Baldwin, G. T. (2016, Jan 14). Relationship between nonmedical prescription opioid use and heroin use. *The New England Journal of Medicine, 374*(2), 154–163. http//doi.org/10.1056/NEJMra1508490

Desai, R. J. et al. (2014, May). Increase in prescription opioid use during pregnancy among Medicaid-enrolled women. *Obstetrics & Gynecology, 123*(5), 997–1002. doi:10.1097/AOG.0000000000000208.

Grossman, M. R. et al. (2018, Jan). A novel approach to assessing infants with neonatal abstinence syndrome. *Hospital Pediatrics, 8*(1), 1–6.

Grossman, M. et al. *Eating, sleeping, consoling (ESC): Neonatal abstinence syndrome (NAS) care tool, instructional manual (1st Edition)*. (2017). Boston Medical Center Center. Published online at: https://docs.wixstatic.com/ugd/55ea1e_f6d23b76d588408eb2f588e523155e79.pdf

Guttmacher Institute. (2017). *Substance Abuse During Pregnancy*. Retrieved online at: https://www.guttmacher.org/state-policy/explore/substance-use-during-pregnancy

Hardt, N. et al. (2013, Nov). Prevalence of prescription and illicit drugs in pregnancy-associated non-natural deaths of Florida mothers, 1995-2005. *Journal of Forensic Sciences, 58*(6), 1536–1541. Retrieved online at: https://www.ncbi.nlm.nih.gov/pubmed/23879385

Heil, S. H. et al. (2011, Mar). Unintended pregnancy in opioid-abusing women. *Journal of Substance Abuse Treatment, 40*(2), 199-202. Retrieved online at: https://www.ncbi.nlm.nih.gov/pmc/articles/PMC3052960/pdf/nihms234989.pdf

Holbrook, A., & Kaltenbach, K. (2012, Nov). Co-occurring psychiatric symptoms in opioid-dependent women: The prevalence of antenatal and postnatal depression. *The American Journal of Drug and Alcohol Abuse, 38*(6), 575–579.

Huybrechts, K. et al. (2017, Aug 2). Risk of neonatal drug withdrawal after intrauterine co-exposure to opioids and psychotropic medications: Cohort study. *British Medical Journal, 358*, j3326.

Jones, H. E., Finnegan, L. P., & Kaltenbach, K. (2012, Apr 16). Methadone and buprenorphine for the management of opioid dependence in pregnancy. *Drugs, 72*(6), 747–757. doi: 10.2165/11632820-000000000-00000.

Martin, C. E., Longinaker, N., & Terplan, M. (2015, Jan). Recent trends in treatment admissions for prescription opioid abuse during pregnancy. *Journal of Substance Abuse Treatment, 48*(1), 37–42. Retrieved online at: https://www.ncbi.nlm.nih.gov/pmc/articles/PMC4648237/

McQueen, K., & Murphy-Oikonen, J. (2016, Dec 22). Neonatal abstinence syndrome. *The New England Journal of Medicine, 375*(25), 2468–79. doi: 10.1056/NEJMra1600879.

Mehta, P. K. et al. (2016, Dec). Deaths from unintentional injury, homicide, and suicide during or within 1 year of pregnancy in Philadelphia. *American Journal of Public Health, 106*(12), 2208-2210. http//doi.org/10.2105/AJPH.2016.303473

Najavits, L. M., Weiss, R. D., & Shaw, S. R. (1997, Fall). The link between substance abuse and posttraumatic stress disorder in women: A research review. *American Journal on Addictions, 6*(4), 273–283. http//doi.org/10.3109/10550499709005058

National Institute on Drug Abuse. (2018, Jun). *DrugFacts: Heroin.* Retrieved online at: https://www.drugabuse.gov/publications/drugfacts/heroin

Stone, R. (2015, Dec). Pregnant women and substance use: Fear, stigma, and barriers to care. *Health & Justice, 3*, 2. http//doi.org/10.1186/s40352-015-0015-5

SAMHSA. (2005). Medication-assisted treatment for opioid addiction in opioid treatment programs. *Treatment Improvement Protocol (TIP) Series, No. 43.* Report No.: (SMA) 12-4214. Rockville MD: Substance Abuse and Mental Health Services Administration (US). Retrieved online at: https://www.ncbi.nlm.nih.gov/pubmed/22514849

Welle-Strand, G. K. et al. (2013, Nov). Breastfeeding reduces the need for withdrawal treatment in opioid-exposed infants. *Acta Paediatrica, International Journal of Paediatrics, 102*(11), 1060–1066. http://doi.org/10.1111/apa.12378

Zedler, B. K. et al. (2016, Dec). Buprenorphine compared with methadone to treat pregnant women with opioid use disorder: A systematic review and meta-analysis of safety in the mother, fetus, and child. *Addiction, 111*(12), 2115–2128 http://doi.org/10.1111/add.13462

Chapter 13: Opioids and Older Adults

D'Ath, P., Katona, P., Mullan, E., Evans, S., & Katona, C. (1994, Sep). Screening, detection and management of depression in elderly primary care attenders, 1: The acceptability and performance of the 15 item Geriatric Depression Scale (GDS-15) and development of short versions. *Family Practice, 11*(3), 260–266.

Nasreddine, Z. S. et al. (2005, Apr). The Montreal Cognitive Assessment (MoCA): A brief screening tool for mild cognitive impairment. *Journal of the American Geriatric Society, 53*(4) 695–699.

Stuppaeck, C. H. et al. (1994, Oct). Assessment of the alcohol withdrawal syndrome —Validity and reliability of the translated and modified Clinical Institute Withdrawal Assessment for Alcohol scale (CIWA-A). *Addiction, 89*(10), 1287–1292. PMID: 7804089.

Sullivan, J. T. et al. (1989, Nov). Assessment of alcohol withdrawal: The revised Clinical Institute Withdrawal Assessment for Alcohol Scale (CIWA-Ar). *British Journal of Addiction to Alcohol & Other Drugs, 84*(11), 1353–1357. PMID: 2597811.

Yesavage, J. A. et al. (1982-1983). Development and validation of a geriatric depression screening scale: A preliminary report. *Journal of Psychiatric Research, 17*(1), 237–249.

For your convenience, purchasers can download and print worksheets and handouts from www.pesi.com/opioid

Index

Made in the USA
Middletown, DE
26 November 2019

79459429R00144